The Political Management of HIV and AIDS in South Africa

The Political Management of HIV and AIDS in South Africa

One Burden Too Many?

Pieter Fourie

Foreword by Alan Whiteside

palgrave
macmillan

First published in 2006 by
PALGRAVE MACMILLAN
Houndmills, Basingstoke, Hampshire RG21 6XS and
175 Fifth Avenue, New York, N.Y. 10010
Companies and representatives throughout the world.

PALGRAVE MACMILLAN is the global academic imprint of the Palgrave Macmillan division of St. Martin's Press, LLC and of Palgrave Macmillan Ltd. Macmillan® is a registered trademark in the United States, United Kingdom and other countries. Palgrave is a registered trademark in the European Union and other countries.

ISBN-13: 978–0–230–00667–6 hardback
ISBN-10: 0–230–00667–1 hardback

This book is printed on paper suitable for recycling and made from fully managed and sustained forest sources.

A catalogue record for this book is available from the British Library.

Library of Congress Cataloging-in-Publication Data

Fourie, Pieter, 1972–
The political management of HIV and AIDS in South Africa : one burden too many? / by Pieter Fourie ; foreword by Alan Whiteside.
p. cm.
Includes bibliographical references and index.
ISBN 0–230–00667–1 (cloth)
1. AIDS (Disease) – Government policy – South Africa. I. Title.

RA643.86.S6F68 2006
362.196'979200968—dc22 2006043210

10 9 8 7 6 5 4 3 2 1
15 14 13 12 11 10 09 08 07 06

Printed and bound in Great Britain by
Antony Rowe Ltd, Chippenham and Eastbourne

This book was inspired by and is dedicated to the memory of baby Johanna, who died of AIDS in May 1999

Contents

List of Figures and Tables

Figures

Tables

Acknowledgements

I would like to thank the following people for their friendship and support:

Kevin Algeo, Betty Amailuk, Khadija Bah, Mary Crewe, Desirée Daniels, Ena de Villiers, Shirin Elahi, Ester Ferreira, Mervyn Frost, Amanda Gillett, Jessica Gomes, Vicky and Suzy Graham, David Hallett, Claerwyn Hamilton-Wilkes, David Harrison, Barbara Heinzen, Botha and Hilda Kruger, Liani Lochner, Suzette Meyer, Nicoli Nattrass, Hulda Ouma, Marlise Richter, Yolanda Sadie, Maxi Schoeman, Magriet Snyman, Desislava Tzoneva, Brendan Vickers, Willie Venter, Euníce Walker and Alan Whiteside.

This book would have been impossible without the tireless and meticulous work of the Palgrave Macmillan editorial team – thank you!

A special word of thanks goes to my mom, Rietjie, whose sacrifices made it all possible, and who taught me not to be blind to the invisible and always to question the knowledge.

List of Abbreviations and Acronyms

AAA	AIDS Analysis Africa
AAG	AIDS Advisory Group
AIDS	Acquired Immune Deficiency Syndrome
ALQ	AIDS Legal Quarterly
ANC	African National Congress
ARV	Anti-Retroviral
ASO	AIDS Service Organisation
ATIC	AIDS Training and Information Centre
AVRU	AIDS Viral Research Unit
AZT	Azidothymidine
CHBC	Community and Home-based Care
CIA	Central Intelligence Agency
CODESA	Conference for a Democratic South Africa
COSATU	Congress for South African Trade Unions
DMF	Dimenthylfomamide
DP	Democratic Party
EC	European Community
EEA	Employment Equity Act
FAO	Food and Agricultural Organisation
GAAP	Government AIDS Action Plan
GDP	Gross Domestic Product
GEAR	Growth, Employment and Redistribution
GNU	Government of National Unity
GPA	Global Programme on AIDS
GRIP	Greater Nelspruit Rape Intervention Programme
HAART	Highly Active Anti-Retroviral Therapy
HDI	Human Development Index
HIV	Human Immunodeficiency Virus
IDC	Interdepartmental Committee on AIDS
IDU	Intravenous Drug User
IFP	Inkatha Freedom Party
IPRs	Intellectual Property Rights
MCC	Medical Control Council
MEC	Member of the Executive Council

MinMEC	Ministerial meeting of the MEC
MOH	Medical Officer of Health
MRC	Medical Research Council
MTCT	Mother-To-Child Transmission
NACOSA	National AIDS Co-ordinating Committee of South Africa
NAP	National AIDS Plan
NARP	National AIDS Research Programme
NCOP	National Council of Provinces
NDHPD	National Department of Health and Population Development
NEC	National Executive Committee
NEDLAC	National Economic Development and Labour Council
NGO	Non-Governmental Organisation
NIP	National Integrated Plan
NP	National Party
NUM	National Union of Mineworkers
OAU	Organisation for African Unity
PAC	Pan-African Congress
PACs	Provincial AIDS Councils
PHC	Primary Health Care
PHRC	Provincial Health Restructuring Committee
PhrMA	Pharmaceutical Manufacturers' Association
PWA	Person living with AIDS
RDP	Reconstruction and Development Programme
SAA	South African Airways
SACP	South African Communist Party
SADC	Southern African Development Community
SAIMR	South African Institute for Medical Research
SAIRR	South African Institute of Race Relations
SAMA	South African Medical Association
SAMDC	South African Medical and Dental Council
SANAC	South African National AIDS Council
SARS	Severe Acute Respiratory Syndrome
STD	Sexually Transmitted Disease
STI	Sexually Transmitted Infection
TAC	Treatment Action Campaign
TB	Tuberculosis
TRC	Truth and Reconciliation Commission
TRIPS	Trade-Related Intellectual Property Rights
UN	United Nations
UNAIDS	Joint UN Programme on AIDS

UNDP	UN Development Programme
UNECA	UN Economic Commission for Africa
UNISA	University of South Africa
US	United States
USA	United States of America
VCT	Voluntary Counselling and Testing
WCC	World Council of Churches
WHO	World Health Organisation
WTO	World Trade Organisation

Foreword

The story of AIDS in South Africa is one of lost opportunities, and the result is that the country has one of the most serious epidemics in the world. In late 2004 the South African Department of Health estimated that there were 6.28 million infected South Africans, the largest national total anywhere. Prevalence among women attending antenatal clinics stood at 29.5 per cent; in the worst affected province KwaZulu-Natal it was 40.7 per cent. Even more worrying, the prevalence continues to rise, albeit, as the Department of Health is quick to point out, at a slower rate.

The first two cases of AIDS were seen in South Africa in white homosexuals in 1982. It was not until July 1991 that the number of heterosexually transmitted cases equalled the number of homosexual cases. Indeed, for the first eight years, the epidemic appeared as a primarily gay, white disease. A number of surveys carried out in the mid-1980s found virtually no HIV in the black population – the only HIV infections were in fact found in migrant mineworkers. But the epidemic was poised.

In 1990 the first national HIV prevalence survey found just 0.8 per cent of pregnant women attending the state clinics were infected. But the rates were to take off. In 1994, at the time of the first democratic election, HIV prevalence stood at 7.6 per cent; at the 1999 election it was 22.4 per cent, and in 2004 it stood at 29.4 per cent. It was consistently worse in KwaZulu-Natal; indeed, here there are pockets where over 50 per cent of women are infected. In Hlabisa in 1992 6.9 per cent of women aged 20–24 were infected in 1992, by 2001 the rate was 50.8 per cent.[1]

There was ample warning of what was happening. As early as 1988 there were urgent calls to pay attention to the potentially devastating effects of AIDS in South Africa. Unfortunately, there were also predictions of imminent catastrophe – epitomised by a privately published book *AIDS Countdown to Doomsday*.[2] The dire warnings detracted from sober calls for attention to the epidemic. My involvement was, in part, a desire to understand what exactly was going on. I had first taken notice of AIDS when working on labour migration issues in the Economic Research Unit of the University of Natal in the mid-1980s. It was clear that migrant workers, mostly male, and, under apartheid, highly circumscribed in where they could live and what they could do, were a group who would be at risk of a disease like HIV and AIDS. They had the potential to carry it back to their homes across the *veld* and *vleis* of Southern Africa.

In 1988 the First Global Impact of AIDS conference was held at the Barbican Centre, London, where I offered a paper on the migrant labour system and HIV and AIDS. At that time South African academics were not particularly welcome in international fora. The paper was accepted, presented and lost – never appearing in the book that resulted from the meeting. It was apparent that AIDS was already a political hot potato. At one of the social functions associated with the conference a doctor from the mining industry informed me that what I had said was totally unacceptable and excessively critical of the South African government. He had checked up on me in 'the files' and I 'needed to watch my step'.

The hysteria around AIDS needed to be countered and, in 1989, I was asked by the Development Bank of Southern Africa to prepare a considered paper looking at the potential impact of the disease.[3] The need for quality information was immense and in 1990 the newsletter *AIDS Analysis Africa* began publication under my editorship. This not only monitored what was going on, but also published detailed analysis by many astute observers. The reason for mentioning this is that Fourie's 'history' is something many of us lived. In the 1990s we would never have believed it possible that we would be where we are today as a nation. The analysis in this book shows that, to some extent, there was an awful predictability to what happened.

There were many voices sounding the warning, as this volume shows. The ANC health desk understood what was going on. The (mainly) left-wing doctors and health professionals planning the post-apartheid health system were deeply aware of the threat posed by the epidemic. Indeed, if anyone wanted to, they only had to look at what was going on in Uganda, Zambia (where in 1996 President Kenneth Kaunda announced he had lost his second son to the epidemic) and other countries north of the Limpopo river.

What went wrong with South African AIDS policy? Many South Africans are baffled. In 1998 then Deputy President Thabo Mbeki was set to lead the response to AIDS; two years later he was engaged in dialogue with AIDS 'dissidents' setting up a Presidential Panel on the causes of AIDS. It smacks of the world of Arthur Dent and Ford Prefect – a 'somebody else's problem field'.[4] There have been noble attempts to understand, most recently the work of William Gumede.[5] But all leave us dissatisfied.

In a *cri du coeur* in his recently published book, Stephen Lewis, a Canadian who has served since 2001 as the special envoy to Africa on AIDS for the United Nations, wrote that 'every senior UN official, engaged directly or indirectly in the struggle against AIDS, to whom I have spoken about South Africa, is completely bewildered by the policies of President Mbeki'.[6] So are we, Dr Lewis, so are we.

In this book Pieter Fourie documents the history of policy failure in South Africa, grounds the analysis in policy theory and explains why the response has been so disastrous. It is not just a history though; as Fourie says, the book has a purpose: 'to identify the reasons for the failure of public HIV and AIDS policies in South Africa – in particular at the level of the national government and thus to improve on the process that is policy-making'.

The reality is that large numbers of South Africans are infected, and increasing numbers are dying. The work by the Actuarial Society of South Africa predicted that in 2005 the number of deaths from AIDS would exceed 350,000, and the number will continue to rise until 2010 and beyond. The Department of Health's own figures show that over 100,000 South African infants were infected in 2004.[7] This is unacceptable: we have the drugs and delivery mechanism to prevent most of these infant infections! We have the ability to provide more treatment and surely prevention should be a national priority.

On a personal level my perception of the epidemic has changed. In the 1980s it was a theoretical concern; in the 1990s the first signs of the epidemic were visible. A visit to Leopard's Hill cemetery outside Lusaka in 1995 left me shaken to the core. By the early years of this decade AIDS and its consequences were increasingly real. It is no longer abstract: it is touching friends, colleagues and staff. In the Eastern Cape lives a little girl whose father worked part-time in my garden, she is an orphan – her father died of AIDS despite the fact that we had started him on ARV therapy. Why was treatment late? Because it was hard to speak of the possibility of HIV infection, something many still refer to as 'this thing'. This is no longer an academic issue, it is deeply personal and as a citizen the failure of my government is also personal.

This book began life as a PhD thesis, an excellent and readable PhD that was a pleasure to assess. The sad truth of PhDs is that they are usually read only by the supervisor, examiners, really, *really* good friends and the occasional parent or partner. This work needs to be read more broadly because it has a contribution to make not only to understanding what went on in South Africa, but also to making future policy.

Rather than trying to summarise its contents or explain its main messages I urge you to read, enjoy and apply the ideas you will find.

Alan Whiteside
Director of the Health Economics and HIV/AIDS Research Division (HEARD)
University of KwaZulu-Natal
Durban, November 2005

Introduction

The South African epidemic

In 1982 AIDS claimed its first two South African victims. Twenty-two years later, at the 15th International HIV and AIDS conference held in Bangkok in mid-2004, the Joint United Nations (UN) Programme on AIDS (UNAIDS) released their most recent statistics for South Africa. These indicated a disturbing increase in the years since the disease was first detected in South Africa. By December 2003, out of an official population of just over 43 million:

- 5.3 million South Africans were HIV-positive;
- 5.1 million of these people were economically active (i.e. between the ages of 15 and 49 years), representing 21.5 per cent of the adult (sexually active) population;
- 370,000 AIDS-related deaths had occurred in South Africa in 2003 alone – more than 1,000 deaths a day; and
- the country had 1.1 million AIDS orphans.[1]

According to a report published by UNAIDS, life expectancy in South Africa is projected to fall from 68.2 years in 1998 to 48.0 years by 2010 as a result of AIDS. The population growth rate is expected to drop from 1.4 per cent to 0.4 per cent annually.[2]

One of the most comprehensive studies into the effect of HIV and AIDS on South Africa was published by ING Barings in April 2000. The report focuses mainly on the impact of the disease on the domestic economy, and points out that:

- HIV infection rates in South Africa will peak at almost 17 per cent by 2006 for the population as a whole. AIDS-related deaths will peak about five years later at 256 AIDS deaths per 100 deaths from other causes.

- The economically active population will be the worst affected, with infection rates forecast to reach 26 per cent. South Africa is already battling with a skills shortage, which will be exacerbated by the AIDS epidemic, raising remuneration and replacements costs for companies.
- South Africa will have a smaller labour force, lower labour productivity, higher cost pressures for companies, lower labour income and increased demand for health services from both the private and public sectors. The report found that the public sector was then spending between R3,000 and R4,000 per AIDS patient per year. This would result in annual increases in health spending in excess of R4 billion by 2008.[3]
- Gross domestic product (GDP) trend growth is forecast to be on average 0.3–0.4 percentage points per year lower than in a no-AIDS baseline.
- South African domestic savings will plummet.
- The lower growth and higher risk profile for South Africa will not bode well for financial markets and may well deter foreign investors.

In addition to the negative economic impact of the disease, South Africa stands to suffer on the socio-political and developmental levels.[4] One effect of the disease will be a sharp rise in the number of families without adult breadwinners. The result will be that the elderly and the very young will have to be cared for by the state, putting great strain on the fiscus, or by older children. AIDS impacts on the lives of people around the sufferers of the disease, leading analysts to talk of people infected as well as affected by AIDS.

The expected increase in the number of AIDS orphans in South Africa, for example, has led some commentators to conclude that the country is on the verge of experiencing another 'lost generation' – a generation of orphans who will have to fend for themselves. This could give rise to further increases in the national crime rates. As the disease rips through society, everyone will become the victims of HIV and AIDS in one sense or another: *all South Africans are affected by AIDS*.

Visually, the South African HIV and AIDS epidemic can be represented as shown in Figure I.1.

When HIV enters a new population it generally spreads slowly at first, then rises rapidly until 'saturation point' is reached, when HIV infection levels start to stabilise. This first (HIV) curve is followed by an AIDS

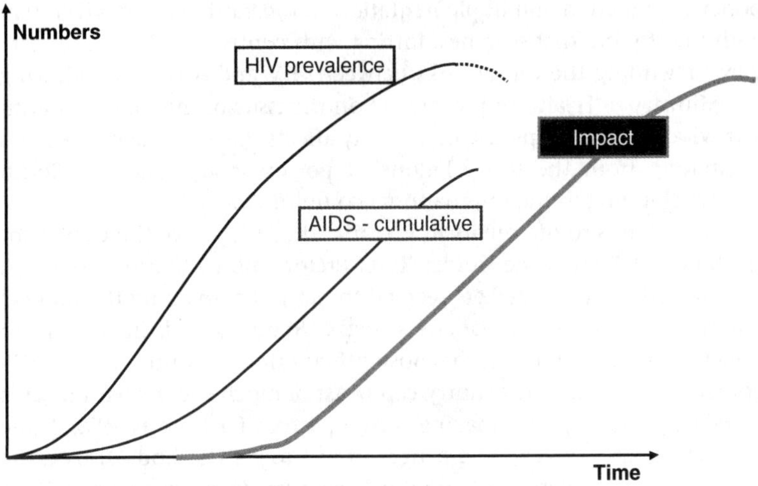

Figure I.1 HIV and AIDS epidemic impact curves

curve about 4–10 years later. The AIDS curve is most dramatically illustrated by a rise in the number of deaths. Between the HIV and the AIDS curves, increasing morbidity levels start taking their toll, with indicators such as work absenteeism and higher household expenditure on health care; the burden of care falls on women and girls in particular. Once AIDS has claimed the lives of HIV-positive people, their absence is felt most directly by the people they leave behind – hence a dramatic increase in the impact curve in the years following heightened mortality levels. Examples of this impact curve include child-headed households and an increase in the number of orphans in South African society.

What have successive South African governments done?

Two facts emerge from this: first, South Africa has a horrifying and growing HIV and AIDS problem; and second, the country has failed to address the issue effectively. Whatever the government policies that might have been introduced to combat HIV and AIDS in South Africa since the 1980s, the statistics cited above and the continuous, exponential rise in HIV infections in this country through the 1990s to the present day demonstrate that the policy response has been a dismal failure.

In addition, the current government in general, and President Mbeki early in his presidency in particular, seemed to be less busy with serious policy formulation and implementation in the battle against AIDS than with nightly Internet searches, flirting with controversial and minority views regarding the causal links between HIV and AIDS, and allowing the Ministry of Health to prevaricate on the issue of the rollout of antiretroviral (ARV) therapies. This not only affects the legitimacy of policies emanating from the top echelons of power; it also damages South Africa's standing in the international community.

In an address to diplomats in Pretoria, the Director of the Centre for the Study of AIDS at the University of Pretoria noted that the country's HIV and AIDS policy-makers seemed to her to be 'roaming the [policy] landscape like packs of leaderless dogs'.[5] She also said, in relation to policy-making, that 'this is the most difficult time in South Africa's AIDS epidemic'. Not that the country can boast of much success with regards to HIV and AIDS policy-making in the past: as far back as 1992, Sadie and Schoeman noted what a struggle it was to get HIV and AIDS on the policy agenda – even to get political scientists to write about AIDS in South Africa. Sadie and Schoeman reviewed the National Party (NP) government's handling of the emerging HIV and AIDS polemic, and pointed out that the previous government's policies had failed to address it appropriately.[6] The reasons for this include homophobic and racist assumptions regarding disease vectors, an exclusivist approach to policy consultation, resultant inappropriate policy formulations, misplaced actions, ineffective implementation and a general lack of legitimacy, all of which compounded the whole problem.

Reviewing the African National Congress (ANC) government's handling of the epidemic during the Mandela administration (1994–99), Marais notes that, although legitimacy became less of a problem for HIV and AIDS policy formulation, structural impediments within state structures, dissonance and a clear lack of capacity between different spheres of government (notably national and provincial government levels) led to the failure of the government to implement its policies effectively.[7] The irony, according to Crewe, is that although the new government did have a good, inclusive and multifaceted AIDS strategy at its disposal in 1994,[8] the structural impediments, together with the fact that South African society was in the midst of a fundamental social constitutional change, distracted policy implementers from adequately addressing this issue.

These problems were compounded by a government which became increasingly belligerent and defensive in the face of criticism. Marais points out how, particularly in the aftermath of the Sarafina II[9] debacle in 1996, the government started to close itself off from constructive criticism: 'these scandals, in fact, showed that politicians were already under pressure to act on AIDS and [were] searching for short-term solution. In that reading, they betrayed, misapplied or miscalculated political will.'[10] The government's response to AIDS became an opera of blunders, embarrassments and scandals: Sarafina II (1996); Virodene (1997); the mystery of the azidothymidine (AZT) decision (1998); mixed messages on notifiability (1999–2001); the courting of scientific dissidents (2000–5); and prevarication on treatment rollout (2003–5).

Referring to President Mandela's record on HIV and AIDS, Marais sardonically notes that, 'measured minute-by-minute, during his Presidency Mandela probably spent more time with the Spice Girls and Michael Jackson than he did raising the AIDS issue with the South African public'.[11] Fundamental to the current as well as previous South African governments' failure to make effective policy with regard to HIV and AIDS is the framing of AIDS as a personal health issue. Marais and Crewe insist that AIDS should, instead, be conceptualised as a public issue which encompasses more than health alone: in South Africa HIV and AIDS are a social, developmental issue and policy responses should not be limited to medical searches for the so-called quick fix, 'holy grail' or 'magic bullet'.[12] One positive development would be, for example, to move public policy-making out of the National Department of Health and into a special unit within the presidency.

Marais notes that the Mbeki government's obsession with finding a vaccine or quick solution to HIV and AIDS might have been brought about by the public's perception of him as 'Mr Delivery' – he needs to perform, and quickly.[13] Instead, policy-makers should address the fundamental issue underlying the prevalence of the disease in this country. This is a *developmental* issue that can be addressed only by focusing on the truly 'South African' situation, namely by bringing the issues of *race* and *culture* into the open, and by formulating circumspect, socially inclusive and long-term strategies.[14]

The purpose of this book

Since the epidemic first made its appearance in 1982, South Africa's policy response to HIV and AIDS has been ineffectual. The rate of HIV infection or incidence level among the populace shows little sign of levelling off, despite the formulation and introduction of several public policy HIV and AIDS interventions by consecutive governments. Analysts are in agreement that national infection rates will only stabilise after 2006, and this will not be on account of effective policies, but rather as a consequence of the natural attrition of the disease: 'saturation point', in the parlance of epidemiologists. By that time, HIV and AIDS are expected to infect more than 600,000 people every year in South Africa, and since these people are – in the absence of ARVs – certain to die within 4–15 years, the imperative to formulate and effectively implement an appropriate policy response is clear.

The history of this policy failure has never been recorded in any comprehensive way. This book is an attempt to plug this gap in the South African literature on HIV and AIDS. It is the purpose of the book to identify the reasons for the failure of public HIV and AIDS policies in South Africa, in particular at the level of the national government. In order to improve on the process that is policy-making, one should evaluate the instances of public policy-making on AIDS in the past as well as in the present, in an effort to uncover which inappropriate or erroneous policies were formulated in the past, and why. Armed with such systematically gathered information, one would be better placed to improve the quality of public policy-making.

It is useful at this point to differentiate between an examination of the policy responses – the actual policy documents – and the policy-making process. There are a number of possibilities:

1 A government may produce good policies that nevertheless fail. It would be odd to say that the only good policies are the ones that succeed. Often good policies fail through the occurrence of unforeseen events.
2 A good policy-making procedure may sometimes produce poor policies. No procedure is going to produce satisfactory outcomes all the time.
3 A bad policy-making procedure may sometimes produce good policies. This can happen by accident, for example. It can also come about through unintended consequences.

All of the above depend on being able to make a distinction between policies and policy-making procedures, and it is indeed the latter that will come under the greater scrutiny in this book.

The structure of the book

The book consists of eight chapters. The current discussion serves to introduce the broad topic by broadly describing the South African AIDS epidemic and providing a 'map' for the rest of the book. The introduction also anchors the study theoretically, by briefly discussing the conceptual and theoretical frameworks of public policy-making, and how these apply to the policy-making process in South Africa in general. Chapter 1 sketches the broader geographical context of the epidemic by quantifying and discussing the vectors as well as the impacts of AIDS in Africa. Particular attention is paid to the link between the epidemic and poverty and underdevelopment.

Chapters 2–4 describe and (extrapolating from and incorporating the policy theory discussed in the next section of this introduction) provide a critical analysis of the policy-making response to HIV and AIDS in South Africa during the period of office of the previous (National Party) government. The main focus is on the years 1987 (when the first legislation was introduced to combat the disease) to 1994.

Following on from this, chapter 5 describes and critically analyses the HIV and AIDS policy-making response of the first ANC government, covering the period 1994–99. This analysis is expanded in chapter 6, which describes and critically analyses the HIV and AIDS policy-making response of the second ANC government, covering the period 1999–2005.

The final chapter concludes the study by providing a summary of the main points discussed throughout the study, and points out the major findings and implications for policy-making in South Africa in general, and on HIV and AIDS in particular. Importantly, the concluding chapter will also discuss the likely road ahead.

Finding our microscope: why words, models and theories are important

Although this book is concerned with a virus, the study of which has long been the preserve of the natural sciences such as epidemiology, virology and medical science as a whole, this study is more concerned with the *socio-political environment* within which the virus operates. More specifically, this book will look at one aspect of the socio-political environment in particular, namely the South African public policy environment and its response to HIV and AIDS. Although the book is not written from the position of medical science, we are still required to find our own kind of tools which can be used to uncover the truth from among all the 'noise' to be found in the socio-political policy domain.

In the remainder of this chapter, we need to do three things that will provide us, as social scientists, with the equivalence of stethoscopes, microscopes and other instruments which we can use to make this study scientific. In the first instance, we need to develop our key *concept*, namely 'public policy-making'; we need to make clear what this means and how the concept is used in this book. The second tool that will be developed is a model of the *process* of public policy-making. Only when we understand what this process entails will we be in a position to measure the way in which policy-making on HIV and AIDS has been made in this country.

Lastly, we need to get a clear idea of the theories that can be used to understand the public policy-making process. Now, although the idea of developing and applying theory might seem tedious, theorising is an invaluable weapon in the arsenal that social scientists have at their disposal. For any single theory or way of viewing the world essentially does two things: it *describes* the world in which we live, and it *prescribes* a path towards a more ideal world. If we are able to identify theoretically the language that various people and governments in South Africa have been using in response to HIV and AIDS, then we will be able to understand their policy descriptions, prescriptions as well as policy-making paths. Understanding the spectrum of the theories of public policy-making that have been used regarding the South African AIDS epidemic can thus prove to be an important tool in understanding why our policy responses to the epidemic have failed so dismally.

A useful definition

Policies are made and implemented by a variety of 'policy actors', including among others private companies, non-governmental organisations (NGOs), multilateral organisations such as the United Nations (UN), universities and governments. It is this last category that we are most interested in, and even then things are not quite as simple as they might seem. 'Government' can refer to different levels of the state, including national, provincial and local governments. In order to make this book as simple and the topic as manageable as possible, we will be focusing almost exclusively on successive *national* government responses to AIDS – from when HIV first appeared in South Africa in 1982, until today.

The definition of 'policy-making' that will be used is provided by Anderson, who defines policy as 'a relatively stable, purposive course of action followed by an actor or set of actors in dealing with a problem or issue of concern'.[15] This definition is useful in that it differentiates between policy as intent and policy as action (accentuating the latter without disregarding the former); it also makes clear that a policy should not be mistaken for a decision (which denotes a specific choice among alternatives). Qualifying this by introducing the public/state realm, Anderson concludes that public policies 'are those developed by governmental bodies and officials'.[16]

There are a few key implications of such a definition: a policy is aimed at changing, achieving or solving something.[17] It does not refer to a random act; the result of chance. Public policies are courses or patterns of action over time of governments and their agents and agencies. They should not be viewed as single, isolated events – it is important to contextualise policies within the greater scheme of things, as continual outcomes rather than individual outputs. As such, a policy is the outcome of a political process that involves negotiation, bargaining, persuasion and compromise – policies should be conceptualised and implemented in a broad enough sense that they need not be replaced and reformulated every year: 'it is clear ... that policy has a cyclical nature and arises from a process over time'.[18]

Public policies in democracies are the result of societal/public demand. The latter may originate from private citizens, groups of individuals, pressure groups, lobbyists, civil society organisations or from within public officialdom itself. These actors demand that public/governmental action be taken to solve a problem or address an issue of concern in society. This issue of concern will most likely be of common interest to the citizens of that state – for instance, a call for the improvement of public roads, to provide anti-retroviral drugs to HIV-positive individuals in government service, or take a position and legislate on the scourge of infant rape.

Public policy should not denote value exclusively as a noun; the study of public policy must also attend to the implementation of policy. In other words, policies should not only refer to government's stated position and intentions *vis-à-vis* a particular problem/issue; it should also focus on the implementation of a plan of action – what government actually does with regard to a problem. Such a policy is concerned not only with government intentions and actions, but also with the *inaction* of government with regard to identified issues and problems. As Anderson states, 'inaction becomes a public policy when officials decline to act on a problem'.[19]

Public policy is also authoritative and based on law. In other words, a policy should ideally be legitimate (enacted or acted upon by a legitimate government) and can be legally enforced by the state (having the monopoly over the legitimate use of coercion). Since public policy is not a singular event, Hogwood and Gunn stress that much policy decision-making is concerned with attempting the difficult task of 'policy termination' or determining 'policy succession'.[20] It is, to paraphrase, difficult to ascertain where one policy stops and another begins. This is compounded by the fact that policies have outcomes that may or may not have been foreseen.[21] At the most basic level, then, public policy analysis is concerned with understanding how the machinery of the state/government and political actors interact to produce public strategies and actions to address a problem.[22]

The public policy-making process

Before turning to the section dealing with theoretical perspectives *vis-à-vis* public policy-making, it is necessary to differentiate explicitly among the various stages of policy-making. Such a differentiation is helpful in that public policy analysts tend to refer to or apply these stages in their models without necessarily clarifying their use, or explicitly stating how one stage follows on another (or not). This discussion will be contextualised by focusing on the policy environment – that vague arena where the boundaries between public and private interface to produce the societal variables that determine the need for (and indeed response to) policy.

Most theorists view the policy process as a series of stages. This is important, since the different values and perspectives brought to bear on each phase of the policy process can determine the definition of the issue at that point. For instance, as mentioned previously, the debate in South Africa on the causal links between HIV and AIDS on the one hand, and poverty and AIDS on the other, may constitute what Heineman *et al.* call a 'wicked problem', on which there is no consensus whether a problem exists.[23] This has significant implications not only during the problem identification and agenda-setting stage, but also for the appropriate drafting of a public policy response, and eventual evaluation and systemic feedback.

This process, or series of stages, should be contextualised within a policy environment; they do not occur within a socio-political vacuum. According to Anderson, the policy environment in its broadest sense includes factors such as natural resources, demographic variables such as population size, race and age distribution, spatial location, political culture, the regime type of the state in question, social structure, class system, other nations, geopolitical position and the economic system.[24] He points out that a state's political culture and the socio-economic conditions will have a significant impact on what are deemed to be important societal issues.

The basic stages in the policy process approach, which will be reviewed individually below, and are illustrated in Figure I.2.

Problem identification

Problem identification is probably the most under-valued stage in the policy-making process. Normally grouped with agenda-setting, many

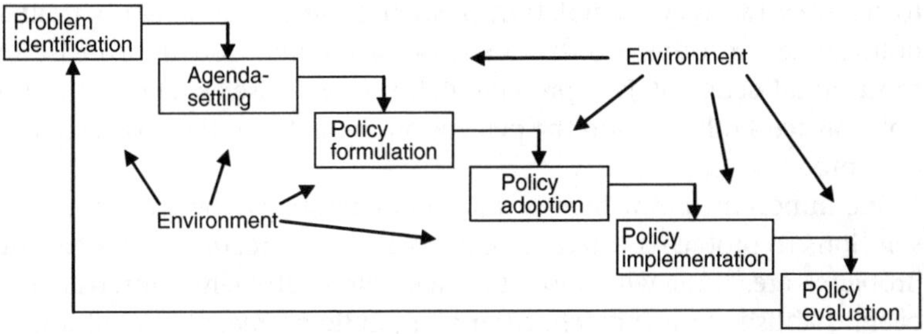

Figure I.2 Policy-making stages
Source: Adapted from Van der Waldt (2001: 94).

analysts ignore this phase in its entirety. Upon reviewing the definition of policy early in the chapter, it is clear that policy-making always occurs in response to a societal ill – it aims at purposefully solving/changing something. The implication is that some issue in society has to be identified for amendment or improvement. If there were nothing to solve, policy responses would not be necessary.

Parsons makes a related point, noting that the genesis of a policy necessarily involves the recognition of a problem.[25] However, not all troubling issues in society constitute problems to be addressed via public policy-making. For instance, HIV and AIDS prevalence might be an issue, but it does not in itself equal an addressable problem. Rather, the actual problem might be the impact of the disease on the economy, in response to which government could design a policy. The accurate definition of the problem is therefore of paramount importance in terms of the drafting of an appropriate policy response.

In order to qualify as a public problem, an issue has first to be deemed unsatisfactory by a significant group in the public domain, and second to be something that can be addressed by government action – if there is no solution to such an issue, no policy would bring about any change and the attempted drafting of such a policy would therefore be a waste of time. Problem identification is further complicated by the fact that one person's problem may not be another's problem.

Furthermore, conditions that are treated as public problems at one point in history may not be perceived as such by a government 20 years later. For instance, the South African government had detailed policy responses to the 'problem' of sexual mixing among the races in 1980; this problem has become a non-issue in contemporary, democratic South Africa. What is crucial in examining what becomes a problem is to see how the very formulation of something as a problem is itself a political act. In other words, this is not a problem-solving exercise in the normal sense: it is a problem-defining exercise, which is itself a political act. Problems and the perception thereof can, therefore, change over time.

The important point here is that public policy analysis cannot offer solutions to problems when there is no general agreement on what the problems are.[26] But who should decide when sufficient consensus has been established on the definition of a public problem? In addition to underlining the inherently political nature of problem identification, this question brings the issue of values to the fore. As Hogwood and Gunn state, 'there is no such thing as neutral analysis'.[27] Values (moral, ethical, political, historical, and so on) are not universal – especially not in a country is sociologically heterogeneous as South Africa.

Agenda-setting

Not all public problems make it onto the public policy agenda. To get on the public policy agenda, a problem must be converted into an issue that the government actually responds to. Cobb and Elder qualify this by differentiating between the systemic public agenda and the institutional, or governmental, agenda.[28] The former refers to those issues on which there is general political consensus as to what merits public attention (for example, high levels of property crime in Johannesburg), while the latter denotes those issues on which the government and its institutions feel compelled to act (for example, the approval of treaties, or government departmental budget requests).

Parsons adds that agenda-building would be facilitated by the conscientisation of large sections of the population about a specific issue; that such a process could push a fairly isolated issue onto the public policy agenda.[29] This can be done by first defining a problem ambiguously in an attempt to encompass as many individuals and interest groups at once; second, by impressing upon one's audience (the public) the dire, long-term effects of inaction on an issue; and third, by keeping the definition non-technical – easy for the general populace to understand and identify with.

Clearly, the media, lobby and other interest groups, and the head of state him-/herself play an important role in establishing both systemic and institutional agenda items, and expanding the issue from a rather contained nature into the ambit of the general public. In addition, individual Members of Parliament, agency representatives and citizens who push policy proposals also act as so-called 'policy entrepreneurs' in the agenda-setting process.[30]

A crisis or cataclysmic event also has an impact on the agenda-setting dynamic – for instance, increased anti-terrorism legislation in light of the 11 September 2001 attacks on the United States, or legislation targeting specific groups in South Africa in light of recurrent race-inspired acts of terror. Changes in quantitative data are another variable impacting on agenda-setting. For example, the South African government in the second half of 2002 decided to rethink its macroeconomic growth targets and policy-making *vis-à-vis* inflation targeting given recently released inflation figures and other econometric data.

But the converse is also possible – that some individuals or groups in society might work against certain issues attaining agenda status. For instance, Anderson mentions that denial of the problem or certain causal links may be used as such a tool – the South African example of casting doubt on the causal link between HIV and AIDS could be seen as an example of this tactic.[31] If such a ploy were to work, an issue could lose its status as a problem to be addressed by government and the issue might then lose its agenda status, slipping from the public policy domain.

Policy formulation

Once an issue has become a problem, and the problem has made it onto the public policy agenda, it is incumbent upon the government to strategise an appropriate response to that public problem. A response, one should add, could be positive (leading to action: planning, drafting and eventual implementation of a new or amended public policy) or negative (inaction – maintaining the status quo). In the actual process of policy design, the technocrats who write the policy need to have an understanding of the problem that would enable them to delineate clearly the overall mission, broadly-stated goals and prioritised objectives of the draft policy or policies. Note the plural here – a cogent strategy would be the conceptualisation of two or more alternative policy responses, giving the decision-makers a choice as to which policy to implement.

In making that choice, these officials would be taking into account the policy environment and the input from various policy entrepreneurs in society. The final choice of policy would take into account the constraints posed to every alternative – and the government needs to decide which policy alternative would, in their opinion, have the most fortuitous outcome and outputs. It is important to note that the entire process is iterative; in other words, one stage of the policy formulation process may not neatly follow on any previous stage: the process may be interrupted, with novel variables impacting on the outcome of the policy formulations at the end. Important in this regard is the impact of scenario planning, forecasting and cost-benefit analyses in general.

Based on the above, the policy decision-makers will decide on their preferred policy alternative. The criteria applied in this last process (which may, in turn, be fed back into the policy formulation for purposes of policy refinement) would then be measured in terms of envisaged effectiveness (is the policy able to solve the problem?), efficiency (how much effort will this require?), adequacy (are societal needs met?), equity (are these needs met across the board?), responsiveness (are those most affected by the problem shielded from any negative future impacts?) and appropriateness (are the assumptions underlying the policy's objectives tenable?).[32]

Policy adoption

This is the stage during which a selected policy, once formulated, is legitimised and formalised. Policy adoption, therefore, has direct correlates with decision-making – who decides on any specific policy alternative, what the variables are that impact on that decision-maker, and so on. Clearly, public policy adoption means political support from the powers-that-be – the government. The latter may adopt a policy and sell it to the public and various individual stakeholders through command, persuasion and bargaining.

Policy implementation

This stage of the policy-making process entails the translation of decisions into action. It is, therefore, distinctly political in nature – dealing directly with the questions of who implements policy, where, when and how. The success of this stage is dependent upon a myriad of variables: the correct definition of the original problem, the accurate identification of causal links, just determination of realistic objectives, and so on – all having an impact on whether or not deviations might occur during the implementation stage. Given the interconnected and co-dependent nature of this and other stages, it becomes difficult – due to the iterative nature of the policy-making process referred to above – to know exactly where the policy implementation phase commences or concludes.

Policy evaluation

At its most basic level, policy evaluation is learning about the consequences (both positive and negative) of public policy.[33] In other words, it is an assessment of all the policy's effects, including its impact on the target situation or group, on situations and groups other than the target (spillover effects), on future as well as immediate conditions, direct costs, in terms of resources devoted to the policy, and indirect costs, including loss of opportunities to do other things.

Government may evaluate its own policies by instructing officials to provide reports, undertake site visits, measure programme effectiveness, conduct public hearings, evaluate citizens' complaints and compare outputs with professional standards. However, Dye cautions that bureaucracies may provide a myriad of rationalisations on why policies did not achieve all their objectives: the impact should be assessed over time and not too early, they are diffuse and general in nature (cannot be quantified), and the research methodology applied in the impact assessment is flawed, not the policy.[34] Government and its agencies need to save face and may therefore not be the best judges of (normative) public policy.

But even where policies are deemed to have failed, they are seldom terminated. Dye explains that 'the most common reason for the continuation of inefficient government programs and policies is that their limited benefits are concentrated in a small, well-organized constituency, while their greater costs are dispersed over a large, unorganized, uninformed public'.[35] In this way, negative impacts may remain hidden from public scrutiny and the public agenda. Also, government officials and other agencies who implement policy may be dependent on the continuation of programmes for their entire *raison d'être*. This leads to a situation where failed policies are repackaged, renamed and maintained.

Theoretical frameworks

In the discussion thus far, much has been made of the argument that public policy-making can be viewed as a process that describes the interaction between various policy-making stages. Analogously, this section will provide an overview of social theorists' varying and intersecting perspectives on policy-making: how these stages are interpreted and placed within specific mental maps that may enable an improved understanding of public policy-making. This does not mean that the book views theorising on public policy-making as a chronological development. Rather, the emphasis here is on the interplay between various levels of analysis, foci on differing policy actors and procedural emphases that the different theories allow.

One should guard against the so-called imperative to choose instantly any single correct theoretical approach, for as Dye warns, 'we doubt that there is any "model of choice" in policy analysis – that is, a single model or method that is preferable to all others and that consistently renders the best solutions to public problems'.[36] Approaching the section with this in mind, the study will distil a model for application in this book. This approach expects to gain from the spectrum of thinking on public policy-making. In other words, combining what can be acquired from most of the theoretical perspectives: simplifying and clarifying thinking about politics and public policy, identifying important aspects of policy problems, focusing on essential features of political life, and suggesting explanations for public policy (as well as – ambitiously – predicting its consequences).

This process/stagist perspective on public policy-making serves as a good introduction to the first theoretical model of analysis: *systems theory*. In brief, it states that public policy-making can be viewed as a phenomenon with four main aspects: societal pressures (defined as needs and demands) determine the political issues of the day, evolving to problem status, which feed or provide inputs into the 'black box' of problem processing and intra-governmental decision-making processes. Once these processes have led to decisions on the creation of public strategies/responses, the latter become policy outputs that are subsequently implemented in society through the organs and different levels of the state. As these policy outputs impact on society, new needs or imperatives may arise, engendering a reappraisal of some policies and issues, which in the final instance may be fed back into the input stage at the start. Visually, this stage/systems approach is shown in Figure I.3.

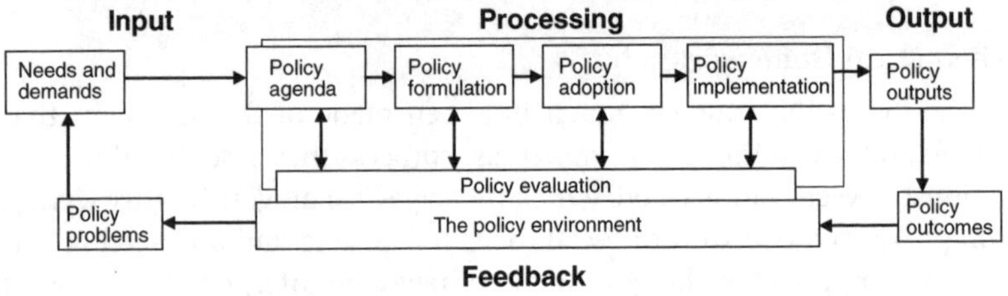

Figure I.3 Amended systems model of policy-making

The main contribution of the systems model is that it assists understanding of the complexities of the process of decision-making. It lacks, to put it bluntly, the public administrator's fixation with political institutions, forcing the analyst to take processes into account. There are, however, some criticisms levelled against the approach. Mainly, the systems model can be interpreted as being too contrived a projection of the way systems work in practice. For example, policy-makers themselves may be the source of demands, and the policy-making process is not as neatly organised as the model implies – it is a complex, elaborate, continuous and flexible process. The systems model is, however, ideal for explicating the multivariant nature of the process, particularly in qualitative analyses.

The second theoretical perspective on public policy-making is that of the *pluralists*, of whom Robert Dahl is the main exponent. Pluralism is an outflow of industrial and post-industrial, Western societies which have liberal constitutions and a clear separation between the powers. Pluralists maintain that power in liberal democracies has become fractured; that it is not and should not be centred in the organs of the state. In fact, they contend that governmental agencies constitute but one of a myriad of interest and pressure groups that might influence the manner in which politics is conducted.

At the level of public policy-making, these theorists view society and its power relations as being made up like a jigsaw puzzle. There is no single group, individual or agency that controls all the power resources in society (pecuniary, knowledge-based, status, and so on). Instead, in the modern state, power has become diffuse and is unequally spread out across the plain of politics.

Not even the government has a monopoly on power. Rather, in the pluralist view, government is but one of many interest groups that make policy demands. In addition, the groups that together constitute society are not self-contained units. Rather, they are composed of individual, cross-cutting memberships. This means that, when policies are made or demands for the identification of policy problems are stated, these groups will contract and expand their memberships – eventually mobilising around issues of common concern. Given sufficient pressure group formation, these issues will then be defined and placed in the public domain as problems – to which government must respond by making and implementing public policies. Accordingly, 'public policy at any given time is the equilibrium reached in the group struggle'[37] – policy-makers are constantly responding to various group pressures: bargaining, negotiating, and seeking compromises amongst those groups.

Critics of the pluralist perspective point out that this approach seems to be so fixated on group interaction that it does not pay sufficient attention to the actual issues that are processed and why such issues are different across sectors and countries – the pluralists are silent on how interests interact to produce policies.[38] Furthermore, detractors claim that pluralist analyses of the policy-making process are prone to using tautological arguments: 'if the approach explains everything in terms of group processes, the account leaves little to be explained because it makes no distinction between cause and effect'.[39] The approach seems to be facile on the level of content explanation, and so bent on demonstrating the interplay between groups that it underplays the importance of the state and its institutions.

As pluralism developed, some theorists came to identify a spin-off of public policy-making, namely *public choice theory*. Its logic is as follows: within a society where there is a plurality of demands on the state, a political marketplace develops in which interest groups vie for their specific positions and issues to be placed on the public policy agenda. Concomitantly, the public sphere/government becomes the target of an 'issue popularity contest'. In democratic societies, the state has to respond to these issues in such a manner that the majority of interest/pressure groups approve of the state's policy agenda. This places the state in a powerful, yet paradoxical position: on the one hand, the state is the object of interest groups' requests for policy action; on the other, the state has to respond adequately enough to ensure that demands are met and needs are satisfied. As Hill notes, 'parties compete to win power, by responding to the demands of the pressure groups'.[40]

Public choice theorists argue that the state grows in power as a result of its response to plural demands – the greater the demand on the government to address policy issues, the greater the need to expand the state to enhance its operational capacity. This in turn enables empire-building in bureaucracies, backed by monopolistic proclivities among state suppliers as a push-factor for state expansion.[41] Public choice theory diverts from classical pluralist theory in its emphasis on the government as a societal actor – classic pluralists view government agencies as powerful, but equal interest groups among many; public choice theory stresses that the state in fact rises above other interest groups in the politics of public policy-making.

Departing from this focus on what motivates governmental expansion and decision-making, *rational choice theory* stresses the importance of the individual in public policy-making. According to these theorists, powerful individuals – those who decide how to respond to public problems – have access to all the information on the parameters of that problem. The decision-maker then applies his/her rationality in an attempt to ascertain which policy alternatives are available for addressing this well-defined problem, through such measures as cost-benefit analyses. Upon receipt of the results of these analyses, the decision-maker chooses the policy alternative that most adequately addresses his/her rationally decided-upon objectives. Rational choice theory – given its emphasis on the quantification of problems and possible solutions – derives from economic theory. Although most analysts of public policy-making respect rational choice for its emphasis on exact problem definition and the finding of alternative solutions to that problem, it is flawed.

For instance, critics point out that the theory assumes too much about individual human behaviour – that individual decision-makers will act rationally, that such rational behaviour is defined by cost-benefit analysis, that the presence of values is underplayed, and that it is naïve to assume that an individual will act in his/her own best interest, or in the best interest of society. Anderson, for instance, is highly sceptical of whether individual decision-makers will have all the perfect information they need about the policy alternatives available to address a problem.[42] In addition, Anderson point out that rational theory is intellectually underpinned by assumptions, values and a methodology that may not be entirely appropriate for the study of social problems: 'rigid and narrow assumptions, mathematical equations, abstractions, and remoteness from reality'.[43] This theoretical perspective does, however, alert the policy analyst to the importance of self-interest in policy decision-making, and provides a better understanding of decision-making processes by highlighting the importance of the individual as level of analysis.

Linked to the impact on conservatism in policy adoption discussed above, and the criticism of rational choice theory that it assumes too much in terms of its own impact on policy change, the *incrementalist* perspective becomes pertinent.[44] In brief, the proponents of incrementalism view actual public policy-making as an arena of compromise. Policy decisions are made in a constricted time-frame – there are pressures on the government to address a problem, and these pressures mount as time goes by.

Policy implementers, therefore, favour an approach where they adjust *existing* policies to suit their needs – instead of doing away with what is available and implementing new policies in their place. The latter is simply too costly – both monetarily and in terms of time. Adapting existing policies also safeguards a government against public criticism. In other words, the state does not need to reformulate policies, running the political risk of uncertain policy outcomes. According to this view, at most policies can be slight alterations of existing ones. In most instances, no grand revolution in policy-making is required to address public problems. Persuasive as it is, this perspective is open to a number of points of criticism.[45] The most apparent is incrementalism's inherent conservatism. Critics point out that due to incrementalist policy-making's search for only a slight, sufficient alternative to existing policies, pressing problems may not be addressed adequately. Also, in doing so, policy-makers tend to legitimise pre-existing policies by merely building on them – not taking cognisance whether or not those policies were flawed to start with.

Elite theory is yet another variant of classic pluralism. Elite theorists agree that political demands within society come from plural sources – interest and pressure groups; they also agree with the public choice theorists that the state might assume greater power than other groups. However, they go one step further, pointing out that not only government and interest groups subsumed under its banner hold political sway. The elite perspective also stresses the elevated power of other identifiable groups, namely the economic, military, political and aristocratic elites.

In contemporary society, the economic elite refers to those sections of society that own the means of production – the so-called 'captains of industry'; the military elite refers to those groups that control the means of coercion; whereas the aristocratic elite denotes those groups (prominent families, for instance) who have attained political clout. In South Africa, the Sisulus and the Mandelas would be examples of such an aristocracy, and in a broader perspective large sections of the returned exiled community within the liberation movements would also belong to it. Most important, however, is the political elite – the group comprising sectors of business, military, economic and bureaucratic society who occupy public office, controlling a state's wealth, technical/intellectual expertise, knowledge and so on.

In the public policy domain, elite theorists maintain that these elites control the agenda-setting process, advancing their own political agendas in determining who gets what, where, when and how. Their proponents within the state bureaucracy determine how public policy is drawn up, what its content is and, in the final analysis, who the prime beneficiaries of policy impact are. Public policies are, in this view, 'the preferences and values of a governing elite'.[46] The policy-making process is, therefore, top-down: the elites determine policy problems and 'sell' these issues to the ignorant populace; policies do not flow from the masses upwards. Concomitantly, policy change occurs when elites re-evaluate their own needs and respond to altered needs by instigating the alteration of state intervention according to their concerns.

Statism (also known as the 'institutional perspective') is a theoretical confluence of elements of elite and public choice theory.[47] Broadly stated, a variant of elite theory notes that elites may congregate in the organs of the government, influencing public policy-making in line with their specific needs. In doing so, the agency of the state becomes a determinant of policy content (with the latter feeding back into the agency in order to reinforce the state elite position). This does not mean, however, that the elites within government agencies have narrowly convergent views on the policies they require; rather, the point is that the state becomes the main stage through which policy is made – this is where politics happen. In this manner, the state comes to dominate political life in society, feeding policy demands and prescriptions to sections of society (top-down), who in turn reinforce the state's legitimacy (*à la* public choice theory) and capacity to react to those problems via public policy-making.

In so doing, government gives public policy three distinctive characteristics:

1 it lends legitimacy to policies, projecting legal obligations into the policies that are made;
2 government makes public policies universal – purporting these policies to apply (both in input and in output) to all the citizens in the state; and
3 the government monopolises coercion in society – only the state can legitimately sanction violators of its policies.[48]

Government, therefore, becomes the all-important progenitor of policy processes, since group theory/pluralism informs us that other pressure/interest groups will then have to defer to the state to have their issues placed on the public policy agenda. However, John notes how some pressure groups may circumvent the state in insisting on certain policies or policy changes.[49] Statism's insistence that the government is all-powerful should therefore be qualified. Clearly, the systems analysts and pluralists are correct in that the social context of policy-making has the potential to shape and mediate formal policy arrangements.

Moving closer to original pluralism and expanding the conception of politics beyond state power, *corporatist theory* describes the political process as consisting of interest representation. This theory views the state and other (fairly limited in number, legitimate – sometimes even state-created) entities as the main representatives of negotiating interests. Economic theorists have viewed corporatism as descriptive of the bargaining within the policy-making process that takes place between government and the market, with the latter being represented by a few encompassing organisations. This relationship between so-called policy networks can be described as differing from one policy sector to another.[50] In order to achieve policy legitimacy, the state requires the support of interest representatives or networks; this strengthens the nature of democracy and so-called democratic corporatism within liberal societies.

The *Marxist theoretical perspective* on public policy-making disagrees. These theorists take some of the premises of elite theory, focusing specifically on the economic distributive power of the state. Marxian analysis of public policy-making takes the concept of ruling class, combines it with elite theory and criticises the public choice, pluralist and other group theories of policy-making for skirting the issue of the (economic) stratification of society. In *The State in Capitalist Society* (1969), Miliband takes as his starting point not the political process itself, but the form of economic organisation or the mode of production.[51] Marxian analysts emphasise that ruling elites (be they part of the state, subsumed under corporatist arrangements or operating through incrementalism's policy change mechanisms) constitute a class that comes to own the policy-making process. They do this to advance their own station in society, and their economic interests in particular.[52]

Given Marxists' contention that political power flows from economic prowess, this serves to reinforce this public policy bourgeoisie's ability to determine the definition of public problems, the policy agenda and policy formulation, as well as to shape policy impacts to their needs. The state is, therefore, in bed with the values and exigencies of capital, which rewards the complacent public policy class by acting to legitimise their government and policy output. Hill notes that the actual class background of state officials is not important, as they are co-opted by capital into joining their ranks. (See public choice theory above for an explanation of how this happens.)[53] The state is not a collection of institutions and functions, but a relationship between classes in society. John criticises this last position, noting that – in their fixation on the class model transposed onto the state and policy-making level – Marxist analysis 'does not explain the variation and complexity of public policy'.[54] In other words, the main criticism against these analysts in the domain of public policy-making is that their (class) level of analysis is too descriptive and self-reifying. It remains overly abstract and does not explain the detail of the actual policy-making process or the multiplicity of actors involved.

So where to from here?

The discussion above demonstrates that a mass of material is available on public policy-making in general and on the theoretical perspectives that try to make some kind of sense of this process. We also have a typology of the key stages by the phase approach to policy-making, and the rest of the book aims to use this material as a learning device to focus policy analysis on certain items that are present in the design of any policy. This does not imply an embrace of any specific theoretical approach; rather, during policy analysis the phase/stage model's key variables serve as reminders of elements to look out for.

In addition to a focus on the stage describing policy-building, this chapter delineates the differing theoretical perspectives on public policy-making. As noted, theory denotes both description and prescription. So where does this leave us in terms of applying the theoretical perspectives to the history of political management of HIV and AIDS in South Africa? Should we stick to the hard-and-fast rule of being obliged to decide upon a single cognitive framework of analysis? The short answer is that the multiplicity of theories leaves the analyst better off – with tools that, if not viewed and applied exclusively, may be combined in an eclectic manner to paint a more complete picture of the AIDS policy-making process. There is no 'theory of all' in the study of public policy-making, and an application of the entire discursive environment of intersecting theories may, in fact, allow us to escape some of the individual theories' more negative implications.

Clearly, some theories are better at explaining specific sections of the policy-making process than others. For instance, systems theory and statism both focus on the process of policy-making, whereas Marxist theory does well at emphasising the economic context of the policy environment. Elite theory, on the other hand, instructs the analyst to remain sensitive to the inimical effects that some elements of the policy-making process might have on democratic consolidation. One can conclude from this that, as Anderson states,

> It seems wise not to be bound too dogmatically or rigidly to one model or approach. A good rule for the policy student is to be eclectic and flexible, and to draw from theories or concepts that seem most useful for the satisfactory and fair-minded description and explanation of political events and policies. The objective explanation of political behavior [*sic*] rather than the validation of one's preferred theoretical approach should be the goal of political inquiry. Each of the theories ... if drawn upon skilfully and selectively, can contribute to a better understanding of policy-making.[55]

This will be the approach employed in this book. After all, theories are utilised to order and simplify reality, identify what is significant, reflect something of the complexity of reality, provide meaningful communication, direct inquiry and research, and suggest explanations.[56] If a careful application of all or some of the theoretical perspectives comes to approximate these ideals more than the strict application of any single theory, then it is imperative for the student/policy analyst to follow this approach. According to Heineman *et al.*, if this can be done successfully, '[policy analysts] will be able to enhance the utilization of rational analysis in policy decisions'.[57]

1
AIDS, Poverty and Development in Southern Africa

Introduction

The introductory chapter has demonstrated that policy interventions can be used by public bodies as well as private companies in an attempt to remedy societal ills. But policy is not as narrow as this – it can be used as a problem-solving tool in a general way. Indeed, any social entity that is governed requires policies from its government. The specific societal malaise that this particular study focuses on is the HIV and AIDS epidemic in South Africa. But this country cannot be divorced from its geographical context. South Africa is politically and economically integrated with the states around it, and as such a transnational phenomenon like the AIDS pandemic can be viewed comprehensively only by placing this country within the broader environment. The problem of regional environmental pollution is as much South Africa's issue as it is Swaziland's; the issue of human refugees created by regional conflicts or famine in sub-Saharan Africa requires political ownership from South Africa as much as from the states surrounding us.

Analogously, it would be analytically limiting to view HIV and AIDS in the region as a motley assemblage of independent instances of infection. For this reason, this chapter aims to be a descriptive point of departure for the analysis of public policy HIV interventions in South Africa. What is all the fuss about? What is the nature and scope of the problem that the South African government has attempted to address since the early 1980s? As such, this chapter serves as a conceptual bridge between the preceding chapter's exegesis of public policy theory's discursive environment and the domestic case studies in chapters 2–6. Again, it should be pointed out that, since the AIDS pandemic is exactly that – a pandemic, cutting across borders – a descriptive chapter such as this would be lacking in analytical focus should it refer exclusively to the domestic South African experience. (That focus is applied in the ensuing analyses of domestic policy interventions.)

The altered conception of 'security' and the introduction of its 'human' angle specifically in the post-Cold War context imply cogent reassessments of issues pertaining to sustainable development and international politics. HIV and AIDS are one such an issue that has, and will continue to have, a significant impact on the dynamics of who gets what, where, when and how in Southern Africa. This chapter addresses the socio-political impact of the disease in South Africa and in the region, using human security as the conceptual looking glass through which to gauge the causes and effects of the unfolding disaster.[1] This is achieved by focusing specifically on the implications for demographic, food, political and macroeconomic security, and the effects on governments' ability to provide essential services. In other words, this chapter provides an answer to the implicit question of why governments in general and the South African government in particular should draft and implement a public policy response to HIV infection among its population.[2] It quantifies the 'fuss' around HIV and AIDS in South Africa and in the Southern African region, describing why it is imperative for governments to respond to the unfolding crisis which is so closely tied to poverty and development in the region.

Human security, development, and HIV and AIDS

Traditionally, the concept of security has been interpreted in militaristic terms as the defence of the state, involving 'structured violence manifest in state warfare'.[3] Since the end of the Cold War, this narrow definition of security has become less relevant.[4]

The term 'human security' was first officially used in the 1994 Human Development Report of the United Nations Development Programme (UNDP). According to this report, the intention of human security is 'to capture the post-Cold War peace dividend and redirect those resources towards the development agenda'.[5] Hubert expands this conceptualisation:

> in essence, human security means safety for people from both violent and non-violent threats. It is a condition of state of being characterised by freedom from pervasive threats to people's rights, their safety or even their lives ... It is an alternative way of seeing the world, taking people as its point of reference, rather than focusing

> exclusively on the security or territory of governments. Like other security concepts – national security, economic security, food security – it is about protection. Human security entails taking preventative measures to reduce vulnerability and minimise risk, and taking remedial action where prevention fails.[6]

HIV and AIDS do not fit into the traditional definition of security. However, as Hadingham argues in terms of the post-Cold War human security regime, HIV and AIDS pose a 'pervasive and non-violent threat to the existence of individuals, as the virus significantly shortens life expectancy, undermines quality of life and limits participation in income-generating activities. The political, social and economic consequences are equally detrimental to the community, in turn undermining its security.'[7] The point is that HIV and AIDS are purported to have a direct impact on the ability of a state to allocate scarce resources in society – as the introductory chapter would have it, the dynamics of who gets what, where, when and how.

In January 2000, the UN Security Council debated the impact of AIDS on peace and security in Africa. The debate was the first in the Council's history to discuss a health issue as a threat to peace and security. UN Secretary-General Kofi Annan told the Council:

> The impact of AIDS in Africa was no less destructive than that of warfare itself. By overwhelming the continent's health and social services, by creating millions of orphans, and by decimating health workers and teachers, AIDS is causing social and economic crises which in turn threaten political stability ... In already unstable societies, this cocktail of disasters is a sure recipe for more conflict. And conflict, in turn, provides fertile ground for further infections.[8]

At the same Security Council meeting the president of the World Bank, James Wolfensohn, said that AIDS was not just a health and development issue, but one affecting the peace and security of people in Africa. While life expectancy in Africa increased by 24 years in the last four decades of the twentieth century, the continent's development gains were threatened by the AIDS epidemic and as a result life expectancy gains were being wiped out. 'In AIDS, the world faced a war more debilitating than war itself ... Without economic and social hope, there could not be peace, and AIDS undermined both. Not only did AIDS threaten stability, but a breakdown in peace fuelled the pandemic,' Wolfensohn said.[9] Unfortunately, these statements cannot be dismissed as hyperbole: HIV and AIDS are now the leading killer in sub-Saharan Africa, mortality rates surpassing people killed in warfare. In 1998 alone, for example, 200,000 people died from armed conflicts in Africa, compared with 2.2 million from AIDS.[10]

Although Africa is late in reacting to the HIV and AIDS pandemic as a security threat, the US Central Intelligence Agency (CIA) has been tracking the disease's impact on human security in sub-Saharan Africa for more than a decade. In 1990 CIA Interagency Intelligence Memorandum 91–10005 instructed the Agency's analysts to track the dissolution of states all over the world by including the effect of HIV and AIDS as one of the variables that determine which states would self-destruct.[11] For these agencies the link between HIV and AIDS and security goes beyond the reality of AIDS as a physical killer: the CIA warns that 'the relationship between disease and political instability is indirect but real'.[12] The UN has picked up on this point, stressing the impact of HIV and AIDS on states' developmental progress:

> [AIDS] is present in a number of countries already facing conflict, food scarcity and poverty, and poses real threats to social and political stability where it is most concentrated – in Africa. The Security Council redefined security as an issue going well beyond the presence or absence of armed conflict, one which affects health and social services, family composition and social structure, economies and food security. There is now broad acknowledgement that AIDS has become a global development crisis, potentially affecting national security in some countries. Armed conflict and associated population movements provide fertile ground for the spread of AIDS, while the epidemic itself can be seen as a risk factor in the breakdown of social cohesion and in social and political instability, in addition to a threat to security forces.[13]

Malan accuses African governments of extreme negligence in their response to the human security aspects of HIV and AIDS – it was only at the Organisation of African Unity (OAU) summit as recently as May 1999 that an African government minister for the first time called the disease a major threat to economic and social development.[14] Holzhausen echoes this sentiment, enjoining African governments to go beyond an admission of the dire impact of AIDS on African communities.[15] He underlines the importance of the insistence in the South African White Paper on Defence in a Democracy that a 'common [i.e. regional, cross-national] approach to security in Southern Africa is necessary.'

At last, the African continent's leaders seem – ostensibly at least – to have woken up to the human security challenge of HIV and AIDS. A UN Economic Commission for Africa (UNECA) discussion document referring to 'key areas for joint African-international action' states that HIV and AIDS 'is Africa's number one survival issue. Without an effective effort to overcome HIV and AIDS, all of Africa's progress in terms of development and governance will be reversed.'[16]

Quantifying the fuss: HIV and AIDS in Africa

The global HIV and AIDS epidemic is far more extensive than initially anticipated. The number of people living with HIV and AIDS at the end of the twentieth century was more than 50 per cent higher than had been predicted in 1991 by the World Health Organisation. As the Worldwatch Institute points out, the HIV epidemic raging across sub-Saharan Africa is a tragedy of epic proportions, one that is altering the region's demographic future. It is reducing life expectancy, raising mortality, lowering fertility, creating an excess of men over women and leaving millions of orphans in its wake.[17]

Due to the long period between infection with HIV and eventual death due to AIDS-related diseases, many Africans remain sceptical about the demographic impact of the disease. AIDS remains distant and unreal, perpetuating denial and stigmatisation. In an effort to make the disease more 'real' – to give it greater visual impact – the following two figures are included. As can be noted from Table 1.1, South Africa is closer to the high prevalence end of the spectrum of states provided here.

Table 1.2 gives projections of life expectancy and population growth in South Africa and six other African countries for 2010. Note that in the case of South Africa, life expectancy is projected to drop by more than 20 years, whilst population growth per annum decreases to less than 1/2 per cent.

One has to keep in mind that the majority of the people cited in Table 1.1 are not yet sick with the effects of HIV and AIDS. They will start dying within the next 5–10 years. The 15–49 year age group is where the leaders of society are found: the governing elite, the moneyed youth, the economically active, the mothers, teachers, agricultural labourers, miners, and so on. What will the effect of their initial morbidity and eventual premature mortality be on the social cohesion, economies and military security of their countries as a whole? How can and should governments respond to the ensuing crisis?

Table 1.1 HIV infection rates in various African countries for the 15–49 years age group, 2003[18]

Country	HIV infection rate (%)
Botswana	37.3
Congo (DRC)	4.2
Kenya	6.7
Lesotho	28.9
Malawi	14.2
Mozambique	12.2
Namibia	21.3
Nigeria	5.4
Rwanda	5.1
South Africa	21.5
Swaziland	38.8
Uganda	4.1
Tanzania	8.8
Zambia	16.5
Zimbabwe	24.6

Table 1.2 Life expectancy and population growth, 2010[19]

	Life expectancy (years)			Population growth (%)	
Country	Without AIDS	With AIDS	Years lost	Without AIDS	With AIDS
Namibia	70.1	38.9	31.2	2.8	1.2
Botswana	66.3	37.8	28.5	1.9	0.2
Swaziland	63.2	37.1	26.1	3.1	1.7
Zambia	60.1	37.8	22.3	3.1	2.0
Kenya	69.2	43.7	25.5	1.8	0.6
Malawi	56.8	34.8	22.0	2.2	0.7
South Africa	68.2	48.0	20.2	1.4	0.4

Explicitly linking the disease to security, the UNECA report underlines the following:[20]

- The epidemic destabilises societies in profound ways. As parents and workers succumb to AIDS-related illnesses, the structures and divisions of labour in households, families, workplaces and communities are disrupted, with women bearing an especially heavy burden. From there, the effects cascade across society, reducing income levels, weakening economies and undermining the social fabric.

- The economic and developmental impact can be especially dramatic. It is estimated that gross domestic product (GDP) growth shrinks by as much as 1–2 per cent annually in countries with an HIV prevalence rate of more than 20 per cent. Over several years, the loss of economic output accumulates alarmingly. Calculations show that heavily affected countries could lose more than 20 per cent of GDP by 2020.
- The epidemic increases the strain on state institutions and resources, while undermining social systems that enable people to cope with adversity. In badly affected countries, education and health systems are compromised, economic output shrinks and state institutions such as the judiciary and police are undermined. In some societies, increased social and political instability can result.
- AIDS thrives in settings already marked by high degrees of socio-economic insecurity, social exclusion and political instability. Individuals subjected to those conditions – migrant workers, displaced people, refugees and ostracised minorities worldwide – face a much higher risk of infection.
- Similarly, it is often the absence of economic security that propels people into sex work for a living, and many end up in prison where they face a higher risk of infection.
- In the past decade, HIV and AIDS have emerged as a major threat in emergency settings. Humanitarian operations can place both relief workers and local populations at greater risk of infection, with children and young people being especially vulnerable. The increased likelihood of sexual violence and prostitution among refugee populations broadens and accelerates the spread of HIV.

The estimated 22 million orphans in sub-Saharan Africa by 2010 are expected to comprise a lost generation with little hope of educational or employment opportunities. Such societies will be at risk of increased crime and political instability as these young people become radicalised or are exploited by various political groups for their own ends – the child soldier phenomenon may be one example.[21] The increase in crime and political instability, moreover, will probably be accompanied by the increased availability of illicit small arms and increased operations by organised criminal organisations in sub-Saharan Africa.

What drives this disease at such a horrific pace in Africa? Are South Africans and other Africans in general particularly vulnerable to HIV? The answer to the last question is yes, given the socio-economic factors referred to above. Africans are not more sexually promiscuous than people in the West or in the greater global North, but poverty, geographical displacement and regional conflicts have become the social determinants that are fanning HIV infection on the continent.

The Jaipur Paradigm has been devised to serve as an analytical model to illustrate the interaction between HIV and society. Analysts praise the paradigm for its simplicity – its central premise is that, in relation to HIV, societies are distinct in two parameters High susceptibility, Low vulnerability distributed on a continuum: susceptibility and vulnerability. Susceptibility is defined as 'those aspects of a society which make it more or less likely that an epidemic will develop'; vulnerability refers to 'those aspects of a society which make it more or less likely that an epidemic will have a serious impact on social and economic Social cohesion organisations'.[22] According to the Jaipur Paradigm, two factors modulate the level of susceptibility and vulnerability of a society: the level and distribution of wealth and income, and the degree of social cohesion. The latter concept is, of course, difficult to quantify, but easy to identify intuitively.[23] Visually, the paradigm operates on two axes, as illustrated in Figure 1.1.

This is all well and good on a theoretical level, but what were the vectors of HIV and AIDS in Africa on the ground? Which specific variables contributed to and continue to compound the rapid spread of HIV on the continent?[25] Analysts point to key factors in explaining the epidemic proportions of the disease in sub-Saharan Africa.[26]

Labour migration

Studies have shown that mobile workers such as long-distance truck drivers have a higher probability of HIV infection than their communities of origin. Migrant labourers – for instance in South Africa during the days of influx control, and those constantly migrating between urban and rural settings – are separated from their families for long periods of time, are prone to visit prostitutes or have multiple sexual partners, become HIV-positive and then return to their primary sexual partners to

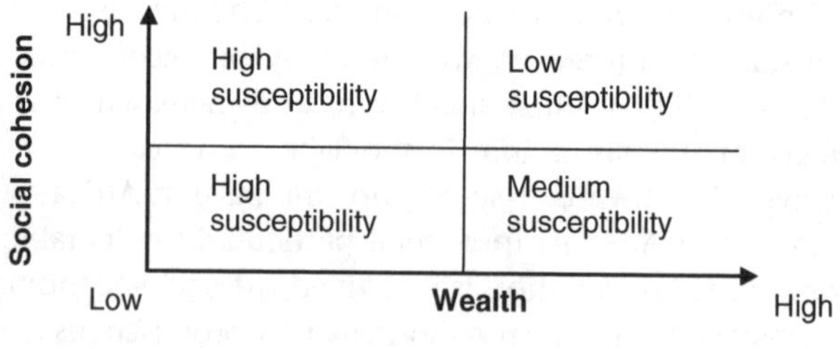

Figure 1.1 The Jaipur Paradigm[24]

spread the virus in those home communities. Decosas demonstrates that the profile of HIV infection in West and Southern Africa is directly related to the regional pattern of labour migration:

> Widening the focus to the entire continent reveals a crescent-shaped distribution of high HIV prevalence extending from Namibia in the south-west along the east coast to Kenya, then via Southern Sudan into the Central African Republic. As in the West African region, the southern horn of this crescent coincides with a zone of intense labour migration to a single destination, South Africa. The northern horn is less clearly related to a single migration focus. Population movements above the region of the Great Lakes are more likely due to displacement caused by war.[27]

Ironically, then, HIV and AIDS have become the Frankenstein of Africans' dream for a better life: the search for greater economic security (jobs, money, housing) is one of the direct causes of the spread of the disease.[28]

HIV and AIDS, the military, war and peacekeeping

War is an instrument for the spread of HIV and AIDS. 'History has revealed time and time again that the Three Horsemen of the Apocalypse – Famine, Pestilence and War – often gallop together'.[29] With more than a dozen violent conflicts, tens of thousands of troops and guerrilla fighters in the field, and some eight million refugees and internally displaced persons, conflict has become a major factor in the spread of HIV in Africa.

UNAIDS warns that military conflict brings economic and social dislocation, including the forced movement of refugees and internally displaced persons, and resulting in a loss of livelihoods, separation of families, collapse of health services, and dramatically increased instances of rape and prostitution. This scenario creates conditions for the rapid spread of HIV and other infectious diseases.[30]

The impact of HIV on civilian populations lies in the high rates of sexual interaction between military and civilian populations whether through commercial sex or in rape as a weapon of war; and in the extreme vulnerability of displaced and refugee populations to HIV infection.

Rape and other forms of sexual violence, such as forced prostitution, are frequently used in war for a number of reasons. 'Rape is an outlet for the sexual aggression of combatants and it is related to the idea that women are war booty; it is used to spread terror and loss of morale; and it is used to undermine women's ability to sustain their communities during times of conflict.'[31]

Refugee populations – many of whom are single women and unaccompanied children – are particularly vulnerable to coerced sex or rape. In the early stages of conflict situations, when a large number of refugees are on the move, their need for food and other basic necessities can be acute. Exchanging sex for money or food may therefore be commonplace. Women, for example, are six times more likely to contract HIV in a refugee camp than the general outside population. 'Among refugee and displaced people it is common for the number of commercial sex workers to increase because women feel they have no other way to keep their families alive,' according to Christen Halle, the head of the UN Department of Peacekeeping Operations (UN DPKO).[32] Over time, established refugee camps attract prostitutes from surrounding communities to cater for the many male refugees without partners.

Young adolescents, with little to do in refugee camps, will often start to experiment with sex earlier than young people in more stable situations. Moreover, amid the chaos and deprivations of the conflict that is the cause of the mass movement of people, materials for HIV prevention such as condoms are in limited supply. Refugees are also likely to have inadequate access to basic health care services, including care for sexually transmitted diseases, thereby further increasing their risk of acquiring HIV through unprotected sex.[33]

Bad blood

The South African blood transfusion services started testing donor blood as late as 1985. The military, like students and church-going civilians, were considered excellent donor populations. The military, at their own request, stopped donating blood for 'security reasons'.[34] Be that as it may, notes Shell, a better blueprint for initiating a pandemic could not be wished for than the map of personnel living on South African military bases.[35]

Regional transport infrastructure

Shell furthermore points out that HIV is not only a camp follower of military campaigns, it also travels in style on civilian aircraft, railroads, highways, roads and spreads humbly by bicycle and on foot.[36] Ironically, Southern Africa's well-developed transport infrastructure – well utilised after the demise of apartheid and the abolition of 'influx control'; and given the stress on economic regionalism and economic integration – has become an excellent corridor for accelerating infection.

A free-riding disease

Tuberculosis and sexually transmitted diseases are endemic in Southern Africa. According to Shell, as many as half the population of sub-Saharan Africa have been exposed to TB.[37] HIV-positive people provide an open window for its opportunistic invasion. With the increasing use of antibiotics – South Africa has one of the highest usages in the world – increasingly resistant variants of TB can be expected to appear in the general population.

When these factors are coupled with the dire implications of the socio-economic indigence described in the Jaipur Paradigm, it becomes clear that HIV and AIDS in Southern Africa are the result of different levels of human insecurity; the latter creating a downward spiral or vicious circle of ensuing military and social insecurities that compound the whole problem. To paraphrase: HIV and AIDS in Africa are not merely a health problem anchored in the sexual behaviour of individuals. Rather, they are the cause and result of human *in*security – the confluence of socio-political variables on a systemic, regional level that should be viewed through a more circumspect developmental lens.

In the following section, the impact of HIV and AIDS on the security of people's public and private spaces is considered – the former referring to the sphere of socio-economic interaction (macroeconomic, governance, as well as the functions of intrastate justice), and the latter denoting the household levels of social interaction.

HIV and AIDS at the macroeconomic level

HIV and AIDS already have a huge and detrimental impact on the economy of South and Southern Africa. Both the production and the consumption levels of economies are affected, with dire implications for the willingness of foreign investors to make any long-term investments in sub-Saharan Africa. In fact, it is becoming increasingly apparent that different sectors within the broader Southern African economy will have to restructure completely to ensure self-preservation.

Economists have identified several major areas of macroeconomic vulnerability. These include effects on the labour supply and productivity, remuneration cost increases, demand changes among households, higher government expenditure, as well as instances of severe risk exposure in key sectors of the economy.

In one of the most comprehensive studies of the impact of HIV and AIDS on the macro-economy of South Africa, Quattek found that '[t]he infection rate among the economically active population peaks at about 25.5 per cent by 2006, well above the 16.7 per cent peak for the total population'.[38] Not only will HIV and AIDS affect the day-to-day quality of life of HIV-positive individuals and their families, the disease will also remove them from their places of work while they are ill, leading to increased absenteeism also among spouses. Where spouses have already died, children will have to be taken out of school to look after sick adults/parents. Household spending power will decrease, labour productivity will suffer, the corporate memory or skills base within companies will literally die out, and the economy as a whole, the state and the private sector, will have to pick up the tab for training new workers, paying health bills, and so on, which will drain the fiscus from any capacity to expend moneys on other essential services.

Some Southern African states have already shown that they simply do not have the monetary and physical capacity to deal with the numbers of people sick with AIDS-related illnesses. The African Eye News Service report that 'AIDS patients in Swaziland are flocking to neighbouring South African clinics after being turned away from hospitals in their hometowns. At least 22 per cent of residents in the small kingdom are HIV-positive and hospitals have begun sending AIDS patients home in an attempt to reserve meagre resources for uninfected people.'[39]

An ING Barings study quantifies the sectoral impact of HIV and AIDS in South Africa as shown in Table 1.3. The latter projects that the consumer manufacturing and retail sectors will be particularly hard hit by the epidemic.

Again, it is useful to separate these figures for their illustrated effect on morbidity (by 2005) and mortality (by 2015). For example, by 2005, just less than a third of all workers in South African mines were HIV-positive; these workers are regularly absent from work, resulting in decreased productivity. Mining companies will have to provide pecuniary resources to cope with the health status in mines, individual households will have decreased income and less spending power, and extended family members will have to withdraw from the workforce in order to look after the sick. By 2015, this pivotal sector of the South African economy will be hugely affected by AIDS: almost eight mine workers will be dead or dying due to AIDS-related disease compared with one 'normal' death. And this is but a single sector of the economy.

The effect will be felt throughout the economy. Quattek projects that 'the average annual trend rate of GDP growth over the next 15 years is

Table 1.3 The sectoral impact of HIV and AIDS in South Africa[40]

Sector	**HIV + per 100 workers (2005)**	**AIDS deaths per 100 normal deaths (2015)**
Agriculture, forestry and fishing	23.2	503.9
Mining	29.3	759.2
Consumer manufacturing	23.0	867.2
Forestry products	20.2	636.6
Chemicals	21.6	632.5
Metals	19.9	658.4
Machinery	21.2	563.6
Construction	23.9	694.6
Retail	21.3	876.4
Catering and accommodation	23.0	601.9
Transport and storage	23.5	652.6
Communication	16.5	528.4
Finance and administration	12.4	479.6
Business services	15.6	788.8
Health	20.0	471.9
General government	24.5	229.1

likely to be 0.3–0.5 percentage points below the rate in a no-AIDS scenario'.[41] The savings constraint on both the macro-economic and household levels will be severe, and only the bravest or most ignorant foreign companies will want to invest in South Africa. As the chief executive officer of DaimlerChrysler South Africa stated in June 2001: 'AIDS is definitely one of the factors inhibiting foreign investments – on top of all the structural issues. When I try to persuade foreign suppliers to invest here, they ask about four things – trade unions, cost of capital, crime and AIDS.'[42]

Of course, South Africa is not the only country in sub-Saharan Africa that is experiencing such odds in its economy. According to Forsythe and Roberts the average company (in heavy industry, transportation, wood processing and the sugar industry) in Kenya was expected to incur HIV- and AIDS-related costs at an average annual loss of US$150,000 in 1992, and by 2005 the annual cost would average US$403,000 per business.[43] Health-care costs, HIV absenteeism and training alone will account for more than 60 per cent of all AIDS-related company costs in this country.

Southern Africa also has a large informal economy – conceptualised as 'businesses that were unregistered and did not have a value added tax (VAT) number'. Such enterprises (excluding a significant numbers of domestic workers) within the sector provided work for an estimated 2,705,000 South Africans in 1999.[44] In 1996, the informal sector accounted for 15 per cent of the total number of economically active South Africans.[45] Wilkins cautions that informal enterprise operators and workers tend to belong to groups (women and young people) who are at high risk of infection with HIV.[46]

Due to the structure and social determinants inherent to its operation, the informal sector is hard hit by HIV and AIDS: 'when the operator of an informal enterprise, and probably one or two other family members develop AIDS-related illnesses, can no longer work and eventually die, the enterprise will die with them'.[47] Also, due to their insular existence, it is exceedingly difficult to reach the informal sector with orthodox anti-HIV and AIDS interventions and programmes. Again, the poorest and most isolated sectors of society are at the greatest risk to be infected and affected by the disease.

HIV and AIDS and food security

In August 1999, the Zimbabwean Commercial Farmers' Union put figures reflecting the decline of the country's agricultural food output at the following: maize 60 per cent, cotton 47 per cent and vegetables 49 per cent.[48] The reason provided for this rapid decline was the loss of workers and workdays due to HIV and AIDS. In northern Uganda, millet and sorghum are left overgrown because labour goes into caring for the sick. In the east of the country, pastoralists are dying before they can transmit skills in animal husbandry. In Namibia – a country dependent on water purification plants for a consistent supply of fresh water – NamWater (the country's largest water purification company) says that HIV and AIDS is crippling its operations and the company is experiencing a loss of productive hours due to increasing absenteeism.[49]

In Malawi, it was reported that the death of the primary male in a farm household will lead to a loss of income of more than 50 per cent for such a household.[50] The UN Food and Agricultural Organisation's (FAO) Committee on World Food Security notes that in the 27 most HIV- and AIDS-affected countries in Africa, seven million agricultural workers have already died from AIDS since 1985. By 2020, 16 million more deaths are likely. The FAO provided figures reflecting labour force decreases in the ten most heavily affected countries, as reflected in Table 1.4. Note that by 2020 South Africa is projected to have lost nearly a fifth of its agricultural labour force.[51]

Table 1.4 The impact of HIV and AIDS on the agricultural labour force in the most infected African countries (projected losses in percentages)

Country	2000	2020
Namibia	3.0	26.0
Botswana	6.6	23.2
Zimbabwe	9.6	22.7
Mozambique	2.3	20.0
South Africa	3.9	19.9
Kenya	3.9	16.8
Malawi	5.8	13.8
Uganda	12.8	13.7
Tanzania	5.8	12.7
Central African Republic	6.3	12.6
Côte d'Ivoire	5.6	11.4
Cameroon	2.9	10.7

Source: FAO 2001.

At the agricultural household level, the HIV and AIDS cycle of destruction goes like this:

> A man is taken ill. While nursing him, the wife can't weed the maize and cotton fields, mulch and pare the banana trees, dry the coffee or harvest the rice. This means less food crops and less income from cash crops. Trips to town for medical treatment, hospital fees and medicines consume savings. Traditional healers are paid in livestock. The man dies. Farm tools, sometimes cattle, are sold to pay burial expenses. Mourning practices forbid farming for several days. Precious time for farm chores is lost. In the next season, unable to hire casual labour, the family plants a smaller area. Without pesticides, weeds and bugs multiply. Children leave school to weed and harvest. Again yields are lower. With little home-grown food and without cash to buy fish or meat, family nutrition and health suffer. If the mother becomes ill with AIDS, the cycle of asset and labour loss is repeated. Families withdraw into subsistence farming. Overall production of cash crops drops.[52]

Bearing in mind that the farm household is the primary production unit in large sectors of Southern African economies, the impact of HIV and AIDS on these units has to be seen within the context that these household units represent a complex system dependent on human capital and remittances. The impact of HIV and AIDS on the human security aspects of this system are manifold: the area of land under cultivation shrinks (land is often allocated by community authorities to families on the basis of their size), agricultural output declines, the crop variety decreases as cash crops are abandoned owing to the inability to maintain enough labour for both cash and subsistence crops, and livestock production declines due to medical costs (the latter often requires the sale of livestock). Shell reminds us that the cost of treating a single terminal case of AIDS with an AZT cocktail each month is equivalent to placing 19 schoolchildren in primary school for a month.[53]

Also, agricultural skills are lost – as Du Guerny points out, the oral tradition of passing on skills of the trade will die with parents – 'owing to the gender division of labour and knowledge, the surviving parent is not always able to transfer the skills of the deceased one'.[54] When parents die, older children are left to fend for their younger siblings (while caring for sick and dying adults). In addition, the FAO warns that agricultural post-production, food storage and processing are impaired.[55] Thus, the security of food and other raw materials between harvests is at risk, including the availability of seed for next year's crop. The FAO report concludes by underlining the systemic impact of HIV and AIDS on agriculture and food security: 'HIV/AIDS does not merely affect certain agriculture and rural development sub-sectoral components, leaving others unaffected. If one component of the system is affected, it is likely that others will also be affected, either directly or indirectly.'

The irony, as noted earlier, is that decreased food production and subsequent hunger might logically lead to the movement of large quantities of indigent populations – not only within their own countries, but across permeable Southern Africa borders. This will exacerbate the movement of people caused by military conflicts elsewhere, again leading to increased vulnerability to HIV infection on the continent as a whole.

Du Geurny mentions a few factors that need to be introduced at the agricultural production level to alleviate the disruptive effects of HIV and AIDS on food security:[56]

- A minimum wage or floor price for a product can guarantee a minimum income to a poor household which, in turn, would lead to migration taking place under better circumstances and conditions. For those agricultural households that already have that critical (subsistence) levels of agricultural production such a measure would, however, be too late. Also, given foreign agricultural producers' insistence on sector liberalisation in terms of World Trade Organisation

(WTO) prescriptions, one wonders whether African states would be able to afford such seemingly protectionist measures.

- The storage of crops so that sales could be better timed in relation to market changes.
- Training and the provision of survival skills are essential for orphans in order to protect them from exploitation and abuse.
- Property rights related to real estate could be adjusted to protect families who would – in terms of customary law – lose their land when the male head of that family dies. Norse echoes this sentiment:

> Governments can act to ensure security of tenure for widows who, under some traditional land tenure systems, would lose land rights upon the death of their husbands. They can strengthen farm support services to ensure that technical advice, credit and labour-substituting production inputs are available. Agricultural research programmes can be redesigned to match more closely the needs of farm families with reduced adult numbers.[57]

Adjustments need to be made that will improve the day-to-day quality of life of those who remain to work the land – women and children. 'They need stronger hoes and lighter ploughs; farming techniques that require less labour, like zero tillage; and instead of expensive pesticides, natural pest control.'[58] Furthermore, some coping strategies, like income diversification, share-cropping and labour-saving technology such as mixing crops, can be beneficial. Communities are evolving ingenious responses, such as sharing farm chores, house repairs and child care, and changing cultural practices such as expensive funerals.

Ostensibly, these options might seem viable as countermeasures for HIV and AIDS or the effects of HIV and AIDS, but the FAO points to deeply entrenched societal beliefs and practices that would render them null and void, or impossible to implement.[59] How can one even begin to address issues related to HIV and AIDS in societies where sexual behaviour is not openly discussed? How can one empower women who survive their husbands in communities with highly rigid hierarchical gender structures? Despite an increasing focus on human security issues, the stigmatisation and marginalisation of individuals with HIV and AIDS or families affected by the disease continue to hamper HIV and AIDS interventions. As recently as December 1998, Gugu Dlamini was beaten to death by her community outside Durban, South Africa when she declared her HIV status.[60] Clearly, the more private levels of human interaction, at the household, community and gender levels, need as much addressing as the human interactions in the public domain. The ideal, surely, would be to move from 'coping mechanisms' to a quality of life that is sustainable – a move to a more encompassing sense of human security.

HIV and AIDS and gender

At the 13th International HIV and AIDS Conference held in South Africa in July 2000 a rather odd sight met men in the toilet facilities: a bumper sticker was stuck above several of the urinals. It read: 'Men and boys, you hold the future in your hands.' Crude, but it served as a reminder of what the socio-sexual determinants of HIV infection in Southern Africa are. Security can be a bad thing if it refers to intellectual safety or ignorance, and what was so pertinent about the sticker was that it forced one to think outside the stereotypical gender box and consider the gender dynamics of the disease. Consider some the ways in which HIV and AIDS are a gendered variable.[61]

Rape

As mentioned above, rape is used as a weapon or tool of aggression by men against women. There are countless examples of rape as a deliberate tool violence. What makes it so applicable within the context of this study is the effect it has on the social security of communities in war-torn areas. Rape, and its use as a vector for the proactive spread of HIV and AIDS, has become a symptom of societal sickness.

Shell mentions the birth of a diabolical new profile of rapists in South Africa: 'Township residents ... term such people "Jack Rollers" which another national authority defined in a glossary as "Township youth who purposefully infect young women with HIV by raping them".[62] This is a relatively new phenomenon and the youth who do this are said to be unemployed and frustrated young men who have found out that they are HIV positive and say that they want to die with others.'

Another dangerous myth that perpetuates rape is the belief that sexual intercourse with a female virgin will cure AIDS. The result, of course, is that HIV is spread violently to this sector of the community. The practical effect is that the epidemic is likely to cause crime in more direct ways. The belief that sex with a virgin can cure HIV and AIDS appears to be widespread in Southern Africa, with 25 per cent of young South Africans not knowing that this is a myth.[63] Moreover, rapists may also be targeting young girls in the belief that being less sexually active, they are also less likely to have HIV or AIDS.[64]

A study conducted among urban South African township youth in 1996 found that for the youth the knowledge that they were infected with HIV or merely believed that they might be infected 'was accepted not only as a death sentence but also as a passport to sexual licence'.[65] That is, some youths argue that they would actively spread HIV among as many people as possible if they themselves were infected with HIV – a philosophy of 'infect one, infect all'. Young women expressed a general fear that men would respond to an HIV-positive diagnosis by raping women.[66]

A study of Tanzanian women found an association between physical violence and HIV infection. HIV-positive women were more likely to have had a physically violent partner. HIV-positive women under 30 were ten times more likely to report violence than non-infected women of the same age group. The strong, consistently positive relationship between a prior history of violence and HIV infection lends support to the theory that violence may play a role in women's risk for HIV infection.[67]

Homophobia

In Africa, homophobia is probably more entrenched than in the West. Homosexual behaviour is considered 'un-African', and homosexuals are stigmatised and socially isolated. HIV and AIDS are also considered a 'white man's disease', and homosexuality is scapegoated as the decadent force that had brought the disease to the African continent in the first place. Despite examples such as a former Zimbabwean president who was tried and convicted because of homosexual practice in that country, the myths and silences around sexuality continue.

The reality of HIV and AIDS in Africa is, however, such that – as Bujra points out – this chiefly heterosexual disease and the gender dynamics that perpetuate it can learn a lot from how HIV-positive homosexual men care for each other.[68] This shatters the image of women as the only caregivers in society and challenges orthodox and accepted notions of what 'masculinity' and 'mothering' are. A human rights culture and values are probably the only factor that can counter the perpetuation of myths, lies and silences around issues of sexuality.

Physiology

Women are physiologically at greater risk than men are of contracting HIV through heterosexual modes of transmission. O'Sullivan notes that:

> [i]n Africa the number of women infected with HIV outnumbers infected men. Twelve point two million African women are living with

> HIV and AIDS as compared to 10.1 million men ... young African women between the ages of 15 and 19 are four to six times more likely to be HIV-positive than young en of the same ages. Women are more easily infected with HIV when they have sex with a positive man than when a man has sex with a positive woman. ... Women's economic, social, sexual and cultural subordination and inequality make frighteningly material impacts on each positive women's life.[69]

Not only do familial relations facilitate the spread of the disease among the female population; stereotypical gender roles place women at greater risk of contracting it from their partners.

Gender roles and culture

In Southern Africa women are culturally disempowered to negotiate sexual intercourse with their male partners; if the latter insists on so-called 'dry sex' (which greatly compounds women's susceptibility to HIV), women have very little say in the matter. Also, women are socially subordinate – they simply do not have any say in whether protection can or should be used during intercourse,[70] access to female condoms is limited, and medical research institutions do not put any great priority on the development of 'stealth' protective measures aimed at the female market such as spermicides and microbicides.[71]

Another contributing factor is the fact that young girls are often married to much older men. This compounds these women's silence: they are materially and socially dependent on men and simply do not have the social and economic resources to claim control over their own vulnerability to the disease. As Ndiaye points out:

> [e]arly marriages place African women in a vulnerable position, as they are passively exposed to risks incurred by having many sexual partners through the behaviour of their husbands. For a man in many African cultures, it is a sign of virility to have multiple sexual partners. Thus, women are often infected by their polygamous husbands or by their partners who adopt risky sexual practices – sex with a number of women, or prostitutes, or with other men.[72]

As mentioned before, in many instances African customary law entrenches women's economic insecurity. In Zambia, for instance, widows of AIDS casualties are often victim to instances of 'property-grabbing' – the law allowing or not acting against in-laws who claim the land of the diseased family member.

Also, society's dependence on women and girls as caregivers within the household makes it impossible or very difficult for females to enter the public sphere and realm of political decision-making. In a sense, then, these traditional conceptions of mothering mean that the 'private' is not allowed to become 'public', and the result is that women remain impotent, suppressed and thus societally and economically insecure.

The examples above provide but a cursory glance at some of the facets of how HIV and AIDS is a gendered disease in Africa. The upside is, however, that it is forcing individuals – men and women – to reconsider their gender roles and to address issues that all relate to a single factor: human rights. If, in fact, feminism is a radical way of saying that women are people, then human rights and the evolution of a human rights culture would be the practical application of that dictum. For only within a human rights culture – a culture of free speech, tolerant of alternative ways of viewing gender relations and societies' rules around such relations – would there be any possibility of particularly women's susceptibility and vulnerability to the disease being addressed.

In order for this to happen, though, men will have to grow up socially; they have to take responsibility for their sexuality, sexual practices and social interaction. African males should no longer be allowed to hide behind customary practice and beliefs in order to perpetuate death. The stakes are simply too high. In saying this, the point is not that there is no room for the state to play a role – that the only way forward is through a change of heart by individuals. Such a suggestion would be wrong: as will become clear in subsequent chapters, states can structure behaviour through various incentive schemes and forms of punishment.

HIV and AIDS and good governance

The possible impact that HIV and AIDS will have on issues related to so-called 'good governance' and sustainable democracy in sub-Saharan Africa have not really been examined in any great depth. The few analyses on this topic echo the CIA's mentioned focus on the impact of AIDS on the dissolution of states. Of course, much has been written on the implications of the disease for governments' abilities to expend resources on essential services with AIDS draining the fiscus, but Willan is one of the few analysts who have attempted to address the potential of HIV and AIDS to undermine democratic governance itself.[73] She highlights a few areas that together might lead to the breakdown in democracy. HIV and AIDS, in her view, can cripple a country's attempts to establish and maintain democracy and equity because:

- The next generation of political and economic leaders is being wiped out.[74]
- Women are bearing the brunt of the disease – they are the primary caregivers and are subsequently removed from the public sphere, and thus from political participation.
- As mentioned above, a magnitude of orphans may pose a long-term threat to stability and development.
- Family structures and social society are breaking down due to their inability to cope.
- The budgetary demand on governments is projected to increase to the nth degree – cutting down on delivery in other sectors of society.
- A crucial tax base is being lost.
- This might lead to decreased respect for government, leading to social unrest as a result of non-delivery and ensuing frustration.
- Citizen support and participation in democratic governance will wane, as more people develop terminal diseases and are removed from the public sphere. This will also affect civil society's capacity to take part in public debates, translating into a loss in society's ability to build a sense of national cohesion.
- The inclination and ability to pay debts such as rates and health bills often dwindle when there is an increase in personal and family illness.

The link between HIV and AIDS and security will depend on what the government does – that is, on its policies. It might become a factor which pushes towards state-building as the bureaucracy and health services are expanded to cope with this crisis.

Although the causal link between these factors and a collapse in governance capacity and democratic social values is speculative at best, these analysts are of the opinion that the future of democracy in South and Southern Africa – infantile and already tenuous – will be adversely affected by HIV and AIDS. Willan argues that, unless HIV and AIDS are regarded by governments and civil society as more than 'mere' health and economic issues, 'democracy itself is threatened'.[75]

Goyer agrees, noting with dismay that the 'relationship between HIV/AIDS and politics is only just beginning to be examined'.[76] In addition to the factors identified by Willan, Goyer points out that the demographic impact of the disease is almost certain to change future voting patterns and political activity – but no one knows what to expect.

Of particular concern is the link between conflict and the epidemic. As noted above, AIDS and military conflict go hand-in-hand in Southern Africa, the one feeding the other. And if, according to Goyer, the link between cross-national military violence and HIV and AIDS is already easy to prove and quantify, why should the disease not have a detrimental impact on security and issues related to governance within states?[77] After all, the disease can well be personified as an abusive husband, as an invading military force: it penetrates societies and kills off the economically viable sectors of society.

A US National Intelligence Council report concludes that there is an undeniable link between infectious disease epidemics (in particular HIV and AIDS) and security.[78] The report found that:

- The impact of HIV and AIDS is likely to aggravate and even provoke social fragmentation and political polarisation in the hardest hit countries in the developing world.
- The relationship between disease and political instability is indirect but real. Infant mortality (likely to double at least in a number of Southern African states because of HIV and AIDS by 2010) correlates strongly with political instability, particularly in countries that have achieved a measure of democratisation.
- The severe social and economic impact of HIV and AIDS, and the infiltration of the epidemic into the ruling political and military élite and middle classes of developing countries are likely to intensify the struggle for political power to control scarce state resources. This will hamper the development of a civil society and other underpinnings of democracy, and will increase pressure on democratic transitions in sub-Saharan Africa.

Income inequality

The economic impact of AIDS after one adult death is greater in poor households than in rich ones, according to a World Bank research report, because households that experience an adult death draw on their assets to cushion the shock of the epidemic. It follows that households with fewer assets can be expected to have more difficulty in coping with the death than households with more assets.[79]

Moreover, while the prevalence of HIV is widespread among all sectors of the population in developing countries, more educated people with higher incomes are in a better position to learn about the epidemic and alter their behaviour to avoid infection. Consequently, even in developing countries, AIDS is taking on the pattern of other infectious diseases in that the poor are more likely to become infected: '[u]ltimately AIDS may become most prevalent in the poorest urban slums of developing countries'.[80]

One of the consequences of the epidemic in high prevalence countries is not only that societies will end up poorer than they would have been without AIDS, but income inequalities are likely to widen. Generally, the poor in Africa are more prone to HIV infection and are least likely to cope with the financial implications of the disease. As a result, the gap between the poor and non-poor is likely to get bigger in many African countries in the next 10–20 years.

The widening gap between the very poor and the rest in society is likely to contribute to rising crime rates in a number of African countries. It is the level of inequality, or the relative deprivation of a group or community in a society, that is an important risk factor for crime frequency. According to the British criminologist Jock Young, widening inequalities of income engenders 'chronic relative deprivation amongst the poor which gives rise to crime and a precarious anxiety among the better off which breeds intolerance and punitiveness towards the law-breaker'.[81] It is no coincidence that South Africa and Brazil – two societies with extremely high income disparities – have extraordinary high levels of property and violent crime.

Conclusion

People are dying. Economies are under threat. The enemy is attacking not only the elite in society, but also the children, the elderly and the infirm. Using the urge at the core of what makes people human – the will to reproduce – it has already infiltrated schools, houses, mines, governments and churches. The threat to Southern Africa's human security is such that those who are not infected, dying and dead are certainly equally affected by the disease. This state of affairs is partly the result of the historical legacy of poverty, creating a confluence of time and space that makes this continent the Armageddon of HIV and AIDS. And the continent is losing its war against AIDS. Yet, denial remains the most prevalent attitude. Academics ignore the issue (for instance, not a single article on the public policy implications of HIV and AIDS was published in South African Political Science journals prior to the early 1990s – since then, these publications have been few and far between), and governments ponder the causal link between HIV and AIDS while the latter is already affecting food security, livelihoods, the sense of community.

What will be the social effects of the missing generation of young adults unable to raise their children? How will intra-African peacekeeping operations be affected by the epidemic that disproportionately affects military personnel? What impact will the virus have on the functioning of state departments in already poorly performing criminal justice systems in sub-Saharan Africa? How will the 30–40 per cent of the adult population who are HIV-positive and dying react when their government decides to spend limited state resources on policing, education or housing instead of building more hospitals and care centres for those infected by the virus?

The sluggish response of African political scientists to this issue until now is an indictment of the academic community – of its 'intellectual *in*security' in dealing with this issue. As Marais notes:

> the debate over [the social determinants and effects of HIV and AIDS] has been lively, but so often imbued with either racism or academic political correctness that the reality of the situation is so often misconstrued and invalidated ... These kinds of epistemological complications render all the more difficult efforts to mount an effective response that answers to the demands of inclusivity, empowerment and 'ownership'.[82]

This chapter is an attempt to provide some qualitative and quantitative insight into the HIV and AIDS problematique – not only in South Africa, but in the region as a whole. Clearly, HIV incidence and prevalence levels are obscenely high, and the nature of how central governments, local authorities and households are and will be affected is only slowly becoming clear.

The question posed in the rest of the book is threefold: first, within the South African context, how have government administrations responded to HIV and AIDS; second, what were and are the gaps in their public policy response to the disease; and third, how should the current government proceed in formulating an appropriate public policy response *vis-à-vis* HIV and AIDS? The conceptual tools developed in the preceding chapter will now be applied to find answers to these questions. In chapters 2–4 the National Party (NP) governments under Presidents P. W. Botha and F. W. de Klerk is the main focus; chapter 5 applies the conceptual public policy models to the Mandela government; and chapter 6 evaluates the first Mbeki administration's strategy regarding HIV and AIDS.

2
The HIV and AIDS Policy Environment in Apartheid South Africa (1982–1994)

Officialdom can never cope with something really catastrophic.
Albert Camus, *The Plague*

Introduction

The focus of this and the following two chapters is the NP government's response to HIV and AIDS. This chapter covers the broad public policy environment in which HIV and AIDS first appeared in South Africa; chapter 3 discusses the biomedical and workplace responses to the nascent epidemic; and chapter 4 concludes the focus on the NP years by setting out the legal and public sector responses.

The first purpose of this chapter is to examine the context of the early years of HIV prevalence in South Africa. This will highlight the societal context of the country in 1982, the year the first two cases of AIDS were reported. The response of the South African government in those days is an essential determinant for how the epidemic would be seen in the years to come. It is thus important to describe the policy environment within which the government was operating, the variables that impacted on possible policy responses, and the normative drivers or vectors of these interventions.

This implies two main areas of focus: a description of how the South African socio-political environment in the early 1980s provided a perversely ideal breeding ground for the rapid spread of HIV infection; and the initial response that set the tone for how the South African government and other key public policy actors would come to view AIDS as a problem, and then respond to such a conceptualisation. Ironically, the context of the initial response exemplified exactly the kind of problems that drove the early epidemic even deeper underground, supporting governmental inaction or misdirected interventions that exacerbated the spread of HIV in South Africa.

Apartheid South Africa: an environment of risk

Apartheid South Africa provided a rich societal Petri dish in which HIV and AIDS could flourish. The epidemics of the past (e.g. Spanish influenza immediately after the First World War) and the present (e.g. SARS in 2003) demonstrate that major epidemics do not crop up by chance. Instead, they tend to occur when circumstances offer a favourable breeding ground to pathogens. As is the case with individuals, a population's immunity to societal ills can be weakened by several co-factors, and South Africa in 1982 was a society most vulnerable to HIV.

This confirms Louis Pasteur's notion that '[t]he microbe is nothing; the terrain everything'.[1] The 'terrain', it is important to note, refers as much to biological factors as it does to non-biological ones, and hence the socio-political context of South Africa in the early 1980s is a significant determinant of the spread of the epidemic. Despite this, Fransen notes that little empirical evidence has been collected about the levels of societal determinants of behaviour and the effectiveness of various policies to bring about behavioural change and reduction of HIV transmission or acquisition: 'Even less is known about such policies from the economic point of view (cost-effectiveness). Among researchers, only a few have tried to start the study of factors underlying risky behaviour and HIV status at population level.'[2]

Since, in Fransen's opinion, this hinders the search for new and potentially effective prevention programmes and policies, the lack of quantitative material would clearly lead to the impotence of pundits of rational choice theory even to start an attempt at drafting a response to HIV and AIDS.[3] The unfortunate fact is that such a lack of data and other supporting information was a feature not only of the 1980s; a lack of epidemiological data and information about behavioural matters continues to be a negative factor in South Africa's policy response to HIV and AIDS to this day.

In 1982 South Africa was governed by a political party bent on racial separation and discrimination. Society was defined by an unequal distribution of resources, widespread poverty, the profligate duplication of civil services, international isolation and regional military insurgencies, the absence of democracy and effective/good governance, domestic political instability and gender inequality. At the time there was widespread ignorance about HIV and AIDS – and given the fact that it was a newly identified pathogen with very few victims, the reality was that policy actors had very little incentive to mobilise public resources to counter its impact. Furthermore, a complex set of cultural factors was playing a catalytic role in the environment within which AIDS was introduced. The social cohesion that is needed to combat HIV and AIDS was absent – and, some would say, continues to be absent to this day.

Instead, there were traditional social practices that fostered infection, a decaying social fabric, great female vulnerability and an economic production system that relied on migratory labour (rural–urban, but regionally as well). All these factors created an environment of risk for the people of South Africa, and this risk was compounded by the fact that although AIDS was first recognised as a syndrome in 1981 and HIV as its cause in 1984, a systematic national and international response to the epidemic did not start to take shape until 1986–7. According to Dorrington and Johnson, this environment of risk was of such a magnitude that 'on any scale of high-risk situations South Africa in the 1980s ranked near the top'.[4]

Some of the key factors that compounded apartheid society's AIDS risk profile are reviewed below.

Risk profile

Biomedical factors

In terms of shaping a response to an epidemic, it is essential to know what kind of epidemic is emerging. Epidemiologically, two strains of HIV emerged in South Africa in the 1980s: the HIV-1 clade remains the dominant strain in the country today, but it has two sub-variants which reflect the kind of society in which it spread in those early days. It thus brings to the fore two kinds of epidemic to which the medical authorities and the government should have responded. Clade B predominated among gay men (the first two AIDS deaths in 1982 were the result of this variety), while clade C has become associated with heterosexual and perinatal transmission. In Karim's view, this suggests the emergence in the 1980s of 'two independent HIV epidemics unfolding in South Africa' – an earlier variety through homosexual transmission, and a heterosexually transmitted variety a few years later.[5] Injecting drug use (IDU) has never been a significant mode of infection in South Africa.

HIV is a 'free-riding' infection, which targets individuals whose immune systems are already compromised by other diseases. In South Africa in the 1980s (as today), tuberculosis (TB) and sexually transmitted diseases (STDs) are rife, particularly among the poor in the community. Almost half of the entire black population has had TB at some stage of their lives, which leaves these individuals immunocompromised for life.[6] Furthermore, high levels of STDs go untreated, for a number of reasons: many STDs are asymptomatic, individuals will often not seek treatment, treatment is ineffective, and sanitation and adequate nutrition are absent.[7] Couple these factors with a political-economic system which did not favour primary health care and rural medication, and the context for vulnerability is clear.

Economic factors

Income is one of the most significant factors correlated with HIV prevalence. The poor – due to an inadequate diet, the need to travel long distances to work, and so on – are most affected by the epidemic. Also, many do not have access to proper treatment for STDs or cannot afford treatment. As Dorrington and Johnson note:

> Of HIV and AIDS admissions to Somerset and Groote Schuur Hospitals between 1988 and 1993, only 48 per cent of heterosexual males had ever been employed, and of those who had been employed, 74 per cent had been employed in unskilled or semi-skilled labour.[8]

Terreblanche notes that black South Africans are particularly vulnerable to HIV because of the legacy of apartheid and the unequal distribution of health and other resources in the 1980s and earlier: this historical framework of systemic exploitation led to a system where 'comprehensive, co-ordinated and effective policies for alleviating poverty and preventing AIDS are not implemented, poor health and [hence] AIDS will remain an important – and ominous – poverty trap leading to the further pauperisation of especially the poorer half of the population'.[9] This reflects the incremental impact of bad policies in the 1980s, echoing what incremental public policy theory might say on the matter.

Ironically, the AIDS epidemic did not escalate in South Africa until the 1990s – it was one of the last countries in Africa to be affected. However, the legacy of apartheid and its ultimate contribution to the cycle of poverty, together with an industrial economic base which promoted migrant labour and exploitation did, in Evian's words, 'ensure that South Africa [would] be no exception and [would] surely face a massive and devastating AIDS epidemic'.[10]

Sexual behaviour factors

South Africa in the 1980s was an exceedingly patriarchal society, and women's disempowerment finds its most severe application in sexual relations. Rape (including marital rape) is endemic, and cultural factors ensure that women have very little say in their sex lives. The inequality between the sexes is one of the key factors underlying the risk factors in society – and South African society is no exception to the rule. Under apartheid even white women did not have equal rights with men – female school teachers and other public sector workers, for example, received lower salaries than their male counterparts. Black women were the most legally disenfranchised sector of South Africa society. Married women were seen as the legal minors of their husbands.

These factors led to a situation where women were not only underrepresented in public life, but were for the most part also powerless in the private domain of their homes. Skewed power relations related to sexual behaviour were not questioned, allowing them to continue unabated. In addition, both homosexual relations and commercial sex work were criminalised in apartheid South Africa, so that homosexuals had no moral or legal recourse in a society that frowned on homosexual activities. Commercial sex workers had (and continue to have) no legal system to call on in the event of abuse or exploitation. These individuals were thus also excluded from an embracing health system.

Compounding these factors, in many instances African customary law entrenches women's economic insecurity. In Zambia, for instance, widows of AIDS casualties are often victim to instances of 'property-grabbing' – the law allowing or not acting against in-laws who claim the land of the diseased family member. Also, society's dependence on women and girls as caregivers within the household makes it impossible or very difficult for females to enter the public sphere and realm of political decision-making. In a sense, then, these traditional conceptions of mothering means that the 'private' is not allowed to become 'public', and the result is that women remain impotent, suppressed, and thus societally and economically excluded. As Mboi emphasises:

> [g]ender expectations/roles are crucial in determining if or how a woman may protect herself, her sexual partner(s), even her unborn child from HIV infection. Within [developing countries] widely held stereotypes about what is 'proper' and 'normal' for men and women regarding sexual feeling and expression severely limit the latitude most women have (or will exercise) for action in the micro-settings where sexual divisions are made. In general 'knowledge', 'pleasure', 'rights' and 'initiative' belong to men, while 'innocence', 'acceptance' and 'duty' are portrayed as 'normal' for women.[11]

Migration patterns

Human migration was a key feature of apartheid South Africa. The apartheid government instituted the homeland system and thus forced black South Africans to move to parts of rural South Africa where they would not be able to find work, so that blacks were obliged to migrate to and from larger urban areas in the search for work. This gave rise to the 'hostel system' which was set up to accommodate migrant workers (who also travelled in from neighbouring countries), and burgeoning networks of commercial sex work to service these hostels. Since the apartheid law prevented workers from bringing their families to their places of work, workers were separated from them for long periods at a time, and in this environment the commercial sex industry flourished. Since commercial sex was criminalised under the NP administrations (and remains so), there were no apparent avenues open to government agencies which might wish to implement HIV and AIDS programmes for commercial sex workers. Furthermore, given their criminal status, sex workers were loath to report their activities to the legal and health authorities, driving this vector for the spread of the epidemic underground.

To illustrate the context of migration, Dorrington and Johnson note that:

- In the decade between 1975 and 1985 alone, more than 3.5 million black South Africans were relocated to the twelve homelands.
- In 1990 more than 2.5 million migrant workers (drawn from rural areas and neighbouring countries) were working in mines, factories and farms.
- In 1989 roughly 40 per cent of the workforce of the Chamber of Mines consisted of migrant workers from outside South Africa.
- In 1995 90 per cent of all black employees in the gold mining industry were migrants, and 89 per cent of those workers were accommodated in single-sex hostels.[12]

As these migrant workers moved back to their homes, they provided an excellent mode of transmission for HIV from their places of work to their families, who might otherwise have remained safe from the virus.

Political turmoil

It is a well-accepted fact that military conflict and the movement of large numbers of military personnel, refugees and even peace-keepers can increase the spread of HIV. South Africa in the 1980s was embroiled in a near-civil war which led to exactly the kind of social dislocation and turmoil that provides an environment for the spread of the disease. The apartheid government followed a strategy of destabilising the region, fuelling civil wars in Angola and Mozambique, and launched military attacks on many neighbouring countries.[13] The African National Congress (ANC) and Pan-African Congress (PAC) set up military bases and other kinds of political presences in these countries, adding to the number of military personnel in particular that were present in those countries.

Inside South Africa, the province of Natal in particular was afflicted by violence and political conflict between ANC and Inkatha Freedom Party (IFP) supporters. Even in the years immediately preceding the first democratic elections in April 1994, South Africa was in the unenviable situation of being 'the only country in the world which had to contend with an exponential rise in HIV prevalence rates in the context of major political transition'.[14] As Dorrington and Johnson note, all of this 'led to a collapse of social cohesion and a disintegration of parental authority, and is a significant factor contributing to the higher levels of HIV prevalence'.[15]

These five factors led Dorrington and Johnson to conclude:

> [t]hat South Africa has experienced such a rapid spread of the HIV and AIDS epidemic should not have come as a surprise to anyone familiar with the conditions in this country prior to 1994. Apartheid left the country with all the ingredients to ensure that it would have the most explosive and extensive epidemic in the world. This, coupled with the mismanagement of the epidemic at virtually every turn, has meant that the country is now facing a disaster which it barely comprehends.[16]

Clearly, apartheid was responsible for much of the structure which determined the patterns of behaviour that led to the rapid dissemination of HIV in South Africa. These patterns in turn precipitated many of the events that journalists reported on in the sensationalist first months and years of the South Africa AIDS epidemic. Summarising the three main apartheid structures that underpin South African AIDS to this day, Fassin refers to *social inequalities*, *gender violence* and *migrations*.[17]

Ostensibly uncomplicated, this is an important point, since it defines the three-headed monster that needed to be addressed and remains to be addressed in combating HIV and AIDS. Government policies regarding the epidemic should, in an ideal world, have focused on addressing these. In shying away (as will become clear in subsequent chapters), the apartheid government's definition of the HIV and AIDS problem became increasingly erroneous. The country is paying the price to this day.

Apartheid – in the extent to which and the duration for which it was allowed to continue – made South African AIDS unique and exemplary.[18] It made the country *unique* in terms of its epidemiological as well as its political specificity – how the socio-political context wrought by apartheid led to the spread of the virus in this country and how the political system underscored the inequities creating the social conditions for its spread. On the other hand, apartheid made South Africa *exemplary* in terms of bringing to light the key variables that drive the disease at the global level: the importance of historical precedents and the social characteristics of ostensibly 'medical' issues. Public policymakers thus have much to learn from how the epidemic started and has been disseminated in this country, since 'South Africa is a society where history has seen the development of high levels of legally entrenched susceptibility [to HIV and AIDS]'.[19]

The normative environment

In addition to the factors describing the high AIDS risk landscape of South Africa in 1982, one also has to take into account the importance of the normative discourses of the time. Given the socio-political pressures present in the early 1980s, it is clear that there were contending ideological discourses, particularly with reference to the governmental regime type required for the future. The political culture in most countries can be classed as individualistic, moralistic or traditionalist[20] – and the normative response of the political culture in 1982 was an important co-factor in describing the AIDS risk environment.

The normative environment is as important as the five factors noted above, since it provides insight into the values permeating South African society at the time. These values are important in determining what centres of authority would be legitimised by ideological and moral constituencies. These contending constituencies become important, pluralist theorists would say, in determining the policies that governments will support, how they will define policy problems, which issues will make it onto the policy agenda, and so on. As Jochelson notes:

> [r]ather than examining disease in a political context as a set of pathogens, or victimizing individuals for 'deviant' behaviour, what is needed is an appreciation of social and historical processes which have shaped unsafe sexual behavioural patterns of today. A political

> economy approach to disease considers the relation of ecological, political and social aspects of disease to the economic transformations wrought by colonialism and capitalism in Africa.[21]

As will become clear, the (often contradictory) values in a society are also essential in determining impressions of where the structural causes of a problem lie, and in doing so, the normative 'blame game' commences. If something – an act or an individual – can be blamed (with moral backing), it becomes an easy target for the building of a mythology of exclusion, moral censure, legal targeting and victimisation. The following sections look at some indicators of the moral-normative environment which, coupled with the factors noted above, provided the socio-political normative context in which the apartheid government was set to respond to the AIDS issue in the early 1980s. This section reviews the context by focusing on the popular culture of the time, as reflected in media reports regarding AIDS in the 1980s, religious and moralistic communities, and traditional societies.

Media reporting and popular culture

As early as 1986 some commentators were noting how the media were exploiting the unfolding AIDS story in South Africa by focusing on its sensationalist value. Here, in a morally conservative society, was a story including aspects related to 'sex, promiscuity, death, blood and the possibility of an uncontrolled pandemic' that would sell newspapers, in the absence of any prominent societal insistence on factual accuracy.[22] The result, in Grundlingh's mind, was 'mythmaking ... a revival and affirmation of prejudices and a new emphasis on conservative morality'.[23] And no story about disaster and victims would have been complete without the allocation of culpability: this was the time of morally-based blame dressed up as scientific reporting, providing public bodies with a good opportunity to latch on to this discourse and act (or refuse to act) accordingly. This was also the time when the AIDS issue would become problematised – in other words, society and the media would conceptualise where the real problem with HIV and AIDS lay, personalise the problem and attack those deemed responsible, instead of targeting the virus itself and the underlying causes of its transmission.

Strasheim was the first media analyst to identify how the social construction of 'news' regarding HIV and AIDS would focus on the apportioning of blame; how the conceptualisation of the problem would be personalised in specific groups of individuals.[24] Homosexuals, black people, commercial sex workers and intravenous drug users became the perpetrators blamed for introducing the virus into society. Homosexuals bore the brunt of society's scorn, and politicians were quick to equate the problems posed by the virus with these individuals who, because of their 'deviancy', were endangering society. In 1985 a prominent member of an opposition political party stated in a newspaper that AIDS was God's punishment for homosexuals' unnatural acts, and such divine retribution was soon projected as just punishment for the immoral acts of intravenous drug users and commercial sex workers as well.[25]

The initial, facile response was thus for the government to support popular notions that the AIDS problem in South Africa was a God-given solution to these outcasts' deviant behaviour, a just punishment that would remove these moral blights from South African society. This meant that government did not have to look towards the impact that their own apartheid policies was having in preparing the ground for further HIV infections in South Africa – they had their scapegoats and government's moral position was underscored by quotes from scripture that enforced the NP government's criminalisation of homosexuality, recreational drug use and commercial sex work. In addition, since the first two South African AIDS fatalities were gay white men, the black community reacted by supporting this moral position: AIDS was seen as a 'predominantly "white" problem'.[26] AIDS thus became associated with 'the Other'; someone else was always to blame and stigmatised – 'blaming other people for a problem as a substitute for tackling the problem itself'.[27] The government was as guilty of this as any other sector of South African society.

Media reports focused on areas where the culpable homosexuals could affect 'normal' South Africa – on 24 February 1985 the *Sunday Times* ran a front-page banner warning of the insidious 'Gay blood peril' in South African blood banks. Strasheim notes how the media, church groups and government ministers acted together to reinforce the association of homosexuals and AIDS: in the same edition of the *Sunday Times* the Minister of Health called on homosexuals not to donate blood; at the same time, calls to make AIDS a notifiable disease started to appear in the popular media.[28] All of this led to a situation where so-called 'social problem groups' felt more marginal, became increasingly victimised, and hid their presence and actions from the rest of society even more. Instead of revealing the societal issues that established apartheid South Africa as a fertile breeding ground for viral transmission, government rhetoric in the media served to stigmatise and isolate those deemed morally and physically guilty of endangering broader society.

This kind of sensationalist reporting and stigmatisation of gays in particular was underwritten by a horrible double standard – the South African media were happy to print bigoted moral views, but professed squeamishness about communicating life-saving strategies to the broader public. As late as 1993 Van Niftrik noted the following about the state of South African AIDS reporting:

> [t]he [government-owned and controlled] national radio and television network is obdurate in its refusal to transmit meaningful AIDS awareness messages. It contents itself with paying lip service to the killer disease by flighting [*sic*: floating?] such watered-down messages as to be obscure to all but the most intelligent – who know all about HIV and AIDS anyway. All but one radio station will not even consider condom ads, and television will only allow material which is so veiled in euphemism that it might as well be promoting a glass of warm milk to ensure a good night's rest.[29]

Ironically, even if the state-run media were willing to report accurately and constructively on HIV and AIDS, its transmission and other factors, the legislative environment governing such publications proved to be a hurdle: the Publications Act was aimed at halting the dissemination of pornographic and politically contentious material, and in doing so it also mired the distribution of information regarding the sexually transmittable nature of HIV.[30]

This leads Strasheim to conclude that 'the AIDS threat [in the mid-1980s was] symbolic – the hysteria [was] over what it [had] been built up to be, not what it [was]. The resultant social reaction to the AIDS moral panic ... made the media reporting of AIDS part of the problem, instead of part of the solution.'[31]

Religious-moralistic responses

The moralistic and sensationalist stance of the media was for the most part supported by the white, Afrikaner churches. Dutch Reformed Church ministers stated on television and from the pulpits that AIDS was God's way of punishing sinful lives, and warned that homosexuals and commercial sex workers should abandon lifestyles that ran counter to God's commandment. In a conservative society, such a response is fairly predictable, and as more became known about the manner in which the virus could be transmitted, a religious mythology was developed to strengthen the church's position. For instance, when it became apparent that unborn children could catch the virus from their mothers, or that individuals could be exposed to HIV via blood transfusions, these individuals and babies were referred to as 'innocent victims':

> This term implies that they deserve our sympathy and some societal acceptance. Conversely, it implies that those who contracted it sexually are guilty and that whether or not they knew of the risk of HIV infection when they were infected, they deserve some social censure. Clearly, double morality was practised here.[32]

Thus in the early days of AIDS it became morally acceptable in the Afrikaner churches to blame the victim – particularly if he/she, due to an unacceptable lifestyle, was 'responsible' for his/her own infection. The virus was not the problem; the victims were. Grundlingh notes that this led to a situation where such a logic could absolve 'the state or social institutions from responsibility for creating social conditions in which AIDS flourished'.[33] The Director-General of National Health and Population Development stated as late as 1989 that 'Transmission of HIV is mainly by promiscuous sexual contact, and it is therefore a social and behavioural problem in the community'.[34]

Instead of examining the specific societal variables that enabled the spread of HIV and some governmental introspection about policies that could entrench it, the government, its agents as well as its church perpetuated the moral mythologies of blame and stigmatisation. Even when, by the late 1980s, it became clear that AIDS was becoming a predominantly heterosexual phenomenon, the NP government and church preferred to exculpate themselves and their own (white) constituents by stigmatising promiscuity among the black population: 'The association of black people with dirt, disease, ignorance and an animal-like sexual promiscuity made it almost inevitable that black people would be associated with AIDS' origin and transmission.'[35]

However, there was a difference between the Afrikaner churches and others. In some instances non-Afrikaner South African church groups realised early on that AIDS would challenge them to re-evaluate scripture and morality regarding sex and sexuality.[36] If AIDS were to be addressed at the structural level – the level underpinning patterns of human behaviour as well as the events reported on by the media – it would be necessary for the churches to review their stance on issues such as same-sex relations, the use of contraceptives (for the Catholic Church in particular, the use of condoms remains anathema), abortion, care for the terminally ill and the criminalisation of commercial sex work.[37]

Condemnation from the pulpit served to stigmatise large sections of South African society, driving risky sexual behaviour underground rather than exposing it and discussing it in a solution-oriented rather than a problem-oriented way. But such a shift would be difficult, and it was only in the late 1980s that theology journals started to address AIDS issues more openly. Calling for Christian non-judgement of and care and compassion for people with HIV and AIDS, Louw, for instance, noted:

> [b]ecause of [the] connection between AIDS and ethics, counselling the person with AIDS is much more complicated than with any other disease. Discrimination and persecution in the light of strong ethical issues make the person with AIDS a vulnerable and most tragic figure. For the most part AIDS patients are stigmatized by society and church.[38]

Clearly, not all churches were as judgemental as the Dutch Reformed and other Afrikaner church groups. In September 1986 the Executive Committee of the World Council of Churches (WCC) sent a message to its communities around the world, for the first time singling out a specific medical condition and calling on the churches to respond to the AIDS crisis with pastoral care, education for prevention and social ministry. The message cautioned against notions of discrimination, stigmatisation, exclusion and righteous blame. In particular, it cautioned against the view that, in focusing on the ethics of prevention, churches should absolve themselves from caring for AIDS patients. In an effort to get away from the notion that treatment undermines so-called 'just punishment' from God, the WCC called for compassion, thus attempting to strike a balance between condemning sinful acts and caring for the infected.

The Anglican Church noted in a 1987 newsletter that '[q]uite obviously promiscuity is both morally and medically undesirable. But it is also very important that Christians should have a deep understanding and compassion for those suffering from AIDS who often endure a great feeling of rejection and isolation.'[39] Unfortunately, the church supporting the apartheid government of the day found it impossible to draw a similar distinction between sinful sexual behaviour on the one hand and the sinner on the other, opting instead to make the victim a perpetrator.

Whereas the Afrikaner churches and the NP government seemed bent on focusing on preaching preventative morality, the other Christian churches started to make a move towards examining the post-infection implications of AIDS. This was an important lesson that the government of the time failed to heed: instead of looking at the implications of HIV infections and making policies to ameliorate their impact early on, the

NP government elected to maintain its focus on moral messages aimed at preventing infections. As the infected individual was, in the opinion of the government, responsible for his/her HIV status, the government felt morally supported in its position to condemn, blame and stigmatise those already infected, and not care for them.

Traditional societies

In addition to the media and religious community response to AIDS in the 1980s, the black section of South African society for the most part reacted in a way that ran counter to what would later be identified as the optimal manner to combat a nascent epidemic. It has been noted that the black community initially saw AIDS as a white problem, affecting the gay community in particular. Since same-sex sexual relations were portrayed as counter to the traditional culture of the black community,[40] the ground was prepared for further obfuscation and mythmaking within this community – denying that AIDS would be a problem in 'traditional' societies which distrusted white remedies and a biomedical response due to the discriminatory apartheid policies of the time. In fact, early attempts by sectors of the medical and civil society communities to inform traditional communities of the dangers posed by HIV and AIDS were viewed as an 'Afrikaner Invention to Discourage Sex'[41] – the AIDS acronym itself becoming the victim of myth, denial and stigmatisation.

In addition to the socio-political reasons explaining why AIDS posed such a danger to the black South African community, there are cultural factors that especially raised black South Africans' AIDS risk profile. In the first place, biomedical response strategies have focused on individual rationality and the rights and privileges of the individual in determining his/her own sex life. However, in traditional African societies:[42]

- The emphasis is more on collective rights than on the rights of the individual.
- Women traditionally do not have the power to negotiate sex with their husbands: it is also the function of the husband to give consent for the wife to be examined by a medical doctor.
- Some analysts would say that the concept of 'fidelity' in a society that tolerates polygamy is contentious. If someone has 20 or 40 wives, the risk for HIV transmission in a community rises exponentially. In a society where there is partnering outside marriage polygamy is not the answer; in such a case it increases the risk. Viljoen notes that 'a man's wealth was measured by the amount of cattle and wives that he had'.[43]

- Condoms are viewed with distrust, since they negate the man's 'right' to pleasure and fertility (particularly in a society where the number of children is an indication of one's wealth), and an infertile wife is viewed as a social outcast.
- Women have little right to counter their husbands' insistence on high-risk 'dry sex', which increases their vulnerability to HIV infection.

These factors serve to underscore the fact that in Africa as elsewhere people are not logical (in terms of the conventional, western conception) and do not necessarily behave in the rational manner that the biomedical response model presupposes: 'You can create general awareness and knowledge about AIDS and its mortality, but that does not necessarily change people's behaviour.'[44]

In addition, it is common in many traditional cultures (as is the case in Afrikaner culture) to establish a link between cause and effect, and then to find a way of punishing a guilty party.[45] In many instances, the victim of a disease would see such an ailment as '*Isidiso*', or 'black poison'[46] – witchcraft is blamed, and the patient seeks the help of a traditional healer instead of consulting a medical doctor. (This is particularly the case in rural areas, where biomedical resources during apartheid were and to this day remain hard to come by.) Zazayokwe notes that such an environment makes it difficult to implement effective educational programmes and other strategies to combat AIDS, since it is 'the tendency of people to blame AIDS on others', and sometimes on metaphysical or supernatural forces (much in the way the Dutch Reformed Church dealt with the issue).[47] Tragically, traditional healers sometimes rely on skin-piercing practices to cleanse the body of ailments, which provide another avenue for the transmission of HIV.

Conclusion

This chapter has demonstrated how South Africa in the 1980s provided an environment of high risk for the spread of the AIDS. Due to apartheid policies the population was politically and economically vulnerable to the intrusion of a sexually transmittable pathogen. To make matters worse, the normative environment underscored the denial, stigmatisation and discrimination required to render an effective response early on almost impossible.

We now turn to describe the response of the South African biomedical community in those early days.

3
Biomedical and Workplace Responses in Apartheid South Africa (1982–1994)

Introduction

Building on the preceding discussion, this chapter provides an overview of how during the NP government AIDS came to be viewed as a behavioural issue that could be tackled only by medical means – government left it to the medical community to respond, the state itself maintaining its distance with moralistic rhetoric that went a long way in entrenching racist and homophobic notions regarding HIV and AIDS. The rhetoric of blame and a focus on 'the Other' became increasingly apparent, and acceptable.

As the medical community responded (and the government failed to address the issues underpinning the epidemic's spread), it soon became necessary for other sectors of society to take action. The private sector started to draw up its own policies to prevent the impact of AIDS – focusing on prevention strategies and other AIDS policy interventions in the workplace. Civil society too started to find its voice – in some instances countering the moralistic discourse of blame stemming from the government, but in other cases reinforcing and building on such unhelpful rhetoric.

As the epidemic achieved a firmer foothold among heterosexuals towards the late 1980s and early 1990s, the HIV and AIDS policy environment started to experience a major shift. In the absence of clear government policies, the courts were swamped by the imperative to respond – case law in particular was used in an attempt to plug legal holes. At first such responses were ad hoc and reactive, but around the turn of the decade a human rights discourse started to emerge. Driven by the medical community, members of civil society and the private sector's responses to the epidemic, and bolstered by the context of fundamental political change, this new legal/human rights approach started to find lip-service in the kind of statements emanating from the NP government and the recently unbanned ANC, as well as the trade unions.

The biomedical response

In the risk environment described in the preceding chapter, and given the government's perpetuation of the moralistic rhetoric that obfuscated rather than exposed the systemic causes of the establishment and spread of the epidemic, the initial response of the biomedical community might have proved seminal in founding a strong response set that could shape the future AIDS policy environment. In setting out what follows, one should bear in mind that the medical community formed part of the public policy environment within which the government was operating. At the same time, the medical community was and remains an important part of the arsenal that governments have in combating HIV and AIDS. This is the sector where the technical expertise and other clinical information reside that can be used to shape a rational response to the virus.

This means not only that the biomedical community forms part of the environment that would shape the public policy response, but public medical bodies also form part of the government agencies that implement those public response sets. In terms of the public policy theories described earlier, this means that the biomedical community could prove fundamental in identifying the biomedical reasons for the presence of AIDS in South Africa, but it also shaped the broader policy environment, assisted in setting the agenda, shaping the detail of policy responses, as well as acting as an agency for those policies' implementation and evaluation.

The biomedical community, therefore, reflects what pluralists refer to as the fractured nature of power and authority in a policy-making environment, forms part of the plurality of demands on the state (as described by rational choice theory) and provides the proof required to build a response model based on biomedical premises, thus perpetuating incremental policy-making. If the state were to act in conjunction with the biomedical community, theorists adhering to statism would have a strong measure with which to explain the public sector response to the epidemic, while Marxist analysts could focus on the more insidious aspects of the financial relationship between the (biomedical) AIDS industry and its relationship with government interests, in other words the annual budget allocated to AIDS specifically.

The following section focuses on the characteristics that defined this multiplicity but also the specificity of the South African biomedical community's response(s) to AIDS in the 1980s.

Contradictory messages

The first feature of the biomedical community in the 1980s was that it mirrored the multiplicity of voices and opinions with regards to HIV and AIDS that materialised in the rest of South African society; in other words, the biomedical community was fractured in both its focus and its message. At first, many authoritative voices echoed the moralistic, reproving positions emanating from religious and traditional societies. For instance, in January 1983 the Chief Medical Health Officer of Cape Town stated that 'the disease only occurred amongst homosexuals and he believed that there were not many of those kind of people in Cape Town'.[1] By the mid-1980s the head of the South African blood transfusion service in Hillbrow, Johannesburg was still using the homophobic language of the preceding few years.

However, other members of the medical profession were attempting to counter the establishment of such an emotive discourse among medical practitioners, pointing out that the focus should be on finding clinical ways of arresting viral transmission, stating that medical personnel should desist from moralistic arguments that incriminated and vilified certain sections of the broader community. These non-moralistic members of the medical profession emphasised the severity of HIV and AIDS, focusing on the dire consequences that an AIDS epidemic would impose on all of South Africa if it were not stopped. In 1986 Andries Brink, the president of the South African Medical Research Council (SAMRC), warned that AIDS might soon spread beyond the homosexual community, and called on all South Africans and the government to be proactive and urgent in their response. In an attempt to counter the moralistic discourse of some of his colleagues, Brink noted that 'Who people are and what they do is irrelevant to the issue – all we want to do is save lives'.[2]

In finding a solution to the AIDS problem, the Medical Research Council's (MRC) newsletter emphasised the need for additional funding for primary research into the epidemiology of South African AIDS. Interestingly, such funding would target 'applied research',[3] with no calls to cross the boundary between the clinical world of epidemiological research and the particular social environment that escalated to the spread of the virus. Hence, in addition to starting out by giving contradictory messages about the disease and playing the moral 'blame game' themselves, some sectors of the biomedical community in South Africa chose to focus on the virus as a clinical entity, de-linked from the rest of the apartheid society.

In doing so, the scientific community contributed significantly in the first few years of South African AIDS in failing to bring the government to book over the social conditions that facilitated the spread of the virus. Clearly, the early response of the publicly funded medical community to AIDS was focused on the perceived needs of white South Africans – there were no clear instructions to the state on how to make policies that would secure the greater safety of the rest of the country. This would not surprise Marxist public policy analysts, who would point to this as an example of the racially inspired collusion between the NP government and its public medical bodies. Pointing out the racist nature of a 1987 Department of National Health and Population Development report related to HIV and AIDS, a medical physician at a state hospital in Natal noted:

> [t]he epidemiological conclusions reached are based on the assumption that South African AIDS is treated on a par with Western AIDS in that the virus has predominantly affected members of the white homosexual community. The report equates South Africa with Israel and Norway in the expectation of AIDS cases, thereby disregarding the black population ... There is a body of opinion that feels that AIDS may provide a solution to many of Africa's problems. This viewpoint will certainly not be hindered by documents such as the one commented upon ... The document concludes that the white homosexual-bisexual male holds the key. I must disagree. AIDS is no respecter of sexual proclivity ... [4]

These criticisms underline how powerful elements within the biomedical community did a disservice to the early battle against AIDS in South Africa by contributing to defining and responding to the epidemic – the HIV and AIDS policy problem – in racist and heterosexist terms.

Absent and insufficient data

In addition to a divisive normative environment, the biomedical community suffered from the absence of quality data about the unfolding AIDS epidemic. This meant that not only did the multivariant medical value perspective keep the medical policy goals shifting; there was also a lack of clarity about the nature and size of what would be targeted for medical as well as other policy interventions. AIDS-related mortalities first occurred in South Africa in 1982, and the virus was isolated in laboratories in the United States and France for the first time in 1984, which made anti-body tests for the pathogen possible.

This meant that by the mid-1980s governments and medical communities had the tools at their disposal to test specific population cohorts for the disease and plan accordingly in an informed and concerted manner. However, the first HIV surveys at South African antenatal clinics commenced only in 1990 – a full eight years after the epidemic first appeared in the country. None the less, as Dorrington and Johnson note, even once these measures became available, 'the government has shown a remarkable reluctance to allow independent researchers access to this data or to explain in detail the methods used to derive the national and provincial figures'.[5]

This was the case in an environment already steeped in mythmaking and blame – surely a properly informed medical community (and the government by proxy) would have been better able to draft an appropriate policy response had accurate epidemiological and demographic data for all of South Africa been available. As mentioned above, in terms of shaping a response to an epidemic, it is essential to know what kind of epidemic is emerging.

As already noted, two strains of HIV-1 were emerging in South Africa in the 1980s: clade B predominated among gay men, while clade C had become associated with heterosexual (and antenatal) transmission. In Karim's view, this suggests the emergence in the 1980s of 'two independent HIV epidemics unfolding in South Africa': an earlier variety through homosexual transmission, and a heterosexually transmitted variety a few years later.[6]

Enforcing the lack of data and thus perpetuating the myths about the virus, the South African government and its medical agencies did not place any great priority on the development of demographic models regarding the impact of the unfolding epidemic: the first quality AIDS demographic model for South Africa was developed in 1989 not by government agencies, but by Peter Doyle of Metropolitan Life (an insurance agency). This tardy response in ascertaining the true extent and nature of the epidemic's spread in South Africa led Dorrington and Johnson to conclude that the politics of demographic and epidemiological data about AIDS in South Africa is, to this day, a feature of the mismanagement of the epidemic under the NP government:

> Part of this mismanagement has been the failure to monitor properly the spread of the epidemic ... Data that is collected as part of the national antenatal seroprevalence survey is only made available at an

> aggregate level. Even then not all the data is published and researchers are expressly barred from access to the detailed data ... [W]ithout detailed data it is not only impossible to understand the nature of the antenatal survey estimates, but it is also difficult to spot and interpret behavioural changes when they do occur.[7]

The absence of data thus had a threefold negative impact. In the first instance, it enforced an environment in which divisive and emotive arguments could prevail; it established and maintained stigmatisation and discrimination. Second, it rendered pre-emptive, appropriate and scientifically supported interventions impossible. Third, the absence of reliable data made it very difficult or near-impossible to measure accurately the impact of any policy interventions. As Webb stated when enjoining the government to attain an accurate model for acquiring data about HIV and AIDS prevalence in South Africa, '[t]hese questions are fundamental to policymakers [*sic*] with the difficult task of budgeting for the immense costs of AIDS in the coming years.[8] Insight now can prevent misallocation in the future.' Unfortunately, medical practitioners and policy-makers had no, very little, incomplete or completely unreliable data to work with: informed public policy-making was impossible.

Blood transfusion services

The South African blood transfusion services used the military community as one of its main sources of serum, but this arrangement came to an end in the mid-1980s – at the military's request. Tests for the HI virus became available around 1985, and in the three years between the first recorded AIDS death in the country and the commencement of the standard testing of blood donations, it has been shown that HIV was transmitted through this channel in about 100 cases.[9] The state acted to introduce the mandatory testing of blood donations due to the recent availability of scientific tests for anti-bodies to the HI virus, yet, despite hysteria in the media, the South African medical community did little to inform the public or the government of the real risks.

The delay between the first appearance of HIV in South Africa and the routine testing of blood donations could be due to the fact that as early as July 1983 the medical director of the Eastern Cape Blood Transfusion Service stated that the Service had not experienced any cases of the disease and that they were 'satisfied that blood donated from homosexuals did not constitute a threat'.[10] In the environment of AIDS myths that emerged in the early 1980s, ignorance and hysteria about AIDS were such that 'by July 1988 a poll revealed that people were still afraid to donate blood because they feared that they might be infected with HIV'.[11]

By 1988, however, the lesson had been learnt and the rhetoric of placation ceased: the *SA Journal of Continuing Medical Education* reported that steps were underway to use blood and blood products rationally, make the donor population safer, and make the product safer at blood transfusion centres. However, instead of focusing on the general risks associated with coming into contact with any blood, the *Journal* emphasised the risk of homosexuals' blood donations in particular, requesting all homosexuals, commercial sex workers and intravenous drug users never to donate blood.[12] The irony was that at this stage the South African AIDS epidemic was shifting from being a predominantly homosexually transmitted disease to being an almost exclusively heterosexually transmitted disease. Due to the lack of epidemiological data, however, the biomedical community had no way of knowing this.

It is important, though, to note that in its response to the danger of HIV transmission via blood transfusions the medical community acted first by attempting to deny the existence of the problem – by placating the general population and minimising the purported risk. However, once the danger became blatant, the blood of isolated groups in society was once again singled out for stigmatisation and censure.

Taking account of the social dimension of the problem

When, by the second half of the 1980s, the dual nature of the South African AIDS epidemic started to become clear (a white, chiefly homosexual epidemic; and a black, chiefly heterosexual epidemic), the biomedical community came to realise that the messages about AIDS that they had been devising and communicating were inappropriate for the majority of the population. This meant that the biomedical response had to interface with traditional societies; apartheid doctors had to enter into a dialogue with the black section of the population.

In February 1987 *Drum Magazine* reported on 'university-trained medicos and chanting bone throwers [putting] their heads together[; t]radition-steeped Africa [meeting] the West to discuss and hopefully find a solution to a threat many consider more frightening than a nuclear holocaust'.[13] The first seminal meeting was convened by Dr Ruben Sher, the head of virology at the SA Institute of Medical Research and a member of the government's AIDS Advisory Group. The medical community thus came to the realisation in the late 1980s that, in an effort to prevent a disaster in South Africa, it needed to adjust its purely Western model with solutions aimed at the white community and expand it to include the non-white section of society. The editor of the *SA Journal of Epidemiology* noted in 1990 that:

> [u]nfortunately current local recommendations for prevention of HIV are based on western ideals which promote the use of condoms, avoidance of so-called 'high-risk sexual activities' and the practice of monogamy – a strategy which is probably doomed to failure because the population at risk cannot identify with them.

Western medicine would go some way in addressing the South African epidemic, but these efforts needed to be combined with a greater emphasis on primary health care (PHC), which focuses on what poorer communities, with little access to biomedical interventions, could do to improve their immunity to HIV infections. For the PHC approach to be effective it would need to include community involvement and an inter-sectoral approach to health education.[14] This meant that the government had to move away from apartheid's prioritisation of the First World segment of society, and readjust AIDS programmes and budgets to supply rural and traditional societies with the appropriate medical resources.

Also, the message projected in the government's AIDS campaigns needed to become more inclusive, more reflective of the kind of society that South Africa is. By 1990 the medical community thus came to realise that they should stop sending conflicting, ambiguous messages, that traditional centres of authorities such as traditional healers needed to be included in AIDS programmes and targeting, that the system of influx control and migrant work ran counter to an effective AIDS intervention programme, and that '[c]ommunity facilitators were too intent on getting "the AIDS message" across, rather than focusing on the issues of immediate social concern to the community, i.e. sexually transmitted diseases and teenage pregnancy'.[15]

The medical community were beginning to comprehend the error in their and the government's initial response to the AIDS epidemic: their AIDS programmes were focused on providing information about how the virus is transmitted, without addressing the issue of human sexual behaviour and the context within which it takes place. The medical information response had been based on the assumption that it is merely necessary to provide people with information, and that rational behaviour would follow. But as the head of the Faculty of Medicine at the University of the Witwatersrand noted, such a strategy was doomed to fail: 'Research amongst cigarette smokers and drug addicts has shown that they are fully informed about the dangers posed by cigarettes and drugs. The problem is not a lack of information.'[16] The medical community by the early 1990s began to realise that their response model to AIDS had been based on flawed premises: Heyns summed up this criticism of the biomedical response model's definition the AIDS problem in South Africa by noting that:

> [t]he biomedical model would ... look for an explanation of AIDS in the field of virology rather than in the realm of human behaviour. In the search for solutions medical scientists would concentrate on the physical mechanisms such as the use of condoms and research would focus on immunisation as well as the development of a cure. Although extremely important, none of the above will stem the epidemic ... What is required is a fundamental knowledge of the disease which also acknowledges that social and psychological factors should be taken into account. Only a change in behavioural patterns will result in an effective slowing down and eventual halting of the disease.[17]

A policy/legal void

This gradual shift in the medical community's perception soon found an illustration in how official sectors of the medical community and personnel started to react to the disease. The first response was for the medical community to start debating the purported positive and negative aspects of making AIDS a notifiable disease. The Dental Association of South Africa appealed to all medical practitioners treating AIDS victims to urge their patients to report their medical condition to their doctors before receiving treatment.[18] In addition, in March 1988 the director of the National Institute for Virology and the MRC AIDS Virus Research Unit in Johannesburg noted that 'The inability to impose public health measures such as notification and quarantine has ... hampered control of infection'.[19]

However, there was a lack of legal precedents and policy guidelines indicating to formal medical bodies how to respond. Van Rooyen lamented that 'the only thing one can do is to await a legal test case, or for legislation to be enacted'.[20] At issue was an emerging conflict between the patient's right to privacy on the one hand, and medical practitioners' as well as society as a whole's purported right to protection from exposure to HIV infection on the other. By the end of the 1980s legal experts were publishing terms of reference in medical journals, setting out their interpretations of issues related to medical consent, the right to information, voluntary screening as well as legal guidelines for medical associations. By 1990 a professor of law at UNISA informed the medical community that 'AIDS has not yet been declared a notifiable disease under the Health Act in South Africa'.[21]

The outcome was that the medical community was left to its own devices: the government simply did not provide the policy/legal infrastructure in which this community could operate with any legal certainty. This led Spier to warn that:

> [i]f running legal battles with trade unions, political organisations and individuals are to be avoided, a treatment protocol needs to be negotiated and agreed upon with all interested parties. Such a policy will need to be realistic and fair ... Unless the industry, together with other affected parties act now, they will have to do so under much more difficult and emotionally loaded conditions later.[22]

Unfortunately, this warning for the most part remained unheeded by the government. As will be demonstrated later, the NP government left it to individual industries and professional bodies to muddle through on their own. It may be the case that the political climate in the late 1980s and early 1990s was such that the government (then just starting to cope with major political changes) was looking elsewhere, prioritising other constitutional developments. In the absence of a political culture espousing individual human rights, the social epidemiology of AIDS implied, and indeed necessitated, a cultural-legal shift that the NP government was unable or unwilling to address.

As Kustner notes, 'the common factor in all these deliberations was the attempt to find a balance between the rights of an individual on the one hand and those of the community on the other hand ... The pendulum had understandably swung far in the direction of the individual'.[23] By the time the South African AIDS problem started to reach epidemic proportions in the early 1990s, attempts to deal with AIDS-related problems revealed voids and stumbling blocks around a few focal points: public apathy, inefficiencies in the delivery of health care services and training programmes for AIDS educators and counsellors, the absence of clear legal operational guidelines for medical practitioners, a legal context based on contested values, and socially inappropriate AIDS information messages and strategies.[24] All this led Hilsenrath and Joseph to conclude that:

> [t]he fluid political conditions in South Africa are generating heightened expectations for change among blacks and fears among

> whites ... The health care community expects a transition and is bracing for substantial change ... Change is necessary to accommodate a new environment and should be directed at two fundamental objectives: (1) The improvement of access by the underserved and (2) The curbing of the rapidly escalating costs of health care.[25]

New institutions for an altered health care environment

The medical community founded a number of state-backed institutions and other formal bodies in order to formulate and implement the initial AIDS interventions described above. These interventions and institutions had a narrow focus on the virology of the HI virus, and for the most part ignored the social aspects of the epidemic.[26] Although the apartheid government's National Department of Health established a small AIDS Advisory Group (AAG) in 1985, the most prominent institutional initiative was the establishment of the MRC's AIDS Virus Research Unit (AVRU) in January 1987 – a full five years after the first reported AIDS fatality in South Africa. The AVRU was the 30th MRC unit to be erected and was sited at the Department of Health and Welfare's National Institute for Virology, and only came about after a special committee (including an overseas expert) had informed the AAG of the need for it. The mandate of the AVRU was to:

- Provide a centre for expertise for studies on the AIDS virus.
- Undertake laboratory-based research work concentrating on:
  - Developing and applying new diagnostic tests to determine the presence of AIDS antibodies and AIDS carrier status accurately,
  - Production of HIV diagnostic probes, and
  - Assisting in broad-based studies on the population prevalence of AIDS in Southern Africa, particularly amongst high risk groups, and to
- Act as a reference laboratory for other researchers.[27]

At the time, the AVRU did not envisage long-term research programmes, since 'the field of AIDS research [was] changing so rapidly that it [was] difficult to pinpoint long-term goals'.[28] This statement is significant, since it demonstrates how the official medical community equated the need for planning with actual outcomes, and also that its main goal was to establish and develop the necessary diagnostic technology for AIDS research. Only a few months into the new initiative, however, the AVRU came to realise that '[western] risk groups need to apply to all population groups in South Africa', providing the first indication of the change in perspective amongst members of the medical community.[29]

In time the MRC came to see its role as including to act 'as a mediator for all other groups involved with AIDS and AIDS research'.[30] It also became the main disseminator of information regarding HIV and AIDS: in the early 1990s the MRC launched a publication, the 'AIDS Bulletin'. The aim was to 'provide an authoritative yet accessible publication which will help to facilitate networking and fill some of the gaps in the information which is currently available'.[31] In the context of increasing criticism from civil society about the government's inaction about AIDS, even after F. W. de Klerk had assumed power in 1989, the MRC formally launched its National AIDS Research Programme (NARP) in January 1992 – a full ten years after the first reported AIDS deaths in South Africa. The NARP was one of six national research programmes in the organisation, and, it is important to note, for the first time provided for some analysis of the socio-political context of South African AIDS. Research projects undertaken by the NARP included seroprevalance studies, demographic projection studies, economic impact assessments, research into education and prevention efforts, and clinical care and counselling research.[32]

In addition to the mainly biomedical research focus of the MRC's AVRU and then later of the NARP, two structures were launched under the aegis of the medical community to combat HIV and AIDS. In the first instance, the South African Institute for Medical Research (SAIMR) established an AIDS Centre in January 1988. The main aim of the Centre was to promote AIDS education by presenting a series of one-day courses targeting different groups.[33] (As noted above, however, the central tenets of this information strategy were flawed.)

Second, after 1987 it became increasingly obvious that a shift towards a more widespread epidemic was inevitable as more became known about the epidemiology and transmission vectors of the virus.[34] The government's National Department of Health and Population Development (NDHPD), focusing on the 'need for information'[35] and channelling resources through the SAIMR, created a number of AIDS Training and Information Centres (ATICS) in the cities and larger towns in the country. It was the task of the ATICS 'to train the trainers, so to speak'.[36]

South Africa's medical community in the 1980s suffered from divisive and inappropriate normative as well as legal frameworks, with the government providing precious little by way of developing a more appropriate and enabling biomedical response model. The epidemiological modelling that came into existence in later years provided too little information, too late, and the institutional structures that were set up came late in the day and were based on erroneous assumptions that disregarded or downplayed the socio-political environment within which the medical community had to operate. For the most part the government left this community to its own devices, undermining rather than enabling this potentially seminal agent for an effective public sector response.

The workplace response

We now turn to an evaluation of the response of key sections of the South African private sector in the early days of the South African AIDS epidemic. As demonstrated in the Introduction, HIV and AIDS affect the quality of life of HIV-positive individuals as well as the people close to them. One of the effects is the impact in the workplace: increased absenteeism, low productivity and the greater risk of infection in the workplace remain some of the aspects that an affected society needs to contend with. Public policies could be applied to address such issues, including the provision of clarity on the legal rights of employers as well as employees, providing guidance to the private sector on the elements that should be borne in mind and included in the preparation of a context-specific or sectoral response, as well as a framework for the introduction of appropriate terms of reference for the insurance industry in general and medical aid in particular.

However, government's reticence in engaging with the medical community was also a feature of how the NP government dealt with AIDS and industrial relations. This meant that (as was the case with the medical community) the private sector for the most part was left to its own devices. The next chapter will discuss the more technical aspects of the legal environment at the time, revealing how the NP government attempted to legislate the AIDS problem into submission rather than dealing with it in a socio-politically circumspect manner. The current section will review the discursive environment and the early response that was evolving within the insurance industry as well as the seminal mining sector.

The medical aid and insurance industry

As the AIDS epidemic started to unfold in South Africa between 1982 and 1992, medical aid coverage was a further exemplification of the fractured nature of society. Less than a quarter of the total population had medical aid: coverage extended to 80 per cent of whites, 40 per cent of Indians, 36 per cent of coloureds and 6 per cent of blacks, and apart from restrictions in the Medical Schemes Act at the time, the trustees of the committees managing South Africa's 250 or so medical aid schemes had virtual autonomy to change their benefits and rules at any time. Taylor states that, '[a]s most of these trustees [were] company-appointed, they reflect[ed] prevailing mores of the employer'.[37] Medical schemes could thus be adjusted according to the values and priorities of those who governed them. As such, the first reaction of this sector of the broader insurance industry was to act in ignorance: between 1983 and 1988 'little knowledge existed in the medical aid industry about the nature or future of the AIDS risk ... Early reports categorised the virus as something peculiar to the white homosexual population, Africa denied it had a problem, and few believed that we would be as bad as San Francisco!'[38]

However, as the heterosexual nature of the epidemic became apparent in 1989–91, initial moralistic complacency among the insurance industry gave way to panic: '[t]he Doomsday roadshow began to have its effect ... The medical schemes responded conservatively, and many imposed the most stringent limits available under the Medical Schemes Act – R600 per family per annum.'[39] Medical aid schemes began to increase their monthly contributions to 25–30 per cent above the inflation rate 'and most adopted the view that AIDS is avoidable (shame about the kids) so why should the healthy moral people subsidise the "sins" of others':

> The doctors responded by submitting accounts for AIDS under 'disguised' diagnoses which were paid innocently by the medical aid. Even if the employer knew, confidentiality was maintained, and this stand-off prevented very valuable data being accumulated. Whilst, important education time was being wasted, the doctors blamed the medical aids, COSATU blamed the migrant labour system, everyone blamed the government and the right-wingers thanked God.[40]

In May 1989 Southern Life eliminated the industry-wide R200,000 threshold for exclusion clauses and began omitting AIDS coverage from all new life insurance policies, unless the applicant submitted to a blood test. Sanlam – one of the largest South African insurance firms – kept a threshold, but cut it. For people applying for term and certain other life insurance worth more than R100,000, Sanlam required a blood test unless the applicant declined AIDS coverage. Some insurance companies opted for limitation clauses instead of exclusion clauses: for instance, rather than excluding AIDS coverage on new policies, Commercial Union would limit the payout on AIDS deaths to eight times the annual premium, no matter how high the coverage.[41]

For its part, the government did nothing to steer the insurance industry in responding to the AIDS epidemic. As the general manager and chief executive officer of the Munich Reinsurance Company of South Africa noted in his review of the first ten years of the South African AIDS epidemic, 'One of the sad chapters of government performance ... has been the initial response to AIDS ... In some instances, there appeared to be initial periods of denial that AIDS was any kind of problem.'[42]

However, concomitant with the change in the perception among members of the South African biomedical community, the insurance industry soon began to realise that they needed to be pragmatic and proactive in the face of the government's reticence to provide AIDS guidelines for the workplace. In March 1989 Sanlam launched a major, country-wide campaign to assist its corporate clients in drafting private AIDS management policies. In doing so, it took the initiative in hosting workplace workshops including members of trade unions and employer organisations as well as representatives of some pension funds.[43] In 1990 *The Businessman's Law* journal, in reviewing the status of AIDS and the South African insurance industry, noted that:

> [n]o review of the present situation and no forecast of the future impact of AIDS can, at this stage, embrace all of its implications for short-term insurers. In South Africa ... we should at least take careful note of what is happening overseas and make tentative plans for what might be in store for us.[44]

From 1992 onwards a more realistic frame of reference started to be adopted: the insurance industry began to draw up treatment protocols reflecting more successful prevention of opportunistic infections, fewer hospitalisations and less aggressive and expensive treatment in the terminal stages. The industry also started to consider alternatives to life insurance, health insurance and pension benefits, as well as the feasibility of a pool of capital for HIV-positive people.[45] In the two years before a new political dispensation came about in 1994, the more inclusive, human rights discourse that emerged within the medical aid community (as well as within the legal community, as will become apparent) also gained a foothold.

For instance, Spier noted that the medical aid industry would have to think laterally in drawing up AIDS education programmes and development benefit strategies aimed at prevention and alternative care: 'The same policies need to be developed in the public sector.'[46] The medical aid industry started to realises that, whatever solution was envisaged, it would have to be communicated to and negotiated with a broad spectrum of community and business leadership, including the trade unions. 'A strategy, however rational, cannot be dictated from above.'[47]

Also, a Medical Aid Administrators' Working Group was established with the purpose of dealing with HIV infection in a more open way, in an effort to create a situation where medical practitioners would no longer need to hide diagnoses from the medical scheme; where patients would no longer be penalised for disclosing their HIV status. In addition to a change in the normative discursive environment, this change of heart was based on pecuniary pragmatism: 'The proof of the pudding will really lie in whether the funders and providers of health care can put together cost-effective packages which their members both want and can afford ... Even for hard-nosed accountants, the prospect of having an employee staying well at work for 5–7 years longer, and therefore contributing longer to his medical aid and other benefits, is an incentive.'[48] In 1991 The Director of Human Resources of Medischeme (the largest medical aid administration in Africa) noted that 'the most pressing need now is for the co-ordination and sharing of the resources, research and energies so as to effectively target our AIDS efforts. The cost of failure will be far greater than the medical bills.'[49]

This shift to a human rights focus and the direct reference to the need for policies consistent across the private and public sectors underscore pluralists' focus on the multiplicity of actors called upon to draw up effective AIDS policies. In addition to the nascent human rights-focused environment, these arguments were based on cost-benefit analyses, echoing the arguments of rational choice theorists.

The mining sector

The South African mining sector and its response to the AIDS threat in South Africa in the 1980s and 1990s are significant for a number of reasons. In the first place, the mining industry played a significant role in the establishment and implementation of apartheid policies, and in doing so, benefited hugely from the highly socially engineered structures that would later facilitate the spread of HIV in the country. As Terreblanche notes, '[f]or 60 years the Chamber of Mines played a key role in institutionalising and maintaining the migrant labour and compound (*kampong*) systems ... Successive white supremacist governments also allowed the chamber to recruit large numbers of foreign migrant workers from neighbouring countries at exceptionally low wage rates.'[50]

Second, the industry was and remains a significant contributor to the South African economy; in fact, for most of the apartheid years it was the industry around which the entire economy was built. Lastly, the mining industry is a large employer of mostly black labour, and as such its early response to AIDS by implication had to take into account the heterosexual environment of the epidemic, addressing the disease in a cultural context that socio-politically was largely impervious to the biomedical approach followed, or rather allowed by, the government.

It might be due to this specificity of the mining industry that, very early on – as early as August 1986 – it came to view the socio-political problematique of the AIDS epidemic in a different way from the NP government. At that time the employment policy adopted by the Chamber of Mines became a sensitive issue between the industry and the government. The latter opted for drafting a policy that would allow for the compulsory testing of all mineworkers in the country, and expelling all workers who tested HIV positive – not only those workers who were too ill to work. Such a policy would have meant the repatriation not only of foreign migrant labourers, but also of those South Africans deemed to be citizens of the so-called 'independent homelands' of Transkei, Bophuthatswana, Venda and Ciskei. Lurie notes that this proposed policy was a product of the apartheid politics of the day:

> the sanctions threat has created an incentive to diminish dependence on foreign miners. If South Africa is perceived nationally as an initially disease-free country beset by the afflictions of foreign black Africans and decadent (i.e. homosexual) Western society, the xenophobia that the State seeks to instil in South Africans will be magnified. Ceasing recruitment should thus be viewed not only as a strategy with little prospect of having a significant impact on AIDS in South Africa, but also as one that dovetails neatly with the State's overall political objectives.[51]

Such a xenophobic policy, in the opinion of Chamber of Mines, would be counterproductive. In July 1987 the difference of approach between the Chamber and the government was at issue during meetings that the Chamber had with senior Department of National Health and Population Development officials, as well as with Willie van Niekerk, then Minister of Health.

In addition to basing its policy on the result of a study of the blood samples of 300,000 miners of all races, Rafel states that the Chamber's policy approach was based on the conclusions of consultations it had with medical and labour experts in South Africa and Western Europe.[52] Repatriation would not be the correct way to control the incidence and spread of AIDS on the mines – only those HIV-positive workers who became too ill to work would be repatriated. Instead, the Chamber would focus on an intensive educational campaign about the disease. The Chamber also decided to pre-test potential workers, to test miners regularly for STDs, and that clinically well HIV carriers who returned home between contracts would not have their disease used as a pretext for terminating their employment.[53]

Thus, although the mines initially chose not to address the more encompassing environment that raised the risk profiles of individuals working on the mines (the hostel system and the migratory labour system, for instance), their insistence on some rights for HIV-positive miners so early in the epidemic in South Africa is quite significant. However, due to pressure from the government, the Chamber stated that it was 'seriously considering' revising its policies in accordance with government's demands. In addition to pressures from the government, the Chamber also had to contend with the powerful National Union of Mineworkers (NUM), which rejected repatriation as a solution to the AIDS problem. Instead, the NUM focused on the deleterious impact that the migrant labour system was having in spreading the epidemic. Rather than repatriation, the NUM called for a human rights approach, insisting that counselling and adequate health facilities, as well as follow-up facilities, be provided for HIV-positive workers. Furthermore, the NUM called for compensation for workers whose working lives had been cut short by the disease: 'Clearly, any changes to the Chamber's AIDS policy would be taken in the knowledge that there could be adverse reaction from the NUM.'[54]

The mining sector maintained its criticism of government's inappropriate policy response to AIDS: in 1989 the Chamber of Mines' medical adviser criticised the government for not taking the threat posed by AIDS seriously enough; yet the mines continued with their system of migrant labour, doing nothing on their own part to counter the hostel system.[55] Despite a minority view that a holistic approach emphasising human rights be followed, by that stage neither the private sector nor the trade unions had come up with a coherent strategy to cope with AIDS – and the management sectors of the major South African companies echoed the government in insisting that education was the only vaccine. This strategy suited big business, engaged as it was with a government blaming homosexuals and black foreigners for the disease on the one hand, and on the other, faced with trade union members who sometimes believed that AIDS did not exist, or that it was a government plot to deprive the non-white population of sex.[56]

The trade unions' focus on the rights of the worker came the closest to an early embrace of the human rights-centred model adopted by the government in later years: the unions insisted that even companies genuinely committed to dealing with the AIDS problem would not get results without proving their bona fides in other spheres, such as showing a willingness to negotiate decent wages and working conditions. The mining sector's early error in dealing with AIDS was that its initial willingness to protect some of the rights of HIV-positive workers did not go far enough. The apartheid context meant that the private sector remained caught between the socially conservative and xenophobic policies of the NP government on the one hand, and demands for profound socio-political change emanating from the trade unions on the other.

The NUM made it clear that they did not share the government's and some members of the private sector's conceptualisation of AIDS as a health problem. Rather, they saw it as a socio-political problem that necessitated a profound rethinking of the entire labour and socio-political context in the country. The NUM insisted on a human rights approach: the provision and design of new housing for workers, new legislation regarding job security, better health services, no patient-specific testing, protection after incapacity, and so on. The NUM stated that:

> [t]he government, business and the unions all have crucial roles to play. Our success or failure [in combating AIDS] will ultimately depend on our ability to confront fundamental issues: employment policy and social policy. In the trade union movement we believe that we have the will to do just this. Does the government and does business?[57]

The drafting and implementation of effective private sector policies to counter the spread and impact of AIDS in the workplace was impossible in this politically divisive environment. To make matters worse, the apartheid context politicised the AIDS epidemic itself, rendering it impermeable to distrusted policy efforts. Prior to real political change in the early 1990s, '[a] broad-based approach by private sector, government, health authorities and non-profit organisations to limit the spread of the disease' remained a distant ideal.[58] But despite the lack of political transformation, the mining industry as well as other private sector industries came to realise that such an approach would be required.

Increasingly in the late 1980s, South African newsletters and journals of business management called for closer co-operation with the trade unions – for a broader social contract against AIDS, including government, business and the unions.[59] In the absence of clear, effective policies from government, however, the Institute of Personnel Management (for one) called on all private sector organisations to develop a corporate policy on AIDS.[60] In early 1989 the Chamber of Mines and the NUM embarked on a process of negotiating a common strategy to tackle AIDS. This meeting was, it is significant to note, the result of a study which argued that migrant labour and the hostel system were the main causes of the spread of HIV on the mines.[61]

However, once the De Klerk government unbanned the ANC and started on the road to profound political changes in early 1990, the private sector was faced with additional problems that made companies less than eager to establish private sector AIDS policies. For instance, despite labour unions' insistence on negotiating a fairer labour dispensation with regards to AIDS, it was clear that the constitutional as well as legal workplace environment would change. The mines and other members of the private sector knew that AIDS would be high on the ANC's as well as the unions' agenda, and hence in some cases wanted to wait and see what proposals would be forthcoming. Also, companies decided to delay drafting private AIDS policies since (in the changed political environment) they did not dare do so without the approval of the unions. Also, according to the Labour Relations Act of 1956, any company policy on AIDS in which the company undertakes onerous obligations could be used against the company in any civil damages suit or in any Industrial Court case.[62]

Once the political changes were announced in February 1990, it is little wonder that – as was the case with the medical as well as the insurance industries – the private sector responded with a single voice: the Chamber of Mines and other private sector bodies called on the government to provide greater clarity on the legality of any responses to HIV and AIDS. Issues that required urgent legal clarity were disparate, ranging from pre-employment screening for AIDS[63] to interpreting AIDS as a physical disability in the workplace.[64] It transpired that the mining industry and the electricity supplier Eskom were the only employers to have taken any significant steps towards confronting AIDS prior to February 1990. However, immediately after February 1990, government did little to inform companies and other industrial sectors of the implications wrought by AIDS in the workplace. *Finance Week* noted that 'it's up to individual companies to initiate and research AIDS policies and programmes'.[65] At the time, the head of SAIMR's AIDS Centre noted that '[p]oliticians appear to believe that the virus will call a moratorium while the political issues are being sorted out. I can assure them that it will not'.[66]

Thus, once the political environment changed in 1990, it became clear that private companies would have to draw up their own policies only in conjunction with the government, the ANC and the trade unions.[67] The establishment of workplace AIDS policies would, however, henceforth occur within a more holistic approach, incorporating 'overall problem-solving'.[68] According to a senior manager at Eskom:

> [t]he current political climate in South Africa is enabling us all to address human rights. There seems to be a higher consciousness around the protection of human rights and whatever legislation emerges from the new political order may favour protecting the rights of workers, who have experienced the brunt of the injustices of apartheid.[69]

Concomitantly, the South African mining industry was in a position and under the political obligation to start abandoning the discriminatory AIDS and other policies of the past. As Hermanus noted, '[t]he first AIDS policy drafted by the Chamber of Mines in 1988 was a logical extension of the practice of "dumping" workers who have become a financial liability to the industry'.[70] Due to the challenge posed by the NUM, as well as the changed political environment which placed a higher premium on human rights after February 1990, however, the NUM and the Chamber in the early 1990s were in the process of negotiating a new AIDS policy. At this stage there seemed to be broad agreement about the rights of HIV-positive workers and the industry appeared to be willing to recognise that the spread of the disease is influenced by a number of social factors.[71]

Conclusion

By early 1994 the private sector and broader workplace response to AIDS was well underway; the only factor lacking was a legitimate government: the lack of credibility of the NP government meant that NGOs and the private sector had to go it alone in framing AIDS policies. However, the non-governmental sector lacked the technical capacity to respond to the epidemic on an appropriate scale.[72]

The next chapter concludes our focus on the NP government's response to HIV and AIDS in 1982–94 by focusing specifically on the legal and public responses during the first dozen years of the epidemic in South Africa.

4
Public Sector Responses to HIV and AIDS in Apartheid South Africa (1982–1994)

Introduction

This chapter concludes the analysis set out in the preceding two chapters by linking the developments discussed and the kind of public policy responses they gave rise to by applying the phase approach to policy analysis as expounded in the Introduction. It is interesting to see how AIDS moved from being a 'mere' health issue affecting a few parochial members of society, to becoming a policy problem affecting the South African population as a whole, an issue calling on, abusing and finding support in the gamut of public policy theory options describing and prescribing such interventions.

AIDS legislation as policy

In the absence of an overall government strategy with regards to AIDS it became incumbent upon the biomedical community as well as sections of the private sector (for example, the mining sector and the insurance industry) to draft their own context-specific and rather ad hoc policies. The apartheid government's strategy regarding AIDS seemed to reflect an unwillingness or inability to deal with the socio-political structures underlying the unfolding epidemic, leaving it to other sections of South African society to muddle through on their own. In doing so, a policy of *inaction* rather than proactive planning and intervention seemed to be the government's approach. The private sector battled with conditions of employment in particular, struggling to come to grips with the implications of AIDS in the workplace.

This section provides an overview of how the legal framework at the time was used (or, indeed, abused) to act as governmental policy by proxy. From the preceding two chapters we know that apartheid laws had criminalised certain forms of sexual relations that acted as a vector for the spread of HIV: homosexual relations, commercial sex work, as well as relations across racial divisions. In criminalising these aspects of South African sexual life, the apartheid government had their scapegoats, as well as an excuse for inaction: in the normative environment at the time, these kinds of activities (including intravenous drug use) were deemed unnatural or morally reprehensible by the public sector, and thus the government's response to the deeper structural causes of the spread of the AIDS epidemic was to stigmatise, isolate and legislate against these forms of sexual relations. This was policy-making by inaction rather than by the drafting of a proactive HIV and AIDS-specific set of programmes.

Having looked at the workplace responses, we now turn our attention to how this public policy of inaction or public policy-making by default played out in other areas of the South African legal context in the 1980s and early 1990s.

AIDS-specific legislation

As noted in the Introduction, government legislation with regards to an issue is not in itself necessarily the same as government policy on that issue. A public policy describes the broad aims and purposes that the government might have in drafting a response to an identified public policy problem, and the enactment of legislation is but one response that the government could have. As such, legislation can be used to reinforce a (tacit or explicit) policy – it operationalises the enforceability of such a policy. As noted above, the NP government defined the AIDS problem in moralistic and racist terms: the HIV-positive individual was – due to his/her own immoral behaviour – responsible for his/her own infection. As such, that individual posed a danger to the rest of the 'normal' or 'innocent' society.

The definition of the AIDS issue as a problem to which blame could be apportioned thus found application in legislation based on an attempt to censure and even criminalise those in whom the AIDS issue became personalised. In the absence of a human rights charter in the normative and highly politicised AIDS policy environment noted above, it comes as no surprise that the apartheid government's lack of an encompassing AIDS policy resulted in an attempt simply to legislate the issue into oblivion. According to Kirby, panic, alarm, banishment, cruelty, public stigmatisation and (significantly) *law* are 'the melancholy companions of disease and epidemics'. It was no different in South Africa – the

AIDS-specific legislation enacted by the apartheid government actually exacerbated the AIDS problem, rather than ameliorated it.[1]

The first AIDS-specific piece of legislation that the apartheid government enacted was the Human Tissue Act (65 of 1983), which the government amended in 1990. In accordance with this legislation, certain groups of people were excluded as blood donors – homosexual males in particular.[2] As noted above, the standard test for HIV only became available in 1985, so the aim of the legislation was to draw attention to those individuals who were thought to be risky donors, and by implication to protect the rest of the population against their unsafe blood. The Human Tissue Act also provided guidelines pertaining to employers' rights and obligations regarding the provision of blood transfusion services. As was the case with the later Immorality Amendment Act (2 of 1988), the effect of this legislation was that isolated and stigmatised groups were driven deeper underground, not declaring their sexual orientation or risky sexual partnering for fear of legal prosecution. According to Burchell:

> [l]egislation aimed at curbing the spread of AIDS ... can be categorized as imposing either direct or indirect control to prevent the communication of HIV to new victims. Indirect action might take the form of criminalizing aspects of homosexuality, prostitution, drug-taking and drug-peddling. It is surely not entirely coincidental that the *Immorality Amendment Act* 2 of 1988, although ostensibly designed to remove discrimination in the field of sexual offences, in fact expands the field of criminality in the area of prostitution and the activities of escort agencies at a time when the fear of the spread of AIDS has begun to take hold in South Africa.[3]

The most significant AIDS-specific legislation of the apartheid government was announced on 30 October 1987.[4] On that day the Minister of National Health and Population Development published amendments to the Public Health Act (63 of 1977) which gave special powers to medical officers of health (MOHs) with regards to HIV-positive individuals. Until then, AIDS was not a notifiable disease, but under the new regulations an MOH who suspected someone to be the carrier of a communicable disease could instruct that person to subject him/herself to a medical examination. The regulations further provided that if a person in the opinion of an MOH was – or could be – suffering from any communicable disease mentioned in the regulations (one of which was AIDS), that person was to subject him-/herself to a medical examination and treatment as could be subsequently prescribed. If a person was found to be a carrier of HIV, the minister was also afforded the power to place that person in quarantine – ominously, 'until he is free of infection'.[5]

These regulations did not render AIDS a fully notifiable medical condition. If it had, all persons who might have had reason to believe that a person had died from it would have had to report this to the local authority. A medical practitioner who treated a person suffering from a notifiable medical condition had to submit weekly reports on the patient to the regional director of health. However, these conditions were not prescribed for AIDS. HIV and AIDS were merely added to a list of 'communicable diseases' provided for in the Public Health Act. The effect was to render AIDS notifiable to a limited extent and to bring into play the possibility of compulsory hospitalisation or isolation of persons suspected of having contracted the syndrome.[6]

Interestingly, however, the amendments to the Health Act also meant that local authorities had the power to shut public service agencies (even schools could be closed) to an HIV-positive individual – even a pupil. The amendments obliged school principals to notify MOHs of the presence of an HIV-positive pupil or staff member. Such notification had to take place even if school principals only *suspected* an individual of being HIV-positive.[7]

Another important regulation published on the same day (30 October 1987) by the Minister of Home Affairs related to diseases which would render foreigners who find themselves on South African soil 'prohibited persons' for the purposes of the Admission of Persons to the Republic Regulation Act. One of the conditions listed in the regulation was AIDS (or infection with HIV). The Act empowered immigration officers *inter alia* to require persons who in their opinion are not entitled to be in the Republic to submit to a medical examination where there was a suspicion that the person concerned was afflicted with a listed disease. The fact that a foreigner would become a 'prohibited person' did not mean that he/she would necessarily be required to leave the country or be deported. The Act did, however, vest the minister with wide powers of deporting non-citizens if he deemed it in the public interest.

Civil rights activists immediately stated their opposition to these two pieces of legislation, warning that the implications – in particular the slant towards making AIDS a notifiable disease – enforced the environment of apportioning blame. This would, in their opinion, serve only to drive the disease even deeper underground, enforcing stigmatisation and discrimination.[8] Once the ANC and other liberation organisations were unbanned on 2 February 1990, these civil rights activists indicated that the legislation could be used against returning political exiles. In short, the legislation could be used to politicise and racialise the issue of AIDS even more.

Significantly, opposition to these measures was such that they became almost instantly unenforceable. Shortly after the enactment of the new measures in the Public Health Act and the Admission of Persons to the Republic Regulation Act, the government announced plans to repatriate 1,000 Malawian miners who had tested HIV-positive and to have all work applicants from Malawi, Zimbabwe, Zambia, Zaire and Burundi tested for the virus. However, the deportation plans were thwarted by doctors, who reportedly refused to disclose the names of infected miners to the government on the strength of the duty of doctor–patient confidentiality.[9] It thus appears as though the changing, increasingly human-rights oriented, normative environment among the ranks of the medical profession was clashing with the government's normative environment and had the effect of rendering the government's AIDS deportation policy ineffective. This is a striking example of elite theory as well as pluralism's emphasis of the fractured nature of power in policy-making and implementation – in this instance the medical elite opted not to enforce governmental measures.

The government's plans to implement pre-employment testing of work applicants from Central Africa did, however, go ahead. In fact, in 1986 and 1987, even before AIDS and HIV were added to the scheduled conditions, all persons seeking employment in South African mines who originated from what the Minister of National Health and Population Development termed 'high risk areas' were tested before being allowed to work in South African mines. However, once the change in the AIDS policy environment moved towards a more human rights-centred approach, the Chamber of Mines altered their policy and entered into negotiations with the NUM on this issue.[10]

As political changes in South Africa accelerated after 2 February 1990, the anachronistic and untenable nature of these pieces of legislation became increasingly apparent. In April 1991, therefore, the apartheid government's AIDS Unit published a policy document pragmatically rejecting the use of coercive legislation in the fight against AIDS – in effect rejecting both pieces of the 30 October 1987 legislation. In June 1991 the government-appointed AIDS Advisory Committee recommended that legislation stigmatising AIDS and HIV be repealed. As a result, in October 1991, AIDS and HIV were dropped from the immigration regulations, and indications were that AIDS may also be removed from the communicability regulations. At that time, Cameron noted that:

> [t]hese changes are important. They signal that the government has accepted that statutory coercion has no useful part to play in fighting the spread of HIV. This is a vital lesson; once South Africans had the benefit of learning through the bitter history of the Immorality Act 23 of 1957, which showed that punitive and stigmatizing laws cannot control the way people behave: they cause only misery and devastation while bringing the law and its enforcers into disrepute.[11]

Elsewhere, Cameron and Swanson noted that:

> [t]he change in the law also reveals an important general shift in the government's approach to the growing AIDS epidemic. By removing the prohibition on immigrants with HIV or AIDS, the government has implicitly acknowledged that South Africa cannot insulate itself from the crisis by establishing a 'cordon sanitaire' around the country.[12]

In short, the government had moved from a position of wanting to pass legislation that criminalised those deemed responsible for spreading HIV and AIDS to a position that appeared to embrace individuals' human rights. There was clearly an implicit shift in the definition of the AIDS issue, and hence the AIDS public policy problem. This shift will be discussed in greater detail below. But first, the impact and changes in South African criminal and case law on the broader legal environment will be evaluated.

Criminal and case law

As is the case in contemporary South Africa, during apartheid it was illegal for commercial sex workers to practise their trade openly, and hence it was very difficult to target this group for AIDS intervention programmes. The same can be said of homosexual relationships, as well as sexual relations across racial divides. In criminalising these sexual relations, the government's response to AIDS was to target specific sectors of South African society and blame them for the spread of the epidemic. The enemy was not a virus; the enemy was the individual who – through his/her own morally unacceptable actions – posed a threat to the rest of society. Such a policy of blame would naturally find application in the use of criminal law: by criminalising the conduits of the virus, government could be seen to be acting in the interests of the greater constituency that they represented – white heterosexuals. It is quite telling that, by the time it started to become apparent that the AIDS epidemic would be a chiefly heterosexual phenomenon – in the late 1980s – the government's emphasis on using criminal law ostensibly to combat the epidemic was also abating.

Criminal law was thus used by the NP government as a way to force individuals to alter their sexual behaviour.[13] In doing so, South African criminal law was used to perpetuate the framing of the AIDS epidemic in 'us versus them' terms: the criminal law environment at the time made all South Africans either vectors or victims of the disease – and if you were a vector, you could be punished for it. De Jager cites two reasons in particular to explain why this application of criminal law did not succeed.[14]

In the first place, the coercive nature of what criminal law implied had the effect of exculpating individuals who might deem themselves 'victims' rather than 'vectors'. In targeting sexual and other outsiders as criminals, the use of criminal law made it possible for the rest of society not to take responsibility for their own sexual acts. Second, the application of criminal law as a tacit policy tool to cope with AIDS was based on the assumption that individuals who spread the disease – the ones being criminalised – would remain in their designated (outlawed) groups, and that criminalisation would be enough to isolate the virus to homosexuals, sex workers, drug users and non-South African blacks. The government assumed that, in targeting these groups by criminalising them, they could protect the rest of society from viral transmission. This was clearly not the case, since by the late 1980s the general heterosexual nature of the epidemic had started to become apparent.

In addition to the government's use of criminal law, the legal precedents of South African case law in the late 1980s and early 1990s provide some insight into how the government came to shape its evolving response to AIDS. In the absence of a comprehensive government policy to deal with the legal aspects of HIV and AIDS, civil law cases were important determinants of the legal culture of South Africa after the democratisation of the country in April 1994. Between 1982 and 1994 there were two cases in particular that would shape the legal and policy environment in the years to come.

In the first of these – the McGeary case of 1991 – a civil court case resulted after a medical doctor disclosed a patient's HIV status to two colleagues whilst playing golf. The plaintiff's position was that his moral right to privacy had been violated by what he deemed his doctor's unprofessional act. In 1993 the South African Court of Appeal emphasised and supported the importance of the South African Medical and Dental Council's (SAMDC) 1989 guidelines on HIV and AIDS, which stated that it was the doctor's duty to protect a patient's right to confidentiality if specifically asked to do so (which was the case here). The case was important in that it bound any future South African policy-making and legislation to the principle of patient confidentiality, rendered the SAMDC guidelines legally enforceable, and considered the HIV-positive patient's right to privacy as more pressing that the actual risks associated with occupational HIV transmission. In setting out his evaluation of the McGeary decision, Cameron stated that:

> [t]he judgement ... has wide-ranging implications for policy-making about AIDS and HIV. In practical terms, it is a resounding affirmation of the right to privacy of the individual who has AIDS or HIV. More generally, it discredits the argument that 'the rights of the few' (i.e. those infected with HIV) must yield before 'the rights of the many' (i.e. those not infected). This opposition, the ruling implies, is false, since the community itself benefits by respecting the private rights of those with HIV. There is in this a significant message to South African decision-makers charged with responding to the epidemic.[15]

The message to South African public policy-makers was that the tide was turning: away from using the law as a tool to stigmatise further and criminalise the HIV-positive individual, towards respecting the rights of that individual, and making policy adjustment accordingly.

The Hansen case of 1992 is the other civil case that had important implications for AIDS policy-making in South Africa. In this case, the plaintiff took the administration of a Transvaal provincial hospital to court because the hospital refused to provide him with free medication for which he had previously qualified, while continuing the free provision of the medication to HIV-negative patients. The hospital's decision was based on pecuniary considerations; in its view the right of a patient to free medication became effectively curtailed if that patient were HIV-positive, because the medication would cost the state too much, especially in view of the fact that the patient would die in the long run. In its decision, the court rejected this argument, stating that all patients should be treated equally, regardless of their HIV status.

The implication of the court's decision was that the government would be forced to cease discriminating against HIV-positive individuals and amend legislation to provide such individuals with life-saving drugs. More importantly, however, was the implication that the government and all

South Africans needed to take personal but also communal responsibility for AIDS. As Chetty stated just after the decision was publicised, '[i]t should become the moral and social obligation of all citizens to take active measures in making war against AIDS, and not against people with AIDS'.[16] As with the McGeary decision, the Hansen case forced the South African legal context and government away from the spirit of blame and stigmatisation to combating the disease as a societal phenomenon that should be tackled by expanding rather than contracting individuals' human rights.

Redefining the policy problem: the move to a human rights culture

Taken as a whole, the evolution of private sector and legal measures to combat AIDS discussed above indicates the emergence of an interesting trend by the early 1990s, which informed the public policy environment: despite the government's efforts to demonise HIV-positive individuals in the workplace and legislate against them in South African society as a whole, the occupational and legal elites refused to embrace and implement governmental prescriptions ideologically. Human resources managers, insurance portfolio managers and the courts rejected the implications of government's tacit AIDS policy, and opted instead to rephrase their own sectoral response to AIDS in a human rights discourse. At the core of this disassociation was a dissonance with government's ontology about AIDS, which stated implicitly and explicitly that the personalised vectors of the epidemic should be held morally responsible for endangering the rest of society.

In doing so, these elites in the implementation of what tacit governmental AIDS policies there were refused to be a party to those policies. Not only does this demonstrate the power of pluralists' emphasis on the multivariant nature of the process of successful policy-making; it also demonstrates that the incrementalists would be wrong in pointing to the conservative nature of policy-making that merely built on existing measures to combat the disease. Instead, this was a policy revolution. The very fact that the elites acted against the prescriptions of the government – discarding their moralistic stance in the process – demonstrates the power of a new mindset based on individual human rights. There was a clear contrast between the way in which the government perceived the reality of AIDS (zero-sum, namely the rights of the many versus the rights of the few), and the way in which the implementing elites came to view the epidemic (namely, that the virus is the problem, rather than the individuals spreading it).

Eventually, even the AIDS elite within the government, the AIDS Advisory Committee, in June 1991 also arrived at this position, which led to the eventual repeal of discriminatory AIDS legislation four months later. In this case, therefore, the analyst perceives a confluence of the manner in which the AIDS problem came to be redefined among the governing policy elites – a veritable meeting of pluralism, public choice theory, elite theory and statism. After October 1991, it was clear that AIDS would be seen less as a health issue, and more as a developmental, social justice and human rights issue.

Reviewing the AIDS legal context of the late 1980s, Cameron warned that, if the October 1987 legislation had been allowed to continue, discrimination against people with AIDS could well have replaced racism as the major focus of opprobrious exclusionary conduct in South Africa.[17] In Cameron's analysis, the 1987 legislation exemplified the three forms of discrimination that there could have been with regards to people living with AIDS:

1 The enactment by the state of repressive laws aimed at inhibiting civil liberties or civic status of persons with AIDS or HIV.
2 The violation by healthcare workers, employers and others of HIV positive individual's first generation rights – the rights to dignity, privacy and autonomy.
3 Denying persons with AIDS or HIV access to a fair share of national resources and wealth, in both the public and the private sectors (second generation rights).

The repeal of the October 1987 legislation as well as the civil courts' decisions in the early 1990s against similar legislation was therefore a major victory for human rights activists, since '[i]t [was] in these areas that the human rights battle around AIDS and HIV over the next fifteen years in South Africa [would] lie. It [would] not be primarily about "first generation" rights. It [would] be the struggle for people with AIDS and HIV to get a fair and rational share of our nation's resources.'[18] In making this statement in the early days of South Africa's transition to a democratic society, Cameron thus foresaw the possibility that the AIDS policies of the future might be built on principles established during that time. In doing so, he implicitly noted how important incremental AIDS policy-making might become in the future, democratic South Africa.

Perhaps it comes as no surprise that this altered conception of the AIDS problematique happened at the time that it did: shortly after the tumultuous political changes announced by the De Klerk government in February 1990. The trade unions in particular found their voice, and it is significant that it was at its 1989 congress that COSATU had made explicit their demands for a more holistic, human rights-centred approach to HIV and AIDS public policy-making, followed shortly thereafter by the Transport and General Workers' Union's similar 1990 resolution on AIDS.[19] The government could no longer afford merely to suppress or disregard its new negotiation partners' views on public policy issues, and it became clear that the normative AIDS environment was swiftly moving away from the Botha government's actions to criminalise the disease and stigmatise those held responsible for its dissemination.

The radically changed political context was underscored by the real need to change South African society's perception of previously proscribed sexual behaviour. For instance, there were calls for the moral approval and decriminalisation of homosexuality, with Viljoen enjoining public policy-makers to 'replace punishment with empathy'.[20] Moreover, AIDS activists and members of the medical elite within government agencies started to put pressure on the government to decriminalise commercial sex work, and to empower women by enacting greater gender equity.[21] These notions were supported by a change within the South African medical community: less emphasis was placed on First World medicine, and more on the notion of 'well-being', primary health care and the need for greater integration among the various schools of thought regarding individuals' rights to health – not only as a medical issue, but also as a developmental issue.[22]

The redefinition of AIDS as a human rights issue reached its civil society zenith on 12 November 1991, when the AIDS Consortium (an organisation representing the width and breadth of the AIDS civil society community in South Africa) adopted its 'Charter of Rights on AIDS and HIV'.[23] The Charter stressed the need to protect individuals' first- and second-generation rights in the context of AIDS, with specific reference to liberty, autonomy, confidentiality and privacy.

After February 1990, and increasingly after the repeal of discriminatory AIDS legislation in October 1991, it became clear that the AIDS problem had been redefined; the AIDS public policy environment had changed, ostensibly irrevocably.

Government

Upon reviewing the NP government's actions and inactions on AIDS in the years following the first incidence of AIDS in South Africa in 1982, three loosely defined phases of AIDS policy-making for the era 1982–94 can be identified. Although it is difficult to provide meaningful, accurate time-frames to policy-making, it is none the less possible to discern a first phase that stretched from 1982 until about 1988. This era is notable for government inaction on AIDS; in fact, Van der Vliet refers to these years as the 'silent' HIV phase.[24]

The second phase of the public response to AIDS was from around 1989 to 1992, and is notable for the government's AIDS policy evolution to a more human rights-centred approach (yet still excluding the majority of public stakeholders in the broader policy environment). The third phase commenced with the establishment of the broadly inclusive National AIDS Co-ordinating Committee of South Africa (NACOSA) in 1992, and the development of the country's first truly encompassing, broadly inclusive AIDS strategy, culminating in the democratically elected ANC government adopting the National AIDS Plan (NAP) shortly after assuming office in 1994. Each of these phases are reviewed in greater detail below.

The 'silent' HIV phase: 1982–1988

In the first few years after AIDS appeared on the South African political landscape the battle against the epidemic struggled – and, indeed, failed – to make it onto the public policy agenda. No comprehensive AIDS strategies or public policies were drafted. A number of reasons account for this, but the most significant was that AIDS did not at first appear to be a truly dramatic threat to South African society. Initially, there was no way of isolating and measuring the prevalence of the disease among South Africans, and very little was known about its possible impact. Also, the virus appeared to have the greatest impact among isolated fringes of South African society, affecting mainly homosexuals, commercial sex workers and intravenous drug users – sections of society who had already been legislated against; indeed, criminalised. There was no great pressure on the government to ease the burden that AIDS placed on these groups; rather, government acted to protect the rest of 'normal' South African society against these 'enemies within'.

As a consequence, it was easier to equate the real AIDS threat to South Africa with these peripheral groups. The policy problem on the public agenda was not to combat a virus that threatened the whole country; rather, the threat was the immoral behaviour of fringe groups who had brought this ill-defined plight upon themselves in the first place. The government's actions were, therefore, fairly predictable: a few pieces of legislation were drafted to restrict the behaviour of those individuals who were deemed to threaten the rest of society – foreign mine workers would be tested, immigrants would be scanned, homosexuals excluded as blood donors, and immigration officials were given powers to deport HIV-positive immigrants. Rather than giving thought to extending the privileges and most basic human rights of blacks, homosexuals, drug users and commercial sex workers, the NP government acted to strengthen discriminatory legislation against these 'enemies'.

In addition, in 1985 the government established the AIDS Advisory Group (AAG) to inform and drive its strategy on HIV and AIDS – a body comprised wholly of white men with leanings towards a narrow biomedical definition of the society-epidemiology interface.

Only towards the end of this era did the government establish a number of institutions to combat AIDS, and these remained exclusive and limited in number. Rather than addressing the structural causes for the rapid dissemination of AIDS in South Africa, these bodies focused on medical solutions, reactively seeking to prevent the spread of the epidemic by way of ill-conceived and societally inappropriate information campaigns.

Limited as they were, it is significant that these latter changes occurred only once it became apparent in 1988 that AIDS had made the jump from the homo- to the heterosexual section of society: the 'gay plague' had become the 'black death' – an untimely addition to the greater NP pathology of a '*swart gevaar*' (black danger).

This politicised the South African AIDS epidemic: the stigmatisation accompanying the virus and institutionalised in legislation was now exported to the broader context of South Africa's race politics – the NP government warned against ANC cadres importing the virus into the country, and the ANC blamed the NP government and Western powers for developing the virus in their laboratories to act as a weapon against blacks.[25] Throw into this political cauldron the normative blame game played by leading South African churches at the time, and it becomes clear how the epidemic became so firmly and irretrievably politicised and racialised.

The country would pay the price for this for many years to come – an illegitimate government would henceforth find it increasingly difficult to secure the buy-in and ownership of their AIDS policies by the majority of South Africans, the AIDS policy problem remained erroneously defined as a personification among certain sections of society, and the narrow biomedical, health-specific policy response became the safest option of policy and decision-makers in the public as well as in the private spheres.

It is little wonder that the NP government continuously fell short of the successful drafting of any comprehensive, circumspect and all-inclusive policy response to HIV and AIDS: the policy environment made it nearly impossible to isolate and address the real drivers of the epidemic, the policy problem remained erroneously defined, and ineffectual, impotent policy responses inevitably followed suit.

Flux and re-conceptualisation: 1989–1992

1989 was an important year in the history of South Africa, as well as in the evolution of public policy-making regarding HIV and AIDS. By that time, it became clear to the government that its 'no explicit AIDS policy' was no longer tenable: the AIDS burden until then had been borne by individual households, the private sector and the biomedical community, but the government was now faced with an avalanche of calls from civil society, the business community and from within sectors of government itself to be more proactive in its approach to HIV and AIDS.

Also, the political landscape was changing: President P. W. Botha's stroke in early 1989 was the first step towards the F. W. de Klerk administration, which formally assumed office in September of that year, as well as the unbanning of the liberation movements and the concomitant birth of the political transition period five months later. The normative public policy environment now had to take greater note of the wishes and values of the government's negotiation partners (the ANC and their Mass Democratic Movement alliance partners), the South African legal system was no longer tolerant of the discriminatory legislation that had existed with regards to HIV-positive individuals in earlier years, and the McGeary and Hansen civil law cases indicated a powerful move towards and was broadly supportive of the ANC and labour unions' insistence on the extension of basic human rights to the majority of South Africans – including people living with HIV and AIDS.

As previously mentioned, government was forced to repeal the discriminatory legislation regarding AIDS enacted in 1987, and the National Department of Health established a number of intra-governmental and other agencies to combat the epidemic. Also, it was clear that the NP government could no longer refuse the call to draft a comprehensive policy on AIDS – putting an end to reactive, inappropriate, ad hoc and ill-conceived strategies that aimed at apportioning blame, or at a biomedical 'solution' to the problem of AIDS. In the early 1990s, therefore, the NP government set out to draft a more appropriate policy on the epidemic.[26]

However, the fact that the government maintained its exclusion of the broader political players, civil society and AIDS activists; that nothing could change the fact that it was an illegitimate government; as well as that it was focusing primarily on constitutional negotiations with the ANC and the other liberation movements – all these factors meant that the AIDS public policy environment remained difficult to navigate, with no comprehensive, inclusive and successful public policy emerging. Despite this, it is important to note that the process of the redefinition of the AIDS policy problem did commence in the three years following the changed political environment of 1989. The successful drafting of a truly democratised public policy on AIDS would depend squarely on this redefinition.

The democratisation of AIDS policy-making: 1992–1994

The redefinition of the AIDS policy problem as a human rights and development issue, and its ensuing repositioning on the public agenda – with the greater need to include the key decision-makers – led, in 1992, to a conference entitled 'South Africa United against AIDS', attended by members of the ruling NP government, key ANC officials, trade unionists, AIDS activists as well as members of the medical community. For the first time the main decision-makers in the South African AIDS arena came together, and this led to the establishment of a truly inclusive body – the National AIDS Co-ordinating Committee of South Africa (NACOSA). The latter would act as a kind of an 'AIDS caucus' where influential and powerful AIDS stakeholders could meet and develop a truly democratic public response to the epidemic. The 1992 meeting that established NACOSA was described by AIDS policy analysts as 'an unusual show of national unity at a time of complex and sensitive political negotiations, well before an election date for a democratically elected government had been decided'.[27]

By 1992 the newly instituted national antenatal HIV surveys made the extent of the reality of AIDS in South Africa clear to the reading public. The normative environment had shifted away from an exclusive conception of the AIDS policy problem, and now emphasised and embraced the need for a human rights-based approach to the epidemic. It was this confluence of a changed policy environment, the inclusion of the majority of important AIDS stakeholders and a sense of urgency that led to the drafting of South Africa's first comprehensive public document on HIV and AIDS: the National AIDS Plan (NAP – also known as 'the Plan'), which was adopted within the first few months of the ANC assuming power in 1994.

The successful drafting of the broadly popular NAP underscores the need for coherent political leadership in the establishment of an appropriate public policy to combat AIDS. According to Barnett and Whiteside, '[a] necessary ... criterion for preventing spread of HIV or turning the epidemic round is political leadership ... South Africa provides an example where absence of clear and decisive leadership damaged prevention activity'.[28] In retrospect the truth of this statement is clear: for the first decade of AIDS in South Africa there was a deficit in the political will and leadership to combat the rapidly growing epidemic appropriately. It was only once that political will came about and was translated into a re-conceptualisation of the policy problem that an appropriate and widely praised public policy could be drafted.

Reflections on AIDS policy-making in 1982–1994

It is not the purpose of this section to restate, re-describe and re-evaluate the policy-making process regarding HIV and AIDS under the NP government – that was done in chapters 2 and 3, as well as in the preceding sections of the current chapter. Rather, the purpose here is to expose more explicitly and summarise the insights of the 1982–94 era of South African AIDS policy-making by reviewing and summarising the key insights that echo the theoretical aspects of public policy-making that were discussed in the Introduction. This theoretically evolutionary/synthetic approach will assist the analyst in identifying the tacit patterns of public policy-making that prevailed at the time and determined the specific issue and problem identification that led to AIDS' inclusion on the public policy agenda.

The first insight worth noting is the truth of Anderson's caution that policy-making does not only refer to the explicit public sector statement of and proactive reaction to an issue or a problem; rather, public policy-making could also be the description of a government's non-action on a public issue or problem.[29] The NP government's handling of HIV and AIDS in South Africa – particularly in the years 1982–88 – is a testimony to such non-action: the government left it to the private sector to respond in any purposive, proactive manner, opting instead to personalise the virus and equate its impacts with the carriers of that virus. Thus, erroneous problem definition right at the onset of the AIDS problem – that morally unacceptable behaviour is the problem and not the socio-cultural environment that facilitated the spread of the virus – exacerbated and fed off the moralistic strictures wrought by this rather narrow problematisation of AIDS. Taking a moralistic stance was thus seen as a sufficient way to handle the issue, acting as an auto-exculpatory mechanism for the public sector.

This initial inaction on the part of the government was the result of and became mutually reinforced by the AIDS policy environment. The second main insight is the fact that, given the particular socio-cultural determinants and drivers of the disease, policy analysts should take particular notice of the social milieu within which AIDS policy problems are defined and policies are made. The policy environment refers to the public–private interface, the grey area where a plurality of interests and actors impacts on the manner in which policies are made. Of particular interest for the first dozen years of AIDS policy-making in South Africa is the perceivable shift in the political culture within which such policies were made.

It is noteworthy how the political culture in South Africa – in particular with regards to AIDS policy-making – shifted under the NP government from an initially hugely moralistic one to a much more individualistic culture in the late 1980s and early 1990s. This shift becomes apparent when one reviews the kinds of AIDS policies that became acceptable, as well as how the moralistic AIDS policies of the early 1980s were later terminated and actually led to policy succession by more liberal, human rights-focused individualistic AIDS strategies.

The third noteworthy aspect of the NP government's handling of AIDS is its underscoring of Dunn's assertion that policy problem identification and conceptualisation occur many times, and keep changing over time.[30] Linked to the point made with regards to a changing political culture in South Africa in the 1980s and early 1990s, this underscores the iterative nature of the policy-making process. The moralistic AIDS problem as identified in 1982 was challenged and eventually replaced with a more socially constructivist conception in the late 1980s, namely that AIDS prevalence in South African society is a result of a virus that free-rides on the social injustices inherent to apartheid South Africa. Interestingly, this re-conceptualisation of the AIDS policy problem was the result of intensive interaction between the policy actors and agents in the broader policy environment, and not only by the government of the day.

This highlights a fourth insight: the fact that the institutional public policy agenda (determined by the government/state and its agents) was challenged and, in fact, usurped by the more systemic policy agenda (as determined by members of the broader civil society, in particular in the biomedical and legal professional communities – in conjunction with the private sector).[31] These 'policy entrepreneurs' thus had an important role to play in the redefinition of South Africa's AIDS problem. Over time, these other policy actors had the impact of successfully counteracting the NP government's move to keep AIDS from the public policy agenda.[32]

Importantly, this exposes a fifth insight: that AIDS policy formulation and implementation under the NP government appear to have occurred as a more bottom-up than top-down response.[33] The government (top-down) initially failed to acknowledge and appropriately address the AIDS problem. Due to the input from other (bottom-up) policy entrepreneurs and actors (as well as a changing international political environment), however, this position changed, and the extra-governmental AIDS policy actors prevailed. The latter acted to delegitimise the government's stance on HIV and AIDS, and this led to the reformulation of the entire AIDS problematique in apartheid South Africa, as well as its place on the public policy agenda. The Hansen and McGeary civil court cases also serve to underline the fact that the policy mechanisms implemented by the government could be challenged from beyond the legislative and the executive branches of public governance: the independent judiciary (and this is important in terms of AIDS policy-making under Mandela and Mbeki later on) seized the hiatus in public policy-making and responded by revolutionising the AIDS policy environment altogether.

Another insight from a review of the NP government's AIDS public policy-making process is the fact that these dramatic changes in the public response to AIDS occurred only once the prevalence of AIDS became measurable, namely once annual antenatal HIV surveys were introduced in 1990. This emphasises the importance of policy evaluation: only once the impact of governmental and other measures against the AIDS epidemic could be measured (and were proved to be ineffectual) did the imperative of policy termination and succession become uncontested. Before 1990, however, there was no empirical evidence to disprove the worth of the measures implemented by the NP government to combat AIDS and HIV positive individuals – hence there was little AIDS policy termination and significant policy succession prior to 1990.

The final key insight worth noting here is the fact that pluralism and its sub-branches of public policy-making theory (public choice theory, elite theory and statism) seem to provide the most appropriate and insightful analysis of the manner in which AIDS policy was made under the NP government. For instance, pluralism is correct in terms of pointing out the myriad of actors and interests that were represented in AIDS policy-making in 1982–94 – the state was certainly not the most significant actor in shaping the public policy response under the NP government. Rather, the private sector, the biomedical community and the legal environment were at least as, if not more, prominent in shaping the response to the epidemic than the government. Membership of these differentiated actor groups was cross-cutting, emphasising the fractured nature of the real power behind policy responses to HIV and

AIDS. In some instances the power wielded by government was actually proactively undermined by these opposing policy entrepreneurs: the biomedical community and legal community as well as other sectors of civil society refused to be the implementers of the NP government's prescriptions regarding AIDS, and eventually influential agents within government (the AIDS Unit in 1991, for instance) worked to undermine and replace these prescriptions.

This creates an interesting confluence in the values and political motives of the forces external as well as inherent to government – eventually creating a powerful elite inside and outside of government that instituted problem re-conceptualisation and eventual policy change. These elites – particularly those in the biomedical, legal and state spheres – were central to adjusting existing AIDS public policies (as well as gaps in public policy-making) during the NP government's incumbency. Conversely, it is clear that rational choice theory certainly did not contribute any insights into the manner in which the NP government made AIDS policies: until 1990 there was simply no mechanism by which the AIDS problematique could be quantified.

Also incrementalism seems inappropriate for the period under discussion: 'although the NP government at first attempted to entrench the AIDS strategies following in the first half of the 1980s, the superficial adjustment of existing AIDS policies soon became unacceptable and impractical. According to Stover and Johnston, 'the groups leading the policy process [in 1992–94] were unconstrained by previous government experience. It was a time of "dreaming and great visions" '.[34]

If anything, 1982–94 is notable for the revolutionary change in the public policy response to HIV and AIDS – away from a denialist, hands-off public response based on moralistic arguments and towards a more proactive, constructivist re-conceptualisation of the policy problem in the late 1980s and early 1990s. Thus, although the NP government policy-making process was inherently conservative, incrementalism fails to explain how the government lost its public policy-making foothold on HIV and AIDS beyond 1988. The radically changed policy environment and the fact that public policy-making went far beyond the ambit of the state translated into a pluralistic, decentralised and rapidly changing policy-making environment. The conceptualisation of a more comprehensive AIDS policy in the run-up to the constitutional changes of 1994, therefore, 'was developed not by a government department but rather by a coalition of forces outside government. These forces, led by the ANC, had the advantage of a strong moral position'.[35]

5

AIDS Policy-making during the Mandela Administration (1994–1999)

> AIDS policy is too important to be left in the hands of technocrats.
>
> Nicoli Nattrass[1]

Introduction

After South Africa's first fully democratic elections in April 1994 the country entered a honeymoon period: after weeks of political violence and nervous negotiations the Inkatha Freedom Party (IFP) had joined the poll a few days before the elections, there was a remarkable absence of any political violence during the actual election, the messianic Nelson Mandela was sworn in without incident as Head of State on 10 May 1994, and a new Government of National Unity (GNU), including former political foes, was legitimately governing a truly democratic country. In short, the 'South African dream' had become a reality: four years of (at times) exceedingly tenuous political negotiations had paid off, and immediately the new political elite had to face the challenges of leadership.

But the new government inherited a polity in disarray: the NP government had created superfluous institutions and wasted money on replicating various state infrastructures in the so-called 'homelands'. Economically, the country was institutionally isolated from external sources of liquidity and close to insolvency. There was an urgent need to integrate the various governmental institutions and structures, get the economy growing, create jobs and foster greater socio-economic equality, finalise the constitution and embark on the challenges of nation-building.

Lurking above all of these immediate priorities was the reality of HIV and AIDS in the nascent South African democracy, but even this challenge did not seem insurmountable. After all, the NACOSA process, as we have seen, had assured that the plurality of HIV and AIDS stakeholders had come together in 1992 to embark on the design (by early 1994) of an ideal national strategy to counter the AIDS epidemic. By the time South Africans woke up to the Rainbow Nation on 28 April 1994, the NACOSA National AIDS Plan (NAP) had been drafted and approved, among other policy actors, by all of the main political parties representing ordinary South Africans. Furthermore, civil society as well as big business had bought into the process, and there were grand hopes that the human rights-centred approach that informed the NAP would bear fruit via swift and effective implementation by a democratic government.

This chapter does not reinvestigate the public policy-making around AIDS that had occurred in the years leading up to the sea-change of April 1994. That was the purpose of the preceding three chapters. Rather, it builds on the lessons and insights of that history – both the history of HIV and AIDS and the history of the public policy response that it evoked. This is done by focusing on the three main phases of AIDS policy-making that are discernible during the Mandela administration. During the first phase – 1994 to early 1996 – the Reconstruction and Development Programme (RDP) was held up as the broad public policy blueprint that would improve the country's socio-political equity. The RDP also served as the ideological foundation of other policy measures, including the NAP. However, within two years (in April 1996) the RDP was abandoned and replaced by the fiscally conservative Growth, Employment and Redistribution Programme (GEAR). It was also at that time that the ANC government had to face the reality that – due to an array of implementation difficulties – the NAP had failed to make any significant dent in the country's rapidly expanding AIDS epidemic.

This introduced the second phase of public policy efforts at stemming the advance of the South African AIDS epidemic. Unfortunately, the two years immediately following the scrapping of the RDP and the re-evaluation of South Africa's public response to HIV and AIDS were marked by a rapid succession of so-called AIDS scandals and other instances of maladministration. As discussed below, the country lurched from the Sarafina II humiliation to the Virodene controversy to the government's wholly bewildering handling of the provision of anti-retroviral drugs to pregnant women.

To make matters worse, the Mandela government confounded its AIDS critics by unilaterally moving towards making AIDS a notifiable disease, despite the fact that both the original NAP as well as the AIDS elite in South Africa had agreed upon and espoused the opposite policy ideals. These events worked against a successful third phase of public policy-making on HIV and AIDS during the Mandela administration, namely, the launch in late 1998 of a renewed cross-sectoral 'Partnership against AIDS'. Sadly, by that time the epidemic had become endemic, and it had become at least as politicised as it had been under the NP government.

This chapter analyses these events by applying the theoretical models developed, evaluated and applied in earlier chapters, and concludes by comparing and extrapolating from the key insights and patterns conceived during the pre-1994 years, given life during the Mandela years, and leading to a mode of policy evolution that we continued to experience until the end of Thabo Mbeki's first term as *de jure* Head of State in April 2004.

The National AIDS Plan of 1994

Idealism versus implementation

As noted in the previous chapter, the redefinition of the AIDS policy problem as a human rights and development issue, and its subsequent repositioning on the public agenda, led, in 1992, to the broadly inclusive 'South Africa united against AIDS' conference – the 1992 meeting that established NACOSA and was described by AIDS policy analysts as 'an unusual show of national unity at a time of complex and sensitive political negotiations, well before an election date for a democratically elected government had been decided'.[2]

By 1992 the normative AIDS policy environment had shifted away from an exclusive conception of the epidemic as a health policy problem, and now emphasised and embraced the need for a human rights-based approach. It was this confluence of a changed policy environment, the inclusion of the majority of important AIDS stakeholders and a sense of urgency that led to the drafting of South Africa's first comprehensive public strategy on HIV and AIDS: the National AIDS Plan (NAP) was officially adopted at Cabinet level in October 1994. It was only once political will had come about and was translated into a re-conceptualisation of the AIDS policy problem that an appropriate and widely accepted public policy could be drafted.

Comparatively, the difference between a human rights approach and a public health approach to HIV and AIDS is shown in Table 5.1.[3]

In retrospect, however, it is clear that by the end of the Mandela presidency in June 1999 the NAP policy framework had failed dismally in achieving its goals. The idealism accompanying the ANC's acceptance of

Table 5.1 The difference between a human rights approach and a public health approach to HIV and AIDS

Human rights approach	**Public health approach**
Only rights issues can mobilise a civil or social movement. Only a social movement can cause the necessary sea-change in cultural moves and behaviours.	Activism is destructive. It is immature, emotional and disruptive; fundamentally irresponsible.
AIDS is a unique case and needs resources dedicated to specialised services, to provide the support and acceptance required.	The more one makes AIDS seem different from other diseases, the more one stigmatises it; the more one diverts resources into a 'vertical' programme.
Confidentiality is a fundamental right to enable people to access the support and resources they will need in order to cope. The timing and order of disclosure is a private and personal prerogative.	Confidentiality is confused with secrecy, isolating PWAs from their families, friends and careers, and vice versa. Secrecy is the ultimate barrier to coping and dealing with HIV.
Support of PWAs will enable eventual disclosure of HIV status, but community acceptance is essential before such openness is feasible: Stigma needs to be tackled first and foremost. Disclosure in the face of stigma is very risky.	Stigma is impossible with large numbers of people known or seen to be infected: The fear itself amplifies stigma. In fact, if handled sensitively and well-timed, disclosure is usually therapeutic; the truth reconciles and dissipates stigma.
AIDS notification will drive the disease underground. Already people are too fearful to be tested.	AIDS notification will drive the disease into the open; it could not be further underground.
Deliberate infection occurs, but it is mostly a myth used to justify discrimination and victim blaming of PWAs. It is projection of responsibility for spread by people not yet, or only recently infected, onto those they assume were infected first.	Deliberate infection is a prominent phenomenon under cover of secrecy, a form of retribution born of anger and despair. It is contributing to our epidemics of rape and child abuse.
AIDS needs to become a chronic, manageable disease, and for this specific treatment needs to be provided, despite its expense.	AIDS is a chronic manageable disease and must be normalised and treated as other chronic infections.

the NAP and its human rights approach in April 1994 and the Cabinet's approval of it as the official public policy response to HIV and AIDS in October 1994 were sadly misplaced.

Despite the claim in 1994 that the NAP was an 'ideal' policy that got everything right in terms of inclusiveness, normative underpinnings and human rights-centred policy prescriptions, the empirical data proved otherwise. Table 5.2 quantifies the unchecked growth in AIDS prevalence figures as derived from both antenatal clinic surveys, as well as national extrapolations that covered the whole South African population.

The data demonstrate that, in terms of absolute numbers, the NAP was ineffective. It was unable to achieve AIDS strategy's primary goal: to lower HIV prevalence and AIDS-related morbidity and mortality among the population over time. The HIV prevalence figure among women

Table 5.2 HIV seroprevalence in South Africa

Year	Women attending antenatal clinics (%)	Total population (%)
1990	0.8	0.1
1991	1.4	0.3
1992	2.4	0.6
1993	4.3	1.1
1994	7.6	1.8
1995	10.4	2.9
1996	14.2	4.5
1997	17.0	6.3
1998	22.8	8.2
1999	22.4	10.1
2000	24.5	11.7

Source: Data compiled from Dorrington and Johnson (2002).[4]

attending antenatal clinics in 1994 was a disquieting 7.6 per cent, but instead of decreasing or even stabilising as a result of the implementation of the NAP during the Mandela government, this figure had more than tripled to 24.5 per cent by the year 2000. Concomitantly, the HIV prevalence figure among the population as a whole was 1.8 per cent in 1994, but this had ballooned by 650 per cent to a national HIV prevalence figure of 11.7 per cent by 2000.

Clearly, something had gone badly wrong. Analysts are in agreement that the contents of the NAP strategy could not be faulted. There is wide agreement among policy and AIDS analysts that the NAP had been the result of an ideal policy drafting process. The contents of the Plan contained all the elements required by HIV and AIDS and policy stakeholders including the World Health Organisation's (WHO) Global Programme on AIDS (GPA) officials, members of South African civil society, business, political parties, AIDS activists and trade unions.

A more politically correct and seemingly socially appropriate policy could hardly be imagined. The NAP came about when the new South Africa's first seminal macroeconomic and developmental framework, the RDP, was being drafted. It can be no coincidence that both the RDP and the NAP were accepted by the ANC a few weeks prior to the April 1994 election. Also, the RDP was written in such a manner that it embraced the normative tenets of the NAP, going as far as elevating the NAP as one of its five key elements. Juxtaposing the RDP and the NAP, the numerous congruencies between the two are noteworthy. The ANC's new Health Programme, the RDP as well as the NAP espoused the following values: policy-making would be inclusive, conciliatory, stable and consensual, focusing on bottom-up, populist measure mechanisms to ensure that all the appropriate policy stakeholders take ownership of the policies. Marais referred to the result of these ideals as a nexus of policies that 'established a comfort zone between conflicting forces and interests'.[5]

These so-called 'pro-poor policies'[6] had a strong developmental slant, with goals to embrace social spending for the sake of alleviating the plight of the indigent.[7] Initially, for example, the RDP base document had pledged, among other things, to:

- shift the health system from curative services towards primary health care (PHC), with free medical services for children under six years and pregnant women at state facilities – by 1998, all South Africans were to receive their basic nutritional intake, thanks to school-feeding and other schemes;
- create 2.5 million new jobs in ten years;
- provide electricity to 2.5 million homes by the year 2000, doubling the number of households with such access from the then 36 per cent;
- provide running water and sewerage systems to one million households;
- provide ten years of free education;
- extend infrastructure through a public works programme, and
- restructure state institutions to reflect the racial, class and gender composition of South African society.[8]

The NAP also reflected the broad policy goals of the RDP by emphasising 'a new division of responsibility for health between the different levels of government' and adopting an intersectoral approach.[9] The RDP-NAP nexus was so strong that one analyst noted that:

> [t]he rational and logical way properly to manage [AIDS] is to contextualise it within the [RDP] paradigm, and to approach the problem with the principles and concepts embodied in the RDP. The RDP concept itself will in the long run do the most to minimise the impact of the epidemic ... [10]

The ANC's National Health Plan of May 1994 explicitly noted that '[a]ll legislation, organisations and institutions related to health have to be reviewed' with a view to ensuring that the emphasis went beyond the apartheid era's focus on biomedical responses, focusing on health and overall well-being instead.[11] To this end, it was envisaged that a Charter of Patients' Rights would be enacted, making PHC central to the nation's health. Importantly, Schneider refers to the establishment of the AIDS policy process during the early days of the Mandela government as existing in the arena of 'high politics' – on a level where strategies and ideals compete and are established as core values, including national self-preservation, and the long-term objectives of the state.[12] Again, this echoes the normative and procedural tenets inherent in the discursive environment of pluralist public policy-making. Since AIDS policy-making entered this high stakes game at such an early stage, with core statal values underpinning it, it is important to evaluate the changes that appeared later on as macro-policy values and policy agenda items shifted around the year 1996.

Although an in-depth analysis of the contents of actual policies is beyond the ambit of this book, a brief overview of the NAP's key elements is in order.[13] In the first instance, the NAP entailed an integrated response to HIV and AIDS and comprised six elements: education and prevention; counselling; health care; human rights and law reform; welfare; and research.

According to Marais, key among the principles adopted was that people living with HIV and AIDS (PWAs) would be involved in all prevention, intervention and care strategies; that the NAP would be guided by recognition of women's vulnerable position; and that confidentiality would be protected.[14] Importantly, the Plan did not view the epidemic primarily as a medical issue, but couched AIDS education, prevention and care in broader, social terms. As important, the NAP also emphasised the imperative for both prevention and care strategies. In later years, a rather contrived dichotomy between the two aspects would appear in the government's public policy statements, as if HIV and AIDS prevention and care were mutually exclusive. In the NAP, however, all sectors of government were to be enlisted in the fights against AIDS. Thus, the NAP's goal and objects were to:

- prevent the transmission of HIV;
- provide care for people infected with and affected by AIDS;
- alleviate the impact of AIDS on communities;
- support people not infected by HIV in their efforts to retain that status;
- provide a forum for all South Africans to become involved in efforts to combat the spread of HIV and AIDS;
- identify resources that could be deployed in the fight against AIDS, and
- ensure that communities were fully involved in all stages of the development, planning and implementation of the Plan.

Lastly, implementation would be guided by the pursuit of three overriding objectives: preventing the spread of HIV; reducing the personal and social impact of HIV and AIDS; and mobilising and unifying national, provincial, international and local resources – again a strong balance between and interlocked system of prevention and care was mooted.

Explaining the failure of the NAP

So what went wrong? Why did this purportedly ideal, near-perfect public policy on HIV and AIDS fail to have any impact on the epidemic in South Africa, as admitted by its own progenitors and the new government? In Marais's analysis the policy implementation environment at the time goes some way to explaining this failure, stating that:

> [i]n the 1990s South Africa was the only country in the world which had to contend with an exponential rise in HIV prevalence rates in the context of a major political transition. In 1990–1994, therefore, what was unavailable was the institutional and political stability – not to mention the political legitimacy of government – necessary to implement a coherent and co-ordinated response .... It is widely held that the difficulties encountered [in 1994–1999] related to questions of process rather than technical content – hence the emphasis on the contextual problems that hampered implementation.[15]

Remarkably, the reasons offered for the failure of the NAP are almost identical to the explanations pointed to for the de facto scrapping of the RDP in April 1996. Taken as a whole, the failure of the NAP can be summed up as suffering from a 'crisis of implementation' – the strategic and operational details of the NAP document simply did not move beyond the problem identification, agenda-setting, policy formulation and policy adoption phases. A number of factors kept the NAP from being effectively operationalised. These are important in that for the most part they were the result either of the legacy of bad AIDS policy responses (active or tacit) during the NP administrations (within the policy environment that this created), or of the specific policy environment which introduced issues that would impact negatively on AIDS policy-making and implementation in years to come.

The sad irony of the NAP was that what had been projected as one of its most positive features seemed to be the direct antecedent of its downfall.[16] The purportedly ideal, rather idealistic, programmatic specifications and policy prescriptions of the NAP fell victim to precisely its idealism: the NAP was not realistic in what it wanted to achieve. During the time when the NAP was drafted via the NACOSA process of 1992–94, the ANC had not yet come to power, the NP's power was steadily following the downward spiral of its political authority, and human rights activists in particular (including two of the National Health Ministers of the next decade) could interact with other AIDS policy actors and agents and draw up a strategy in a context wholly divorced from the day-to-day realities of governance. The NAP came about and was accepted by the ANC caucus in early April 1994 as its main policy strategy to deal with HIV and AIDS before the party was exposed to the harsh realities of government.

The NAP in its original form was thus the expression of a wish-list; the ultimate luxury afforded to policy-makers who had been operating outside of the harsh constraints of budget realities and any real consideration for implementation capacity during a time of radical political and institutional transformation. Moreover, there was precious little accountability required of the essentially unelected group that made up NACOSA. The context of 1992–94 meant that the NAP accepted in April 1994 was almost inevitably festooned as a moral script, with serious consideration of whether it was practicable or not left by the wayside. It was the AIDS equivalent of the ANC's Freedom Charter of the 1950s, a document espousing laudable, 'high political' values – the difference being that the NAP gave little thought to the programmatic practicalities that would face its implementers.

Also, one has to bear in mind that the NAP came about during a parallel ideological battle between those in favour of retaining elements of apartheid versus those who wanted to create a wholly transformed society. The progression of the constitutional negotiations being held in Kempton Park at the same time, and the moral high ground of the constitutional transformationalists (as well as their prowess at the negotiation table) meant that the NAP was couched in a zero-sum moral discourse: one was either for a radically changed approach to combating HIV and AIDS in South Africa, or remained stuck in the morally discredited AIDS interventions that had been practised and implemented by the NP government. Given those odds, it is little wonder that the NAP so strongly and unquestioningly embraced the human rights-centred approach; that it had such an idealist slant – without sufficient thought of counter-ideological arguments or the constraints of practicalities.

As a result, it can now be said that the new government took on too much. In keeping with the developmental focus of its other flagship macro-policy, the RDP, it became generally understood that the new government would be at the helm of national developmental efforts. It was primarily up to the government to provide for the poor, change the look and feel of South African society, and ameliorate societal ills – including HIV and AIDS. In the discursive environment of the RDP, and despite lip-service to the involvement of civil society and the ANC's political alliance partners, the government would take on the primary responsibility to improve all South Africans' quality of life. The idealism of this position is less important than the immense pressure on and role that it presupposed for the South African state.

It might be that the ANC's central mistake in the first few years of coming to power was its overwhelming urge to improve all of South Africa; to be everything for everyone. Instead of focusing on a handful of governance or policy issues in which it could make a realistic, considered difference, the new government aimed to do justice to the spirit underlying the Mandela era: to provide 'a better life for all'. One of the members of NACOSA, Helen Schneider, echoes this sentiment:

> [i]n retrospect, one of the problems with the NACOSA process was that it loaded too much on government's shoulders – there was a belief that things would just happen much more effectively than they did. In a way we couldn't have done better at the time, but there should have been a rapid process of reviewing, a constant process of assessing and asking questions. That didn't really happen, not even within government.[17]

The implications of such a government-centred mindset are twofold. On the one hand, the world of AIDS activism would welcome such an approach, since it presupposes the critically important strong political ownership of the AIDS problem (which purportedly had worked particularly well in Uganda under President Museveni).[18] On the other hand, however, some analysts point out that this places too much of a burden and responsibility on the government.

The primarily sexual nature of HIV transmission means that any grand societal behaviour modification needs to happen at the individual, coital level, and no government can realistically or successfully take overall responsibility for individuals' sexual behaviour – in fact, such a political proclivity would come dangerously close to the intermestic policy environment between what is 'public' and what is 'private'.[19] As noted in the discussion on the apartheid years, under the NP government there had been broad policies aimed at policing sexual mixing, much to the antipathy of human rights and anti-apartheid activists all over the world. The new government was adamant that it would not repeat those mistakes, yet its adoption of the NAP and the statements surrounding what government hoped it would achieve meant that the state was setting itself up for failure – and attack – as will become clearer later on in this chapter.

There were four key sets of resources that the new government could employ in combating AIDS. These included: government officials; existing public structures and institutions aimed specifically at reducing the spread and impact of AIDS; fiscal resources, or public money; as well as the newly established context of co-operation between government and civil society.

In the first place, the new government was the result of and institutionally supported by a so-called 'sunset clause', as negotiated during the Kempton Park process. Marais notes that the clause:

> provid[ed] for a period of compulsory power-sharing in the form of the GNU, an offer not to purge the security forces and civil service of 'counter-revolutionary' elements, and the willingness to establish (during negotiations) a set of Constitutional Principles that could not be violated by the final Constitution.[20]

This meant that civil servants who had served under the NP government would not lose their jobs. In other words, the new government was in the fortunate position that, although the ANC had no experience of governing South Africa, it had a cohort of experienced public policy implementers at its disposal. In theory, this opened an opportunity for the new government to make use of existing expertise (also on HIV and AIDS) in its public sector, and to use this resource in order to drive the implementation of the NAP. However, this supposed resource proved to be a double-edged: many of the public sector workers who had served under the NP were now either paralysingly unsure of their own positions, leading to low overall morale and productivity, or plainly unwilling to assist their new colleagues and political masters in implementing the NAP.

One explanation could be the reported bitterness among some civil servants about having to vacate comfortable positions and train their former 'enemies' in the liberation movements in the skills of governance.[21] Unfortunately, there was also an explanation focusing on racism: that the 'old guard', on quasi-racist grounds, were tacitly refusing to co-operate fully with the 'new guard', and in the process making the state impotent in its efforts to implement the NAP as well as other public initiatives.

The idealism of the NAP process thus did not find sufficient application in the actual implementation capacity expected of the new government; this capacity had been taken for granted, but now failed to pay off. It became clear that the GNU would have to learn to muddle through, with AIDS only one among a host of pressing issues on the public policy agenda.[22] These difficulties at the personal level of public sector work undermined the possibility of the new government making effective use of the existing public institutions that had been established to combat the AIDS epidemic. Chief among these bodies were the ATICS – ready-made AIDS centres in urban (mostly white) areas with solid experience and resources to provide some level of preventative as well as treatment input to ordinary South Africans. The ATICS were all but abandoned by the GNU – they were viewed as part of the apartheid era, reflecting the values of that time.[23] Unfortunately, the demise of the ATICS meant that the government, in addition to losing these institutional structures, lost the human capital that the ATICS had enabled: the corporate memory, skills and the people employed there.[24]

These individual and institutional level constraints were exacerbated by the transformation process underway within the state: South Africa prior to 1994 had one central government and four provincial administrations, but in the democratic dispensation after 1994 the state had to adapt to a new unitary government (incorporating the former apartheid 'homelands'), as well as nine provinces. In addition to the institutional and procedural headaches that this implied, it soon became apparent that the 'GNU' was an institutional misnomer: there was very little effective communication between the central government and the various provincial governments, but in addition the new mechanisms for the devolution of powers and responsibilities were untested and – in the first few years of the new government – this implied little effective central–provincial co-ordination.[25]

The effect of this on the public battle against HIV and AIDS was that there was an overall impotence in the public sector, with the provincial governments left in a policy vacuum: not only did they rarely receive enough money for their individual health budgets;[26] they increasingly appeared to lack the capacity to spend the AIDS funds that they did have. As Marais observes:

> [a]ccording to the Plan, the engine room of the HIV and AIDS response would be located at provincial level. But the architects of the Plan had not reckoned with the quasi-federal system that was agreed upon at the political negotiation table. With the exception of

> the housing sector, national government was to allocate to the provinces lump sum budgets that provincial governments then had to divide up between different departments. Strictly speaking, national government could not decree the amount of funding any provincial government had to spend on, for example, health, let alone the amount it wished to see destined for HIV and AIDS work. To be sure, provincial decision-makers had to operate within a framework of nationally determined policy priorities and frameworks, but their subsequent decisions about actual spending were insulated from national 'interference'. This has meant that provincial health departments are tasked with implementing health policies and programmes that are often devised at national level … . Many provinces also regarded the national directorate [of HIV and AIDS] with suspicion and were reluctant to accept joint programmes and decision-making. On occasion, materials provided by the national directorate were rejected because 'proper consultation' allegedly had not occurred. Often muted and disguised, this feuding allowed a process of mutual blame to occur – with the national department accusing provinces of failing to deliver and the latter retorting that lack of consultation and unrealistic directives stymied their work. Similar feuds raged between the provinces and local authorities.[27]

Little co-ordination of human capital at different levels of government meant that the state's capacity to implement an effective AIDS policy became even more of a fiction. Increasingly, the GNU was centralising the governance of health and other public sectors. The first sign of this was that, instead of situating the NAP in the Office of the President, for the sake of urgent implementation and overall checks and balances (as had been agreed upon in the NAP), the ANC government established an HIV, AIDS and STD Directorate inside the National Department of Health. According to Marais, the original NAP had envisaged that:

> AIDS was to be transported beyond the realm of medicine and converted into a social and political issue. Simultaneously, in terms of treatment, services and an ultimate cure, it was still lodged in the medical field. The one area of action was the expanse of broader society; the other was a district of specialised expertise. Straddling these two realms was the belief that rational behaviour would halt the epidemic's spread … . What still eludes us is how to merge the paradigms of the medical and the political, the scientific and the social. There

> have been attempts to do so, but flawed ones ... [T]he Plan was prevented from attaining its goals by incomplete understandings of the social, cultural and ideological terrains on which it had to work.[28]

Situating the governance of AIDS in the National Department of Health thus undermined a critical goal of the NAP: to change the conception of the AIDS policy problem away from being a public health issue, and establish it as a developmental and human rights issue. This let the Office of the President off the hook: although President Mandela had paid lip-service to making HIV and AIDS a central part of his lead projects, the Minister of Health would, once again, become the main institutional policy actor and agent in the state's battle against AIDS.

> [T]he location of the Plan in the Department of Health highlighted the tension between the medical and social understandings of HIV and AIDS. The emphasis would be on the biomedical, behaviourist model of health intervention. This model hinges on aiding and persuading individuals to make certain behavioural choices *despite* the constraints created by social status. It is an approach that avoids looking at the complex social transactions people perform in order to position themselves as advantageously as possible in society. Essentially, it is a rationalist approach that sees behaviour as the outcome of transparent predictable and consistent decisions that can be altered by new, equally rational, inputs. Applied to HIV and AIDS it runs into two problems: HIV and AIDS are a disease that seems to defy rationality, and the approach shows a profound lack of knowledge and understanding of stressed social behaviour.[29]

Significantly, this undermined the relationship between South Africa's HIV and AIDS civil society and the government, and counteracted the spirit underpinning the NAP's mission to facilitate inter-and cross-sectoral co-operation. Instead of taking on the AIDS issue at a macro yet powerful presidential level, it was left to the Health Ministry and other individual government departments to co-ordinate activities. The distance that had opened between the government and civil society on this issue was later played out in the discursive environment and AIDS actors' willingness and ability to redefine the AIDS policy problem – as discussed below, the schism between civil society and the state presaged a battle between the government's increasingly obdurate position on the importance of prevention, versus civil society's insistence on access to treatment for people who were already living with the virus.

The Health Department under the new Minister of Health, Dr Nkosazana Zuma, and the government as a whole did not respond well to criticism of this and other matters. An increasingly intransigent Health Minister insisted on loyalty to the transformation process in South Africa – deeming any questioning of or negative comment on her department's actions on HIV and AIDS as either party-politically disloyal or racist (particularly in the case of media criticism). Such obduracy foreshadowed the further deterioration of the relationship between the HIV and AIDS civil society and the Health Minister and government, in effect re-politicising and re-racialising the AIDS policy problem. A siege mentality had developed within the government, and it soon became a permanent feature of the gamut of the AIDS policy pathology. As Nattrass points out:

> [i]nstead of acting quickly and efficiently to solve the implementation problems, South Africa's political leadership initially engaged in disastrous high profile 'quick fix' solutions. When these failed, and as HIV prevalence increased, the government went on the defensive by questioning the cost-effectiveness and affordability of AIDS interventions requiring the use of antiretrovirals.[30]

Summarising the contextual issues that worked against the effective implementation of the NAP, Schneider notes the following as key issues:[31]

- the delayed development of programme infrastructure at both national and provincial level post-1994 (McIntyre supports this point);[32]
- the lack of experience of new cadres in policy implementation through a large bureaucracy (as opposed to project implementation through NGOs) combined with a culture of non-delivery inherited from the old structures;
- the inability of a state undergoing restructuring at every level to prioritise AIDS in the face of multiple other, more visible priorities;
- failure to capitalise on infrastructure developed prior to 1994;
- implementation too narrowly focused on health sector rather than cross-sectorally as recommended by the Plan;
- weakening of NGOs by the loss of leadership to government/state structures;
- difficulties in defining and co-ordinating roles and responsibilities between different levels of an evolving federal system;

- conflict between stakeholders around unilateral policy development by senior government officials, and the lack of consultation with, and representation from, the broader AIDS community.

In addition, the NAP itself had the following weaknesses: it was a detailed blueprint for implementation developed prior to a massive change in the political and overall policy environment. With the exception of one provincial AIDS co-ordinator, the core members of the task teams who drafted the Plan did not lead its implementation post-1994. Seven of the nine provincial co-ordinators were not involved in the process at all. Institutional or policy-making memory was lost, as was ownership of the Plan. Furthermore, it focused on the technical content of policy, but did not pay sufficient attention to processes of policy implementation, in particular to how various actors could come together to support implementation. It also relied too much on government rather than on mobilising the multiplicity of actors outside of government. As Schneider notes, 'calls for political leadership not only place an inappropriate emphasis on the agency of national political leaders, but also project them as always willing and able to take the best possible courses of action to address the problems of HIV'.[33]

A comedy of errors

Despite the failure of the NAP, it was not abandoned or even amended. Pundits of the incrementalist school of public policy-making theory would, however, point to a possible incrementalist policy shift in focus in a national review of South Africa's response to the AIDS epidemic published in mid-1997. The review was entitled 'Review the Past, Plan the Future, Work Together', and contained very few surprises relating to government's broad AIDS policy prescriptions. The review findings highlighted the need for:

- political leadership and public commitment;
- meaningful involvement of people living with HIV and AIDS in policy formulation;
- responses to be interdepartmental and intersectoral;
- widespread capacity building;
- close co-operation with the TB Programme, and
- an urgent address of human rights abuses and the reduction of stigmatisation.[34]

In short, the review contained nothing new and very few additions that would point to formal, incremental policy addition or shift regarding HIV and AIDS. It merely reiterated the spirit and the letter of the original 1994 NAP. Due to the stated 'ideal' nature of the original NAP, this is hardly surprising – why would any government tinker with the content of a programme that enjoyed the support of all the main AIDS policy stakeholders? The most glaring error of the 1997 review was that it repeated the key mistake of the NAP: it ignored the actual AIDS public policy environment. Instead of a short-term revision of the NAP or any profound evaluation of its implementation difficulties, the National Department of Health started to do exactly the opposite: they shifted in emphasis from implementation to devising guidelines, with the stated goal to develop capacity and improve co-ordination.[35]

By that stage, however, the broader policy-making environment itself had shifted: in April 1996 the government announced that the RDP office would close. Despite the government's reassurances that the developmental focus of its main policy documents would not be abandoned, the ANC opted instead to maintain a greater distance from the programmatic practicalities required of its pro-poor policy. In the place of the RDP, the GEAR was to be the new macroeconomic keystone of the government. This programme, announced in June 1996 after remarkably little co-ordination among the broader corporatist policy environment as well as little consultation with the ANC's main political alliance partners, would lead to an exponential rise in the power of the Ministry of Finance in determining spending priorities in the affairs of state, as well as determining actual policy priorities. From a policy perspective this has important implications: the pro-poor values and developmental policy slant of the RDP would make way for a much more financially conservative, Washington Consensus-based model.

The government thus moved from a pro-poor policy-making stance to a pro-growth macroeconomic policy stance – with the latter couched in the discursive environment of employment creation and low budget deficits. The low social spending implied by such a policy shift arguably had the greatest impact on the critically important health sector. Instead of prioritising spending on social and health services, the government's policy discourse now changed to one of combating dissaving (as spending on social services would be viewed) and emphasising fiscal discipline rather than tolerance of budget deficits. This move foreshadowed a significant institutional shift – in terms of HIV and AIDS policy-making and spending priorities, it led to the tacit redefinition (yet again) of the

AIDS policy problem, which would become much clearer a few years later: the monetarisation of AIDS. The door was now open for the rhetoric of rational and public choice as well as Marxist public policy theories to be applied with regards to HIV and AIDS, and the power wielded by the National Department of Finance implied, in Marais's analysis, that AIDS as a public issue was transformed to a mere policy 'add-on'.[36] In financial terms it simply became less important to the government to spend money on an issue that did not dramatically enough or directly (in the visible short term at least) affect the numbers surrounding economic growth and employment creation.

The first phase of public policy-making on HIV and AIDS under the Mandela government effectively came to an end in 1996. Indicators of the shift to a second phase of AIDS public policy-making include: the demonstrable failure to implement the NAP of 1994 effectively; the move from the RDP (abandoned in April 1996) to GEAR (announced in June 1996); and the emergence of an AIDS policy environment defined by public scandal.

Not counting the failure on the part of the government to implement the NAP, there were four so-called AIDS policy scandals or polemics between 1994 and 1999. These included: Sarafina II in 1996; Virodene in 1997; the AZT decision of 1998; and the gradual move on the part of the government away from an entrenchment of the human rights-centred HIV confidentiality principle, to making AIDS notifiable.

The first scandal to hit the AIDS policy-making environment of the new government was the so-called Sarafina II debacle. In the 1970s and 1980s the South African playwright Mbongeni Ngema came to prominence with his anti-apartheid stage productions. Among these was a play (and later a musical film starring Whoopi Goldberg) titled *Sarafina*, which told the story of a young girl from Soweto and her struggle and that of her peers' for political freedom. The play as well as the film were very popular internationally, emblematising apartheid's dying days. In 1995 the National Department of Health put out a tender for the production of a stage play with the aim of informing young people across South Africa about the dangers of HIV and AIDS.

After meeting with Ngema, senior health officials awarded a R14.27 million tender to the playwright for a stage production. Despite the fact that this constituted a significant portion of the national AIDS budget, the Minister of Health fast-tracked Ngema's appointment, which led to criticism from the official opposition in Parliament as well as from the white-owned media that the correct tendering procedures had not been followed. In addition, AIDS activists questioned the wisdom of the play's (now entitled Sarafina II) central messages, deeming it inappropriate and ineffectual.[37] One of the main objections that the South African AIDS civil society had was that they were not consulted on the content of the play.[38]

There were thus two sets of criticism against Sarafina II: the content of the play and its key messages were attacked for falling short of the intended target market, undercutting its value, and the political opposition and the media pointed out that regular tendering processes had not been followed, and questioned the amount of money awarded to Ngema. As Kitching noted:

> [t]he Minister of Health ... cannot justify spending R14.2 million – one fifth of the already limited national Budget and more than the total provincial budgets – on fighting AIDS. Further efforts by the minister and her Director-General, Dr Olive Shisana, to justify this has also led to a political crisis of morality [translated from Afrikaans].[39]

Other critics were less kind, with Eichbaum noting:

> when the Department of Health embarks upon a R14.27 million exercise to fund a single stage production mounted by a person with an established track record of overspending on mediocrity and, in the process, sidestepping every known convention and procedure for the awarding of such a contract, one's hackles must inevitably rise.[40]

In the months that followed, government's relationship with civil society as well as the opposition and the media rapidly deteriorated. The sad irony was that the AIDS civil society in South Africa was for the most part comprised of former ANC and other anti-apartheid activists. The breakdown of relations between the government and civil society thus came down to a clash within the former broad South African liberation alliance. As the government's opposition to the questioning of the wisdom of Sarafina II increased, so did ASOs become increasingly involved in the politicisation of the issue.

In the process, Crewe noticed the entrenchment of a politically dangerous stance: the creation of an 'AIDS orthodoxy' inside government, and in the National Department of Health in particular, with anything falling outside that 'orthodoxy' deemed counter-transformationalist, disloyal or even racist.[41] The danger of such a stance is that the AIDS policy environment became a new terrain of high political struggle, with various policy actors and agents within that environment vying for the 'right' to make statements regarding the epidemic – going as far as fighting each other for the right to define the policy problem itself.[42]

Health Minister Zuma assumed a particularly combative position, citing racism on the part of the media and opposition parties when they questioned or criticised the Department of Health's actions. In particular, Zuma accused her detractors of abusing the technical details of a tendering process, and highlighting that issue mainly due to the fact that the tender had gone to a black person.[43] A year later, President Mandela referred to the Sarafina II affair as one of the main failings of his presidency.[44] In the end, the play was never produced, and the government wrote off its expenses years later under the Mbeki presidency. Importantly, though, Sarafina II embodied a divorce between government and AIDS civil society from which South Africa is yet to recover. As Phila notes:

> [The Sarafina II storm] has left much political and economic damage in its wake for the department [of health] and the young democracy. The credibility of minister Zuma and senior department officials has been severely damaged ... The policy work of the department was put on hold as this controversy unfolded ... Further, the reluctance of some members of the health portfolio committee and Parliament to ask difficult questions of the ministry of health during its investigations raises serious questions about the role of Parliament in ensuring transparency and accountability within government.[45]

The combative posturing of both the National Department of Health and civil society meant that the shared vision of the NACOSA process two years earlier had all but died. Sarafina II introduced and solidified a defensiveness in the government, henceforth rendering AIDS policy-making reactive rather than visionary or pro-active. Importantly, analysts would refer to the saga as the birth of 'anti-intellectual' AIDS policy-making in South Africa. This approach ran counter to the 'pro-knowledge stance' of extra-governmental AIDS activism in South Africa, and would become a feature of the public management of the epidemic until the end of the first Mbeki administration in April 2004.[46]

The next polemic to make headlines was the government's championing in 1997 of the purported anti-AIDS drug Virodene P058. This was developed by scientists attached to the University of Pretoria, and was touted as a home-grown 'miracle cure'. However, despite the fact that the drug had not passed the Medical Control Council's (MCC) clinical trials, the Minister of Health facilitated a meeting between the scientists and Cabinet, with the government giving the Virodene scientists a standing ovation at the end of their presentation.[47] Then Deputy President Mbeki himself became involved in the saga by publicly pushing for the MCC's fast-tracking of the drug's approval.

Given the political sensitivities following the recent history of Sarafina II, the reaction of opposition parties and the South African media was predictable: great opposition to the government's blatant interference in an epistemic community (biomedical science) where they did not belong. To make matters worse, the media claimed that the ANC had a financial stake in Virodene's development – emphasising vested party-political interests. The MCC deemed the drug to be insufficiently clinically trialled, and declared it unfit for human consumption. The MCC was able to demonstrate that Virodene was, in fact, a derivative of an industrial solvent, dimenthylfomamide (DMF). This 'independent' medical control body was then lambasted by the Minister of Health and eventually (in 1998) disbanded and reconstituted by the National Health Department.

The Virodene saga is significant in that it opened up the government to a new line of criticism regarding its handling of HIV and AIDS as a public policy issue, namely, that the government was interfering in science and not focusing on what they were supposed to be doing: governing the country and implementing policies. Critics pointed out that the National Department of Health rode roughshod over established scientific principles such as peer review and other procedural guidelines, pushing for the drug to be prescribed despite the fact that its clinical trials had not gone beyond the superficial first phase level. Criticism from the opposition Democratic Party (DP) and the South African media of the purported financial stake that the governing party had in the development of Virodene was countered by allegations of racism. The Minister of Health went as far as to intimate that the opposition wanted black people to die, and hence was opposed to any possible solution to the AIDS epidemic. Instead of focusing on the clinical properties of Virodene, and rather than respecting scientific due process, the AIDS policy environment was racialised and politicised once again.

The irony of the history of Virodene was that the same government and the same prominent deputy president who was pushing for its registration as an anti-AIDS drug were discounting scientists' and other critics' position that the drug was toxic. Mbeki would in the next year as well as in later years use the same argument against the wholesale provision of AIDS drugs such as AZT and Nevirapene, even though these drugs had been clinically proved to be effective.[48] Again, this underscores the deepening willingness on the part of very senior government officials to insist on monopolising the right to define the AIDS policy problem itself, discounting any position that countered their AIDS orthodoxy. As a result, the combative stances of the government and the broader 'AIDS world' in South Africa were further entrenched.

Within the context of Sarafina II, this meant that any constructive engagement among the actors that constituted the broader AIDS policy community (as pluralists would call it) became increasingly impossible. The government accused all outside of the state that their arguments were based on short-sighted racism, while the AIDS civil society found an easy policy scapegoat in the hardening governmental position. The spirit of NACOSA was now truly dead and buried, with no one taking responsibility for combating HIV. Instead of opposing a virus, the AIDS community in South Africa was in effect at war with itself. The site of the struggle for a new South Africa had moved from apartheid to AIDS, but the same activists who had fought with the incumbent government against apartheid were now antagonistic to their former cadres.

The National Department of Health and the Office of the Deputy President had touted Virodene as a possible African solution to an African problem, but they ended up with proverbial egg on their faces. Instead of owning up to the fact that it was not in their expertise or interest to 'play science', the government's anti-intellectual stance deepened, and soon the media, opposition parties and AIDS activists were pointing to the government's mismanagement of the AIDS epidemic as symptomatic of a general failure on the part of the ANC to govern effectively.[49] Of course, the greatest disservice of all was done to the fight against AIDS itself – not to mention PWAs.[50] The government increasingly demonstrated a willingness to want to define the AIDS policy problem without consulting any other policy actors, and in the search for a quick-fix solution to the epidemic, arrogant mistakes were made. Unfortunately, Mbeki's own enthusiasm to question the science of AIDS did not stop there; the government had not taken the lessons of Virodene to heart.

Not that the government got everything wrong. Although it criticised the state's handling of AIDS policy implementation, the National Health Review of mid-1997 noted great successes in the public sector's management of sexually transmitted infections (STIs) in general. In addition to the factors noted above, the review was, however, explicit in censuring the government for their centralised decision-making. It was clear, though, that the National Department of Health did not see itself as an equal partner with other actors in the AIDS field (as had been foreseen in the NAP of 1994), and the state as a result remained for the most part closed to criticism. This led Crewe to observe that, although the Review was critical of the government's AIDS management and policy implementation, the NAP remained in place, it was not amended and the recommendations of the review were never implemented.[51] It is no surprise, therefore, that the AIDS policy environment at the time was defined by growing distrust and general belligerence among policy actors.

The third main area of AIDS policy contention during the Mandela administration appeared on the public agenda in late 1998, when the government through the National Department of Health announced that it would not provide AZT to HIV-positive pregnant women, even though in clinical trials held in Thailand and elsewhere, it proved to be effective in limiting vertical, mother-to-child transmission (MTCT) of HIV.[52] The government's decision was therefore directly counter to the information provided by science, the spirit of the NACOSA process, as well as the letter of the NAP of 1994. At first the government gave financial justifications as their main reason for ceasing the provision of AZT to combat MTCT – it was, they stated, simply not cost-effective to purchase expensive drugs which had limited efficacy. Significantly, this can be identified as the invocation of a rational choice theoretical justification for a public policy decision. The Ministry of Finance supposedly did cost-benefit analyses and came to the conclusion that the provision of AZT was not affordable on a large scale. This reasoning was immediately questioned by economic experts,[53] who provided solid evidence to the contrary, showing that it would in fact be more expensive in the longer run not to implement MTCT programmes by providing AZT to pregnant women.[54]

For instance, in 1998 the MRC published a report stating that:

- An estimated 64,398 paediatric HIV infections occurred from MTCT in South Africa in 1997.
- This represents 11 per cent of the estimated global total.
- Approximately 37 per cent of these might be prevented through a national programme which includes short-course AZT.
- The estimated total cost of the national programme is around R164 million.
- This is equivalent to less than 1 per cent of the national health budget.
- Therefore, a national programme to reduce MTCT of HIV infection in South Africa would be an affordable, cost-effective and potentially cost-saving public health intervention.[55]

According to Nattrass:

> [t]he health ministry persisted with this discourse of unaffordability despite medical and economic research showing that the costs of MTCTP were more than offset by the cost-savings associated with reduced numbers of HIV-related paediatric cases. Nono Simelela, chief director (HIV, AIDS and STDs) in the Department of Health, argued ... that those advocating MTCTP programmes were 'cherry-picking' and that this was a 'luxury' that the health ministry could not afford as it had to respond to the health needs of all South Africans. In other words, the concern was that money spent on MTCTP was money lost to other parts of the health sector.[56]

In addition, it became known that the government, and the Department of Health in particular, were not actually able to spend their existing health budget (including the MTCT component). The state's argument that it could not afford to implement its MTCT programme, therefore, did not hold water – and this fallacy was quantifiable. Detractors of the government's position were doubly justified: in the first instance, economists could prove that the affordability excuse was untenable, and in the second they exposed the government's inability to spend its existing health budgets. When it appeared that the government could not prove their case based on the monetarisation of priorities, their justification for their decision on AZT changed yet again: the affordability argument was replaced by the National Department of Health questioning the efficacy and the safety of the drug itself.

In fact, the Health Department started to attack the merits of the drug on the grounds of toxicity, stating that it would be irresponsible to provide AZT to HIV-positive women. Significantly, this was the same government that less than a year before had discounted scientific proof of the toxicity of Virodene in an effort to bypass peer review and other biomedical processes to register a home-grown quick fix to the South African AIDS epidemic. The difference with AZT was that it had been proved effective by international peer-reviewed clinical trials. Again, the government questioned the science of AIDS despite evidence to the contrary.

In terms of the theory of public policy-making the rhetoric surrounding the monetary arguments used by the government as a whole and the Finance as well as the Health Departments in particular to justify their decision not to provide AZT are significant. Marxist theorists would point to the nexus of exploitation between those elements who own the means to produce a good that is to be used by society as a whole and governments' co-option by these capitalist forces. In the case of the Mandela government's early management of MTCT technologies (the drugs), however, the government itself used Marxian rationalisation for their policy decision. For instance, when it became clear that government was unable to implement public policy on MTCT effectively, the politics of blame resurfaced.

The manner in which this happened was played out as follows. In the first place, the government cited the unaffordability of leading AIDS drugs as a reason not to provide AZT. Instead of owning up to the figures demonstrating the state's *under*-spending of its AIDS budget, the government (in line with public choice theory) invoked a confluence with rational choice theory by attempting to quantify the (un)affordability of AZT, and then utilised the rhetoric of Marxist public policy theory by blaming large pharmaceutical companies (like Glaxo Wellcome) and their ownership of the intellectual property rights (IPRs) of ARVs in an effort to apportion ultimate responsibility to these nefarious outside (capitalist) forces. This is an important point, since it would become a major feature of the Mbeki government's handling of the AIDS epidemic in years to come.

As a consequence, the South African government – like the NP government before them – turned to AIDS policy-making via legislation in order to operationalise policy documents. The National Department of Health in 1997 passed the Medicines and Related Substances Control Amendment Act (the Medicines Act), enabling them to parallel-import ARVs from third countries instead of paying what the government called 'exorbitant' fees to large pharmaceutical firms in exchange for drugs. In addition to parallel imports, the legislation enabled the government to activate compulsory licensing, which would transfer pharmaceutical technologies to local manufacturers, making it cheaper to produce ARVs locally.[57]

These measures were legal in international law and in accordance with World Trade Organisation (WTO) specifications, but were challenged by the large pharmaceutical companies, which decided to take the government to court. The matter became a political hot potato for US Vice-President Al Gore, who was then running for office. In the end, the pharmaceutical companies withdrew their case and unilaterally offered to lower prices of ARVs, making it affordable for the government to provide AZT and other ARV combination therapies to ordinary South Africans.

The furore surrounding the Medicines Act of 1997 will be discussed in greater detail in the next chapter, but at this stage it is important to note how the South African government played a game of (unknowingly) using one public policy theoretical discourse against another. Rational choice theory and Marxist theories regarding public policy-making were utilised to justify state behaviour, and in the process the government, to some extent at least, managed to provide some space for policy-making unity between itself and members of the South African AIDS civil society. The latter were united in their opposition to the pharmaceutical companies' court case against the government.

However, it is significant that this unity and the application of these rationales were not sufficient to provide the policy environmental unity required to put AIDS policy implementation back on a co-ordinated, cross-sectoral track. The government was also willing to use arguments of AZT's supposed toxicity when seeking to exculpate their own actions, or failure to act. The government's stance against the pharmaceutical companies did, however, succeed in garnering international support for its broader, anti-capitalist position, and this is widely credited for the loosening of IPRs regimes around ARVs which followed early in the new millennium.

Another important consequence of the government's AZT decision was the establishment of the Treatment Action Campaign (TAC) in December 1998. The TAC was founded by AIDS activists specifically to act as a watchdog on the provision of treatment to PWAs.[58] Although this introduced an important player into the South African AIDS policy environment, it also led to a further hardening of government versus civil society stances: in later years the TAC would use civil disobedience campaigns to create a critical mass against the ANC government's AIDS policies. Unfortunately, such a radicalisation of South Africa's AIDS civil society also translated into a crystallisation of government's focus on the value and strategy of prevention, versus the broader AIDS civil society's insistence that treatment priorities were as important. At the national political level, the party-political aspect of this drama came to the fore when the NP-controlled Western Cape provincial government announced in early 1999 that they would, unilaterally and against the wishes of the central government, implement the rollout of MTCT programmes, including the provision of AZT at certain public locations.[59] This did not, however, end the drama, and the government's AZT decision remained a feature until the end of the Mandela administration in June 1999.

The third and shortest phase of public policy-making during the Mandela administration commenced in October 1998, and came to an end with the swearing in of the first Mbeki presidency in June 1999.

What differentiates the few months between October 1998 and June 1999 is the announcement on 9 October 1998 of a new 'Partnership against AIDS' by Deputy President Mbeki.[60] In an effort to renew the government's commitment against HIV and AIDS, the Mandela government had organised for the President himself to address the nation in a live television broadcast on 9 October and to announce the latest iteration of the NAP: the 'Governmental AIDS Action Plan' (GAAP). AIDS activists were disappointed by the Deputy President's television performance – he was seen as wooden, and cold towards the children surrounding him on screen.

In addition to being a public relations disaster, Mbeki was at the last moment asked by Mandela to stand in for him – again, AIDS activists took this as a sign that the Mandela government did not prioritise HIV and AIDS at the most senior governmental levels, and the fact that Mbeki seemed welded to the teleprompter led to criticism of the government simply going through the motions; lacking honesty. A month before the televised event, the government held an AIDS crisis summit to launch the Partnership against AIDS. However, the Minister of Health was late, and Mbeki made only a brief appearance as he was on the way to open a World Athletics meeting. Opposition parties suspected the partnership was a pre-election ploy.[61]

The government had hoped that the limited level of co-operation with the South African AIDS civil society that came as a consequence of the government's popular resistance to pressure from pharmaceutical companies regarding the Medicines Act of 1997 would gather momentum after the performance of October 1998. But the opposite happened: a mere two months later the TAC was established largely in response to the government's decision not to provide AZT to pregnant women. The short-lived truce between the government and civil society came to a dramatic end in April 1999, when the government announced its intention to make HIV and AIDS a notifiable medical condition. Again, this flew in the face of what had been agreed in earlier years. The NAP had been drafted as part of an evolving human rights-centred approach to AIDS, with the issue of patient confidentiality forming a central part of this culture.

Significantly, the proposed notifiability measures were similar to those the NP government had introduced in 1987. This was surprising, given that (as noted in the previous section) the NP government was forced to withdraw the regulations a few years later. According to the Mandela government's proposed measures, medical practitioners would be required to: report their findings to the local authorities or the Department of Health within 24 hours; provide information on age, sex, population group, date of diagnosis and any available information concerning the probably place and source of infection; and communicate their findings to the immediate family members and the persons who are giving care to the person in respect of whom the report is made.[62]

This fourth 'scandal' did not, however, come as a surprise to many AIDS policy observers: in November 1996 the then Director-General of Health, Dr Olive Shisana, had expressed her unhappiness with the culture of 'secrecy' surrounding AIDS. Shisana was at the time jeered by AIDS activists for comparing the incipient danger of AIDS to the sensational and fast-killing Ebola virus. Again, this was seen as government insensitivity towards PWAs and interpreted as wholly inappropriate, strengthening stigmatisation and driving the epidemic deeper underground.[63] The NAP had been explicitly opposed to making AIDS a notifiable condition, and at the time of its adoption government and civil society in South Africa were in agreement on this issue.

Furthermore, the Health Review of 1997 had warned against making AIDS notifiable, and a dramatic illustration of existing prejudices in South Africa against PWAs was the murder in December 1998 of AIDS activist Gugu Dlamini, who was beaten to death by members of her community after she made her HIV status public.[64] In addition to citing human rights concerns, experts cautioned the government against making AIDS notifiable in resource-constrained environments where there is limited access to health care and HIV testing, and noted that notification is not an efficient way of collecting information on AIDS.[65]

The fact that the government, in light of all these prior agreements, admonitions and events, was on 23 April 1999 still willing to gazette its unilateral intention to make AIDS notifiable drove the wedge between itself and civil society even deeper. The October 1998 armistice abruptly ended, and the AIDS civil society in South Africa declared open season on its own government. Government countered – disastrously – by citing racism as being at the heart of such criticism. Also, Shisana's earlier position that opponents of making AIDS notifiable belonged to a Western, gay-centric subculture that did not fit in the South African context angered human rights activists.[66] The AIDS Advisory Group (AAG) (originally set up by the NP government in 1985) asked for a meeting with senior Health Department officials to clarify matters before the government's April 1999 statement, but the state responded by disbanding the body without warning. Again, this move angered AIDS activists outside of government; they accused the state of being unaccountable, undemocratic and intolerant of criticism:

> High-ranking civil servants in the ministry of health routinely present themselves as being trapped between civil society and their impetuous political masters, and warn activists and medical practitioners not to 'offend' the politicians and to be 'constructive'. Whether intentional or not, the impression is created of a political leadership so concerned about status that it is prepared to act out of pique when criticised. This rather infantile approach to political debate and civil society mobilisation does not bode well for democracy or the rational resolution of AIDS policy debates.[67]

This position echoed the Parliamentary Health Committee's earlier anxieties about the manner in which Minister Zuma was managing her portfolio:

> [i]n its report, the health committee lists several points of 'particular concern' about the department, raised in Parliamentary hearings and the media, which reinforce the Public Protector's portrait of a badly governed bureaucracy. The points include: transparency, accountability, adherence to public administration rules and regulations, sound preparation of new policies, development of a culture of consultation in policy development and proper reporting to Parliament.[68]

The details of these events are less important than the insights they provide into the broader AIDS policy environment of the time. The manner in which the South African government and the AIDS civil society in particular related to them is instructive. For a start, the scandals were telling of the relationship between government and civil society. After the conceptualisation of the NAP in 1994 there were great hopes of the new democratic government and AIDS service organisations (ASOs) in civil society working together and co-ordinating their activities in order to combat the epidemic. By the end of the Sarafina II debacle, however, it was clear that a rift had opened between these two sets of policy agents – the idealism of the NACOSA process had all but dissolved.

When reviewing the history of these scandals, it again becomes clear how the politics of blame and the concomitant (re)politicisation of AIDS became an even stronger feature of the public policy environment in the second half of the 1990s. As noted above, the blame cast on government's failure to implement the NAP, as well as the public sector and civil society's increasingly antagonistic and uncompromising positions, can be seen as a feature of the fact that government was given and had taken on too much of the responsibility to 'save' South Africa from AIDS. The government became an easy scapegoat for those outside the public sector, and hence the state started to seek out scapegoats of its own.

Reflections on AIDS policy-making in 1994–1999

As was the case in the previous chapter, it is not the purpose of this section to describe the policy-making process regarding HIV and AIDS under the Mandela government. Rather, the purpose is to expose more explicitly and summarise the insights of the 1994–99 era of South African AIDS policy-making by reviewing and summarising the key insights that echo the theoretical aspects of public policy-making discussed in the Introduction. In doing so, the phase/stage approach acts as a useful heuristic, enabling one to gain insights into how public policy-making with regards to AIDS found application under the Mandela government. This theoretically evolutionary/synthetic approach will assist in identifying the tacit as well as the more apparent patterns of public policy-making that prevailed at the time and determined the specific issue and problem identification that led to AIDS' inclusion on the public policy agenda.

Mandela's government closed in the midst of an AIDS furore. The first five years of democratic South Africa came to an end riding a wave of discontent and policy contestation around HIV and AIDS, with various policy actors vying for the right to make statements on and define the AIDS problem itself. It is a sad irony that the hope and optimism that had been established in 1992–94 during the NACOSA process could not be followed through with appropriate and effective implementation strategies. As noted above, in terms of its content, the NAP of 1994 appeared to be the perfect blueprint of an AIDS public policy. However, the Mandela government's failure to implement the Plan effectively can be seen as an indictment of policy actors' and agents' inability to translate that substance into something appropriate, effective and sustainable. Proper analysis of this failure is useful to public policy analysts in enabling learning and insight; it can assist the analyst in moving beyond the impotence of failure, in order to gain insights into how not to proceed in future.

As had been the case with the NP government's handling of HIV and AIDS, the first insight to be gleaned from the Mandela years is the primary significance of the policy problem identification phase. Under the NP government, AIDS as a public policy problem was first defined in moralistic and later in biomedical terms. Finally, as South Africa entered the transition period of 1990–94, AIDS was cast as a human rights issue. The NACOSA policy formulation process was supremely influenced by the conception of HIV and AIDS as a developmental issue, taking into account the socio-political context of the epidemic. This developmental focus was further entrenched by the Mandela government when, notionally at least, it viewed the AIDS policy problem as an issue to be tackled under the aegis of the RDP. However, as soon as the new government came to power, the realities of government started to have an impact on the ANC.

Instead of implementing the NAP in a manner reflective of the AIDS policy problem conceptualisation as described in the discursive environment of the first few months of the new government, the tacit tension between the idealism of the ANC government's high political human rights approach and the realities of a public health response came to a head. The latter usurped the high political environment, with the new government finding it easier during the first tumultuous months of its administration to revert to a stricter yet unexpressed biomedical response set; the situation of the NAP in the National Health Department was the first illustration of this policy incongruence. In short, the rhetoric of human rights and a developmental approach to AIDS was maintained at the same time as the government fell back on the ways of the NP past. What this meant in reality was that there was no change – no real policy termination in terms of the implementation of AIDS public policies as South Africa transformed from an apartheid to a rainbow nation republic.

This rendered the so-called ideal or perfect content of the NAP inconsequential: the NAP became a beautiful document, written for all the right reasons and involving all the appropriate policy actors, but utterly powerless to have an impact on the ground. One lesson of this is that problem identification, agenda-setting and policy formulation can only be as significant or powerful as allowed by the actual implementation phase. If the latter remains stuck in the manner in which implementation had been managed in the past, any novel policy is rendered ineffective. In this sense the theory of incrementalist policy-making and implementation is descriptive of the death-knell of AIDS policy-making during the Mandela administration: while it is true that the AIDS policies of the NP government were terminated or at least radically transformed through the NACOSA process, the actual implementation phase of the new policy remained congruent with the manner in which AIDS public policies had been formulated and implemented under the previous government.

There is a related insight, namely that despite the fact that a plurality of policy actors were involved in the formulation of the NAP (and this to a large extent validates the position of pluralist theorists), the broad alliance that had drafted the NAP collapsed as soon as it came to the policy implementation phase. Significantly, however, the government's detractors are for the most part wrong in exculpating the AIDS community outside of government. As discussed above, the South African AIDS civil society found it quite convenient to put the onus of responsibility for policy implementation solely on the new government. Unfortunately, the policy environment created by the RDP mindset facilitated the transfer of this duty onto the government, and it is no surprise that the new ANC government would place the ultimate responsibility with the National Department of Health – after all, this is the way things had been done in the past. This is where the AIDS corporate memory of the new state was located. Then, as accusations, blame and recriminations entered the public policy environment via the media, a lasting schism appeared between the government and civil society. The policy directive deduced from this is that it is essential to involve all policy stakeholders not only at the policy formulation stage, but also at the policy implementation phase. Both the state and civil society were responsible for the failure to do so.

The result of these two fault-lines in the policy problem identification, formulation and implementation phases translated into a battle that came to a head during policy evaluation: since government had taken on the mantle of policy implementation on its own (despite rhetoric to the contrary), it became defensive and rejected civil society's eagerness to comment on implementation strategies (and failures). Conversely, civil society – given that they had been part of the team that drafted the policy response in the first place – felt justified in wanting to redefine the policy problem. This situation very quickly corrupted the entire AIDS public policy environment, leading the policy actors to fall back on the positions of the past. Claims of racism or disloyalty once again entered the policy discourse, re-racialising and re-politicising the AIDS policy issue.

Viewed in this context, it is little wonder that this policy issue so quickly fell victim to a rapidly hardening anti-intellectual policy stance: government became frantic in its search for a quick-fix solution to the epidemic, and the rapid succession of different AIDS scandals (Sarafina II; Virodene; the AZT decision; the reversal of the notifiability position) backed the state into a corner. Soon the relations between the Mandela government and AIDS activists had deteriorated to such an extent that the state had nothing to lose by questioning the tenets of epistemic communities where they did not belong: medical science itself. In the process, the government utilised all tools at its disposal to deflect outside criticism: as discussed above (and reflective of rational choice theoretical underpinnings), first certain assumptions and tools were utilised to discredit the findings of peer reviewed science, and when this was unsuccessful an ethical discourse was used to rationalise the non-provision of ARVs.

Underpinning these dynamics was a single significant fact: the Mandela government had taken on too much in going it alone in the battle against the epidemic, and soon the everyday practicalities of this error caught up with the state. In response, not only was AIDS racialised and politicised; it was monetarised as well. The AZT decision in particular was rationalised on the grounds of fiscal affordability, and this would become a central feature of the Mbeki government's policy response to the epidemic. All the policy noise and confusion stemming from the policy environment created a situation where government and the rest of the South African AIDS community defined the AIDS policy problem in increasingly antithetical terms: where the government prioritised prevention strategies, civil society emphasised the need for treatment; where government reverted to a public health response, civil society underlined the centrality of a human rights approach. Increasingly, the AIDS policy environment became one of several paradigms talking past one another, with very little room for negotiation. The sad consequence was that the Mandela administration thus echoed the destructive dynamics of the NP government's AIDS management: the politics of blame regained its place on the 'high political' plane.

The distinguishing feature for public policy theorising can be summed up as a tension between respectively the discursive and the practical levels of public policy theories' ability to describe reality and prescribe policy ideals. This can be clarified as follows: the discursive environment of the Mandela government's public policy response to HIV and AIDS remained one of pluralism – the NAP policy environment never ceased to pay lip-service to the fractured nature of political power, emphasising the plurality of AIDS policy actors and agents and their respective interests. However, at the practical, pragmatic level AIDS policy-making and implementation in 1994–99 moved away from pluralist descriptions to a more exclusively state-centric path. Public choice theorists would be correct in pointing out that the state itself attempted to centralise and even monopolise the right to address AIDS policy-making as a moral function of government. In doing so, the Mandela government in general and the Health Ministry in particular used the discourse of what can be identified as rational choice theory – in particular as they monetarised the policy stakes and rationalisation involved in the provision of ARV drugs.

However, critics of the government's strategy to quantify the benefits of AIDS prophylaxes have pointed out that this (most probably unconscious) application of what can be identified as rational choice reasoning was based on erroneous and manipulated data. Rather, these critics would underline the impact of aspects of elite theory that emanated (again unconsciously) from within government – particularly as the state increasingly claimed for itself the right to define the AIDS policy problem, as well as its blatant interference in the science of AIDS. In doing so, the state's discourse can be identified as that of one other public policy theory in particular: Marxian theoretical analyses of the AIDS public policy environment were applied in an effort to deflect the growing crescendo of blame cast on the government by the South African AIDS civil society.

Government did so by blaming outside forces – large pharmaceutical companies in particular – for its inability to solve the domestic AIDS issue. The impact of AIDS on South African society was laid at the door of international capitalist interests, in particular companies' profits from selling essential AIDS drugs. Sadly, the discourses of these theories of public policy-making and implementation were unconsciously used in order to reactively justify behaviour and rationalise policy failures, rather than to be applied as tools to facilitate policy modification and the improvement of overall policy implementation.

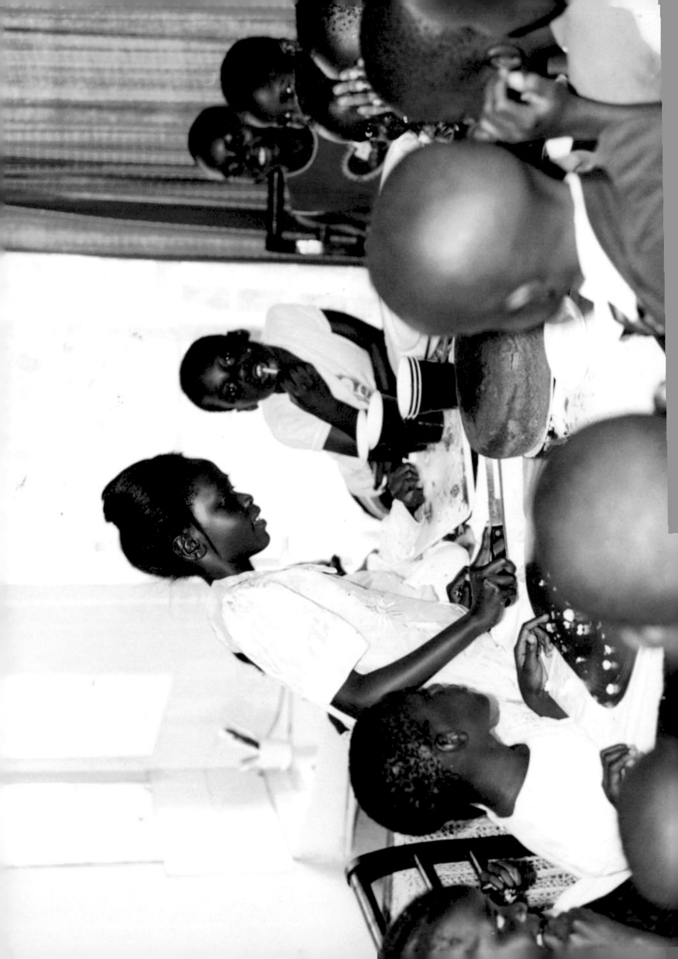

6
AIDS Policy-making during the First Mbeki Administration (1999–2004)

AIDS is a devious disease – it thrives on divisiveness.
The Washington Post, 15 March 2001

Introduction

When Thabo Mbeki became South Africa's *de jure* Head of State in June 1999 he was faced with intense demands on policy-making and governance. The ANC's support in the national election of 1999 grew to 66 per cent (an increase from 62 per cent in 1994) and the President set about to project himself as South Africa's 'Mr Delivery'. Whereas Mandela had focused on nation-building and political reconciliation, the Mbeki presidency was determined to operationalise its election promises of 'a better life for all'.

However, the first Mbeki administration came to be overwhelmed by the reality of HIV and AIDS. As noted in the Introduction, at the 15th International HIV and AIDS conference held in Bangkok in mid-2004, UNAIDS released their latest statistics for South Africa. The data demonstrated that by December 2003 5.3 million South Africans were HIV-positive, and 370,000 AIDS-related deaths had occurred in South Africa in 2003 alone – the equivalent of an 11 September 2001 attack on South Africans every three days.[1] Yet no 'war on AIDS' has been declared analogous to the Americans' 'war on terrorism'.

In terms of the AIDS policy environment, Mbeki inherited the socio-political baggage of his predecessor. The state–civil society relationship had become strained after the Sarafina II debacle of 1996 and remained so, failing to capitalise on the rapprochement around the government's legal case against the large international pharmaceutical companies in light of their litigious proclivities following on the enactment of the Medicines and Related Substances Control Amendment Act in 1997. But this was just one choppy wave of AIDS discontent that the new president's government would have to face in the next five years – in fact, there are five main features of the first Mbeki government's handling of the AIDS public policy environment.

First, the human rights culture nascent during the final years of the apartheid regime was entrenched during the Mandela period, and could now be utilised to its fullest potential. After its establishment in the year before Mbeki took office, the TAC would now come to utilise the new national constitution and the legal environment that it created with the aim of ensuring PWAs' rights *vis-à-vis* essential drugs. For this reason, the first theme of the Mbeki government's handling of HIV and AIDS would be the *culture of legislation and litigation* that came to accompany the public management of the South African AIDS epidemic. As discussed below, the significance of this for the role of the state in coping with AIDS became clear in the way in which civil society in particular stepped up its willingness to bypass the national government and go straight to the courts in order to achieve their goals, creating a kind of 'public policy by litigation'.

The second important feature of the Mbeki government's management of AIDS is perhaps the most controversial, particularly for the way it has been portrayed in the local and international media. Within four months of taking office, Mbeki started to question the scientifically established causal link between HIV and AIDS, exacerbating the anti-intellectualism that had been a characteristic of the Mandela government's AIDS management. The President's so-called *denialism* and polemicisation of the science of AIDS (which, as noted in the preceding chapter, started with the Virodene fiasco) further politicised and racialised the issue of AIDS in South African politics, and at the public policy level many observers would come to criticise the government for confusing the very conceptualisation of HIV and AIDS as a public policy problem, thus unduly and irresponsibly manipulating the policy agenda.

This crisis did not end during the first Mbeki government, but it did set about events that can be identified as the third main theme of the government's management of HIV and AIDS: its handling of MTCT and Highly Active Anti-Retroviral Therapy (HAART) programmes in particular. As mentioned above, the newly established human rights-oriented legal environment afforded civil society in South Africa the opportunity to challenge the Mbeki government on its implementation of South Africans' constitutionally enshrined right to health. This legal environment, coupled with Mbeki's denials, his practice of pseudo-science and his continual questioning of the AIDS statistics came to a head in the shape of the TAC's battle to ensure the public availability of MTCT prevention programmes and ARVs in particular. Underpinning this struggle between the AIDS civil society and the South African government are varying positions on where fiscal priorities should lie (in zero sum terms): with AIDS *prevention* programmes or with AIDS *treatment*. Government has taken the former view, with the TAC and other members of the South African AIDS civil society emphasising the latter. Again, this is a significant consequence of the dynamics established in the last years of the Mandela government.

This issue provides a natural introduction to the fourth discernible theme of the Mbeki government's management of the South African AIDS epidemic: the monetarisation of AIDS. Increasingly, AIDS pundits from within the government and civil society began to emphasise the costs of AIDS – in terms of the costs to the South African society and economy, as well as the costs associated with an appropriate publicly funded response. Importantly, the previous chapter indicated that the public monetarisation of AIDS in South Africa commenced in the mid-1990s, when the ANC government under Mandela enacted legislation to force large pharmaceutical companies to make ARV drugs available in South Africa and the rest of the developing world. The more contemporary monetarisation of AIDS can be analysed within that context, and Marxist and rational choice public policy theories in particular come into play, as will become clear. In fact, questions around the affordability of ARVs have become one of the main themes in the modern South African political context.

The last major theme that this chapter addresses is the ongoing attempt to reappraise the structural variables that drive the epidemic. Since AIDS first emerged in South Africa, the morality and ethics of the state's response have been under the microscope. The thematic golden thread that runs through all the rhetoric surrounding the disease points in a single direction: culture and race. In possibly an ambitious effort to make sense of the AIDS public policy environment, the chapter's penultimate section focuses on these thorny issues. What does the history of dealing with HIV and AIDS tell us about South African society? How have the South African government's conceptualisation who is to blame, who the enemy is, and how one should respond as a society had an impact on the state's capacity to respond – and vice versa?

The chapter closes with an exposition and analysis of public policy theories, and how they are and can be applied (and abused) in an effort to shape the public sector response to AIDS. In particular, the chapter seeks to find an answer to the moral and highly political question of how the state is supposed to respond to this epidemic. Is it right to ask the government to do so much?

The institutional and legal context

'The HIV and AIDS/STD Strategic Plan for South Africa, 2000–2005'

Within the first month of the Mbeki presidency the institutional wheels were set in motion for the creation of the new government's key policy document on HIV and AIDS. At a planning meeting held early in July 1999 the government decided that the NAP of 1994 should be 'revisited and revised'[2] – not, it is important to note, abandoned altogether, but (as pundits of incremental public policy-making would describe it) amended in accordance with the AIDS policy challenges the new government now faced. As had been the case with the National Health Review of 1997, the Mbeki government realised that it would not be necessary to scrap the NAP of 1994 – after all, that policy document had the backing of all the main AIDS policy actors, both inside and outside government, and was widely lauded as an ideal policy for South Africa. Hence, at the meeting it was agreed that a committee would be appointed and charged with the development of a five-year HIV and AIDS/STD Strategic Plan. Task teams were established to review existing goals and objectives for the designated priority areas, and after follow-up meetings in September and October 1999, a draft document was presented to the Inter-Ministerial Committee in November, with additional comments solicited from all government ministers. The final document, the 'HIV and AIDS/STDs Strategic Plan for South Africa, 2000–2005' (the 'Strategic Plan') was completed in January 2000.

The Strategic Plan stated that all government departments, organisations and stakeholders would use the document as the basis to develop their own strategic and operational plans so that all the initiatives for the country as a whole could be harmonised to maximise effectiveness and efficiency. It was the aim of the Strategic Plan for every government ministry and every sector to have dedicated HIV and AIDS focal persons. In addition to reaffirming the majority of the key principles and programmatic imperatives referred to in the NAP of 1994 and in the National Health Review of 1997, the Strategic Plan made specific reference to a number of (public) institutional structures that would drive the programme's implementation during the Mbeki administration.[3]

These structures included the creation of a South African National AIDS Council (SANAC), the interdepartmental committee on AIDS (IDC), the health ministers of each of the nine provinces (MinMECs), a committee consisting of all provincial heads of health (the Provincial Health Restructuring Committee (PHRC)), provincial AIDS councils (PACs), a Directors-General forum, as well as a reconfirmation of the seminal role of the Department of Health's HIV, AIDS and STD directorate.

As was the case with the NAP in 1994, the content of the Strategic Plan was praised for its holistic approach and comprehensive grasp of the issues that needed to be addressed in order for South Africa to prevail in the battle against AIDS. However, again the breakdown between the (ideal) programmatic prescriptions and institutional structures of the Strategic Plan on the one hand and the implementation of those strategies on the other hand very soon became all too apparent. Once again, the Strategic Plan appeared to be unable to overcome the ANC government's crisis of implementation, of moving from policy conceptualisation to operationalisation. This chapter will discuss in greater detail the policy environment which curtailed the successful implementation of the Strategic Plan below, but at this stage it is worth examining some of the criticisms levelled against the actual Plan.

Reviewing priority area 4 of the Strategic Plan two years after it was made public, Heywood noted that 'the inertia and invisibility of the SANAC for most of 2001 prevented [the devising of implementation strategies] from taking place'.[4] Although South Africa had developed one of the most progressive and far-sighted policy and legislative environments relating to HIV of any country in the world, Heywood expressed his frustration that 'the policy environment has still not catalysed implementation'.[5] The government's decision to oppose the decriminalisation of commercial sex work as well as its reticence to roll out ARV therapies and MTCT prevention programmes at public facilities (a problem which continues to this day) was also taken as an indication of the unwillingness on the part of the state to act on the prescriptions of its own Strategic Plan.

This poses an interesting question: in drawing up an AIDS policy framework that says one thing, but then explicitly fails to act on it, what is the Mbeki government's true policy on HIV and AIDS? As will be noted below, this question became a refrain throughout the entire first Mbeki administration. The main point at this stage is to note that there appears to be a disquieting inability (some would say unwillingness) on the part of the South African government to implement all the prescriptions of the Strategic Plan.

Illustrating this, Hickey *et al.* also note that the Strategic Plan was 'criticised for lacking a clear commitment to treatment options, such as the provision of ARV therapy, as well as lacking clear and measurable plans, timeframes and a dedicated budget for implementation'.[6] They also point to a fault-line inherent in the Strategic Plan specific to difficulties at the interface between national and provincial policy implementation:

- The provinces – without being provided with adequate resources – have tended to be primarily responsible for the implementation of policy.
- Provincial programmes lack an independent evaluation system.
- There appears to have been little inter-provincial collaboration or communication.[7]

The official provincial government AIDS response, created in November 1999 and entitled the 'National Integrated Plan' (NIP), further illustrates these challenges. The NIP focuses on the Life Skills programme in primary and secondary schools, the voluntary counselling and testing (VCT) programme, and the community and home-based care and support (CHBC) programme, and is jointly delivered by the health, education and welfare sectors (government's so-called Social Cluster). It is funded separately from the regular budget process. However, Hickey as well as Agenda 53 have found that the NIP struggles in implementing and co-ordinating broad policy objectives and decision-making on HIV and AIDS budget allocations, has cumbersome administrative structures, and struggles to develop the capacity for effective implementation.[8] An illustration of this is that, as *SAPA* reported, 'in the first year of the NIP, the provinces managed to spend only 36.5 per cent of the total HIV and AIDS grants available to them from the central government'.[9]

Some of the most vociferous criticism against the Strategic Plan is centred on the particulars surrounding the creation in January 2000 of SANAC. In terms of the Strategic Plan, SANAC was the natural product of the government's stated commitment to an inter-sectoral approach to AIDS. 'Furthermore,' Strode and Grant write, 'SANAC had to replace the AIDS Advisory Council, as it was not a multi-sectoral body and only made up of technical experts.'[10] The Strategic Plan describes the role of SANAC as:

- advising the government on HIV and AIDS policy;
- advocating for the effective involvement of sectors and organisations in implementing programmes and strategies;

- monitoring the implementation of the Strategic Plan in all sectors of society;
- creating and strengthening partnerships for an expanded response amongst all sectors;
- mobilising resources for the implementation of AIDS programmes, and
- recommending appropriate research.

The Strategic Plan also provides that SANAC is to be made up of 34 people, 16 of whom are from government and 17 from various sectors of civil society. The 34th member and chairman of SANAC is the Deputy President. Once again, on paper the creation of SANAC could not be faulted: it could potentially heal the wounds and animosity created by the Sarafina II and other AIDS scandals during the Mandela administration; it could be an effective interface between central government (via the presence and chairmanship of the Deputy President) and the AIDS civil society in South Africa, providing the institutional vector for the efficient implementation of the programmatic features of the Strategic Plan. The reality, however, turned out very differently. Within weeks of its launch SANAC became the target of a barrage of criticism from both the South African media and the vast majority of members of the country's AIDS civil society: its membership was unilaterally appointed by the government, the majority of SANAC members were government officials, there was an all but total absence of scientists, clinicians and pharmaceutical company representatives, and the AIDS Consortium (a network representing about 200 NGOs) were wholly excluded.[12] As Trengove-Jones notes:

> [t]hrougout 2000 we saw mounting tensions within what could only ironically be termed a 'partnership' against AIDS. Designed in part to give new urgency and impetus to the partnership, [SANAC] was launched early in the new year, top heavy with government ministers and lacking almost any significant NGO representation. The rift this caused only widened through the year until the gap between the government and NGOs had grown to the point where, in October, the AIDS Law Project and the TAC gave notice of their intention to take the government to court over its refusal to implement programmes for MTCT prophylaxis.[13]

In an independent review of the SANAC, Strode and Grant found that:

- It has proved to be ineffective in advising the government on any matters of great policy significance.

Table 6.1 Outline of the 'HIV and AIDS/STD Strategic Plan for South Africa' (2000–2005)

The primary goals are to:
Reduce the number of new HIV infections (especially among youth)
Reduce the impact of HIV and AIDS on individuals, families and communities

Four main areas constitute the Strategic Plan:

Prevention
Goal 1: Promote safe and healthy sexual behaviour
Goal 2: Improve the management and control of STDs
Goal 3: Reduce mother to child transmission
Goal 4: Address issues relating to blood transfusion and HIV
Goal 5: Provide appropriate post-exposure services
Goal 6: Improve access to voluntary HIV testing and counselling

Treatment, care and support
Goal 7: Provide treatment, care and support services in health facilities
Goal 8: Provide adequate treatment, care and support services in the community
Goal 9: Develop and expand the provision of care to children and orphans

Monitoring, research and surveillance
Goal 10: Ensure AIDS vaccine development
Goal 11: Investigate treatment and care options
Goal 12: Conduct policy research
Goal 13: Conduct regular surveillance

Human and legal rights
Goal 14: Create an appropriate social environment
Goal 15: Develop an appropriate legal and policy environment

Source: Adapted from Smart and the Strategic Plan.[11]

- Its structure does not allow it to monitor the implementation.
- Its structure does not allow it to interact with other stakeholders or any non-members.
- Its structure has not enabled it to form strategic partnerships with other organisations.
- Its meetings are closed, making it all but impossible to hold SANAC accountable through the normal democratic channels.
- It is for all intents and purposes managed by the Department of Health.

- It is unable to make an impact on the outcome of key decisions that are made.
- It has no capacity to monitor the implementation of the Strategic Plan.
- It is not bringing political commitment to the HIV and AIDS response in South Africa.[14]

Criticism of SANAC thus centres on the fact that it is not representative of the South African AIDS community, as was envisaged in the Strategic Plan. On the contrary, it is viewed as an exclusive, government-heavy institution created to rubber-stamp and legitimise the National Department of Health's (questionable) response to the AIDS epidemic. Many members of South Africa's non-governmental AIDS elite are calling for the scrapping or radical reconstitution of SANAC.[15] Similar criticisms have been levelled against the IDC; problems remain that keep this institution from carrying out its mandate. These include insufficient links between the IDC and the Directors-General social cluster, the junior position of most IDC members, lack of communication between IDC members and their senior management, insufficient resources allocated to HIV and AIDS programmes within departments, and insufficient project management and monitoring in many departments. Also, due to a high turnover in staff, skills building is an ongoing need; there is a lack in programme management skills.[16]

Legislation and case law

Earlier it was noted how legislation had been used by the NP government in an attempt to compensate for a lack of AIDS-specific programmatic public policy initiatives. This situation changed under the Mandela government, where the NACOSA process led to the drafting of the NAP of 1994. Legislation then became a complementary tool in the state's arsenal in the fight against HIV and AIDS, particularly in so far as it reflected the establishment of South Africa's culture of human rights. As Forman *et al.* note,

> [l]egislation plays a critical role in achieving health reform goals, and has a multidirectional and dialogic relationship with policy. On the one hand, legislation depends on the development of policy to guide its nature and content. Yet health legislation can also express and formulate health policies, and through statutes and regulations it can shape the way that health policy is translated into health programmes

> and services. Legislation however plays a distinct role from policy, and serves to coordinate health sector activities, and to create a management and administrative framework for the development of health care systems. It establishes structures and mechanisms to put policy into practice and provides for sanctions should the policy (encapsulated in the legal provisions) be breached. Health legislation creates certainty with respect to what is expected from various role-players and what the user of health services can expect.[17]

In particular, legislation was used to regulate the workplace and to create a fair and non-discriminatory environment for individuals to apply for and retain employment. Echoing the human rights principles set out in the Constitution of 1996, the Labour Relations Act, Basic Conditions of Employment Act and the Employment Equity Act were but three pieces of legislation introduced during the Mandela administration that contained specific measures to safeguard the rights of HIV-positive individuals. The human rights approach of such formal legislation was also reflected in the case law that was evolving: again focusing on the world of work, several cases came before the courts which further entrenched the rights of PWAs, and a powerful legal foundation was established for the protection of patient-doctor confidentiality, as well as the protection of the rights of HIV-positive employees and job applicants. As will be discussed below, litigation is becoming an increasingly important strategy in civil society's, institutions' as well as individuals' efforts to force the government to stop prevaricating on the provision of MTCT prevention and ARV therapies.

During the first Mbeki administration several important pieces of legislation as well as case law came to fruition or were introduced, which further served to entrench a human rights approach to HIV and AIDS. As noted in the previous chapter, the Medicines Act of 1997 was the first and had the highest media profile – both domestically and internationally. In brief, the Act contained provisions that would make it possible for the government to parallel-import ARVs, and to issue compulsory licences to local pharmaceutical manufacturers to produce generic AIDS drugs at a fraction of what it would cost to purchase from their foreign patent holders. Such measures are legal under the WTO TRIPS rules (of which South Africa is a signatory), but the Medicines Act became controversial when the US-based Pharmaceutical Manufacturers' Association (PhrMA) (representing 39 pharmaceutical companies) decided to take the Mandela government to court in 1998. During the second half of the Mandela administration the US government placed immense pressure on the South Africans to honour the patent rights of the American companies that developed the drugs, going so far as to put South Africa on the US 'Super 301' watch list.[18] Many observers accused the US of bullying or racketeering in an effort to put profits above the rights of PWAs, and eventually the issue became a political and public relations disaster for the US government.

The South African government (under Mandela and in the early years of the Mbeki administration) did manage, however, to put the issue of PWAs' rights to essential drugs on the international agenda. The issue also garnered wide support from sectors of civil society, and the TAC and COSATU in particular established links to drive popular resistance and demonstrations against the PhrMA court action.[19] In April 2001 the PhrMA decided to withdraw their case and this led to great elation among South African and international AIDS communities, who hailed the move as a victory for human rights in the context of HIV and AIDS. The South African government had triumphed in a David vs Goliath struggle against big business. However, their joy was short-lived: at the news conference following the PhrMA's announcement, the South African Minister of Health, Dr Manto Tshabalala-Msimang, announced that the drugs were too expensive to parallel import or to manufacture locally. The alliance between the South African AIDS civil society thus came to an acrimonious end, with the latter accusing the government of not being willing to honour their promises to make these drugs available to PWAs.

> To date, little has come of this victory, a failure which, as a *Business Day* editorial at the time suggested, would leave the impression that government is more interested in scoring points off the multinationals than providing care for millions of poor HIV and AIDS sufferers.[20]

This introduced a phase of severe conflict between particularly the TAC and the South African government, as will be discussed in greater detail below.

However, the drama surrounding the Medicines Act of 1997 did serve a number of purposes:

- The government succeeded in putting the issue of patients' access to essential drugs on the global policy agenda, and in doing so, aligned itself with global human rights and AIDS activists.
- The PhrMAs' retreat was seen as a moral and legal victory for PWAs, further entrenching a human rights-centric approach to drugs provision, particularly in the developing world.

- It paved the way for South Africa and other developing countries to declare AIDS a health emergency, and to activate the TRIPS provisions that would ensure parallel importation and generic manufacturing of AIDS drugs.[21]
- However, the South African government's bizarre about-turn on applying the Act served to drive a very deep wedge between civil society and the state. The government's explanation of fiscal constraints was viewed as an unjustified cop-out. In Buch's analysis:

> having led the world with its challenge, South Africa announced that it would not be implementing what it had fought for. This made the victory somewhat hollow ... *Government's AIDS policy is solid, but its actions and signals have been mixed.* [Emphasis added][22]

In addition to the conclusion in 2001 of the furore surrounding the Medicines Act of 1998, there were three developments in AIDS-specific legislation that were significant during the first Mbeki administration. First, in August 1999, Chapter II of the Employment Equity Act (EEA) 55 of 1998 came into effect. Chapter II is specifically aimed at eradicating unfair discrimination in the workplace. Among other measures, the EEA prohibits anyone from unfairly discriminating against an employee on the basis of his/her HIV status.[23] Furthermore, medical testing prior to employment is outlawed, and the Act makes a point of listing HIV status as a ground separate from the ground of disability. According to Du Plessis, 'the EEA is the first piece of legislation in the world that offers protection specifically to persons living with HIV from unfair discrimination and unauthorised HIV testing'.[24] However, there was some criticism of the more recent versions of the Act, which do not go far enough in expressly prohibiting insurance companies from discriminating against PWAs;[25] such criticisms have led some legal experts to note that a review of the EEA might be in order.[26]

Second, in 2001 the South African Law Commission drafted a Bill for the Minister of Justice which provides for court-ordered compulsory HIV testing of persons arrested in sexual offence cases. The draft Bill presented the government with a legal conundrum: under South Africa's legal constitution, one is innocent until proven guilty – including in cases of sexual assault or rape. However, the draft legislation would force an accused sexual offender to undergo a medical test to ascertain his HIV status.[27]

Third, in January 2001 the government retreated on its intention (gazetted in the first half of 1999) to make AIDS a notifiable medical condition. In their explanation, the Department of Health cited the burden of stigma as its main consideration. The government also noted that they did not have the infrastructure in place to enforce any notifiability regulation or legislation.[28] This change of heart was a victory for human rights activists, who noted that measures or legislation to make AIDS notifiable would have clashed with human rights standards: '[t]he regulations would have required non-consensual disclosure of AIDS status to a broad range of health care workers, as well as to immediate family member and caregivers'.[29]

Besides these developments in the legislative context, the first Mbeki administration also saw some advances in the field of case law affecting HIV and AIDS. As noted earlier, the TAC and the AIDS Law Project in particular set an important precedent during the Mbeki administration in using case law to force the state to provide MTCT prevention and ARV therapies at public facilities. This will be discussed in greater detail below. However, two instances of the use of case law regarding HIV and AIDS merit mention at this stage.

Interestingly, both cases dealt with applicants for work at South African Airways (SAA). These cases were first brought before the South African courts during the Mandela administration, but concluded during the Mbeki administration. In the first of these, *Hoffman* v *SAA*, the applicant contended that SAA had unfairly discriminated against him on the basis of his HIV-positive status in rejecting his application for employment as a flight attendant. In 2001 the court ruled in favour of the applicant, noting that the SAA's employment policy was in contravention of the applicant's right to equity. In September 2000 the Constitutional Court had upheld Hoffman's application, 'alter[ing] the legal landscape concerning AIDS in the workplace in Southern Africa'.[30]

In the second case, *'A'* v *SAA*, the applicant had also been refused employment by the SAA on the basis of his HIV status. The case was one of the first such cases to be heard in the Labour Court, and the SAA's pre-employment HIV testing policy was successfully challenged. 'A' was awarded R100,000 as compensation, with SAA unconditionally admitting that the exclusion of 'A' from the position of cabin attendant on the grounds of his HIV status was unjustified.[31] Both cases have set important precedents in the South African legal system as well as in the HIV and AIDS public policy environment, enforcing the human rights of job applicants, as well as the measures set out in the EEA.[32]

Denialism and obfuscation: Mbeki enters the fray

According to Barnett and Whiteside, a necessary, but not sufficient, criterion for preventing the spread of HIV or turning the epidemic round is political leadership.[33] This must begin at the highest level if there is to be success nationally. However, South Africa provides an example where absence of clear and decisive leadership damaged prevention activity.

Political leadership refers to proactive and effective action from the top echelons of government to drive the battle against the epidemic. This includes the Head of State as well as key government functionaries and departments. In the South African context, it was noted in the previous chapter that President Mandela, by his own admission, did not provide such leadership; unfortunately, most analysts agree that President Mbeki has not fared better. On the contrary, there seems to be a prevailing judgement that, as far as AIDS is concerned, Mbeki did more harm than good during his first five years in power. Statist theorists would point out that the Head of State has significant power and authority in determining and driving the public policy agenda, and hence the fight against HIV and AIDS – President Museveni's successes in Uganda are usually held up as an example of the positive impact that a national leader can have in reducing a country's HIV prevalence. Unfortunately, the majority of individuals belonging to the South African AIDS community are of the opinion that Mbeki has done more to obfuscate the AIDS public policy environment in this country, rather than facilitating and enabling an appropriate response.

This reputation became established even when Mbeki was Mandela's deputy: his first foray into the AIDS arena came in 1997 when he supported Virodene as an alleged cure for AIDS. Despite scientific evidence to the contrary, Mbeki pushed for the registration of the drug, and when the MCC refused, this medical peer review body was first excoriated as being racist or 'counter-transformationalist', and then unceremoniously disbanded and politically reconstituted. Mbeki never distanced himself from Virodene or changed his stance, and drove the wedge between mainstream AIDS science in South Africa and the government even deeper when, a year or so later, he questioned the efficacy of AZT – yet again making statements that flew in the face of established medical science, as well as scientific evidence. As a consequence, the Mandela government refused to offer AZT to women who had been raped.

Mbeki's 'discovery' that AZT might have negative side-effects was gleaned during Internet searches, and Crewe believes that these debates around the safety of ARVs led him to the so-called dissident views on the causal link between HIV and AIDS.[34] Dissidents are a small and diverse minority group of scientists and other individuals, some of whom do not believe that HIV causes AIDS, others who believe that HIV does not exist at all, and a third group who believe that HIV is the cause of AIDS but that it is all a plot by the pharmaceutical companies to sell drugs. These dissident views were repeatedly refuted in the 1980s and 1990s by clear scientific evidence that the HI virus exists, that it has been isolated and indeed photographed, and that it leads to immunosuppression and eventually the physio-pathological syndrome called AIDS.

However, the Virodene and AZT sagas during the Mandela administration created a public policy environment around HIV and AIDS which manifested in a hugely defensive and obdurate government – not in all cases reflecting the views of technocrats and lesser functionaries, but certainly among the political elite within the state. Instead of establishing a culture of free and open exchange between the government and AIDS civil society in South Africa, this served to entrench a growing mistrust and eventual disgust and overt antagonism (even several instances of litigation) between these two groups that are so critical to the fight against the epidemic. Eventually, these fault-lines manifested within the governing alliance (ANC-SACP-COSATU) itself, with the latter two members of that alliance censuring the ANC government for aligning itself with discredited views beyond the fringes of mainstream science.

A brief chronology of Mbeki's mounting assault on AIDS orthodoxy during his first tenure as Head of State reads as follows:

1999

- In late October, in a speech before the National Council of Provinces (NCOP), Mbeki refers to the alleged toxicity of AZT and requests his new Minister of Health to undertake further investigations about its safety and efficacy.
- The ANC's annual report notes that AZT would not be made available at public facilities.

2000

- Early in the year, the formation of a Presidential AIDS Panel is announced. The panel includes mainstream and dissident scientists in an effort to explore opposing viewpoints on the causal link between HIV and AIDS. From then onwards, official AIDS discourses on its causation refers to the causal link between HIV and AIDS as a 'thesis'.
- In February the President questions the orthodox aetiology of AIDS, earning a rebuke from the chair of the South African Medical

Association (SAMA), which represents 17,000 South African doctors, including 75 per cent of all doctors in active practice in both the private and public sectors.[35] Mbeki also rebukes the head of the MRC, Professor William Makgoba, for failing to read a particular article about the toxicity of AZT.

- In March a presidential spokesman, Parks Mankahlana, accuses a large pharmaceutical company of being 'like the marauders of the military industrial complex who propagated fear to increase their profits'.[36] One month earlier Mbeki had told the ANC's parliamentary caucus that drug companies were financing the TAC, which was now 'infiltrating' the trade unions.[37]
- In April Mbeki writes a letter to world leaders (including the British Prime Minister Tony Blair and the US President Bill Clinton) in which he hails AIDS dissidents as modern-day Galileos. The White House finds the letter so bizarre that at first it doubts its authenticity.[38] There appear to be cracks within the ruling ANC on this issue, with the MEC for health in Kwa-Zulu Natal attacking AIDS dissidents for abusing their access to the president to spread lies and confusion.
- Between June and October the President and the leader of the official opposition, Tony Leon, exchange letters on the subject of AIDS. Mbeki reiterates his doubts about the efficacy and safety of ARVs. In subsequent letters to Leon, Mbeki refers to 'hysterical' estimates of the incidence of AIDS by epidemiologists and the 'insulting' theory that HIV and AIDS originated in Africa.[39]
- In June 2000 the President opens the 13th International AIDS Conference in Durban, reiterating his doubts about the South African epidemic, and saying that poverty and not HIV is the main contributing factor to AIDS. Earlier, in response to journalist Charlene Smith's public appeal that South Africans exercise some cultural introspection about the high incidence of rape and sexual assault in the country, Mbeki accuses Smith of launching a blatant racist attack on the new South Africa.[40] Five thousand scientists sign the Durban Declaration, reiterating the mainstream scientific view regarding HIV and AIDS, but the President's spokesman later notes that the declaration is fit for the dustbin, and that it is an 'elitist' document.[41]
- In September, in an interview with *Time Magazine*, Mbeki casts doubts on whether HIV (if it exists) is the only contributing factor to AIDS. Later in the month, in a statement to Parliament, Mbeki states that a virus cannot cause a syndrome – echoing the anti-intellectual statements of dissidents. After his statement to Parliament, the SACP and COSATU call on Mbeki to stop raising questions about the causes

of AIDS in public. The ANC health portfolio committee in Parliament sends a confidential memorandum to the Minister of Health urging her and Mbeki to make a public statement stating that HIV causes AIDS.[42] After an ANC National Executive Council (NEC) meeting later on in the month, Mbeki announces that he will make no further public statements on the issue. Behind closed doors, however, Mbeki continues his crusade, and if newspaper reports are to be believed,[43] in late September he addresses the ANC's parliamentary caucus, stating that the American intelligence agency (the CIA) and large drug companies were behind a conspiracy to discredit him. Mbeki allegedly also accuses the TAC of being funded by these drug companies, and that they were leading the local assault against his Presidency. He also states that it was not clear to him whether his own Cabinet supported him against the drug companies.

- In early October, the ANC's NEC publishes a statement staying that Mbeki was the target of a massive onslaught against the ANC and the government. The statement criticises the SACP and COSATU for supporting views contrary to those held by Mbeki. However, the statement also announces that government policy on AIDS would continue on the 'premise' that HIV causes AIDS. The AIDS issue is taken up in electioneering in the Western Cape.[44] Responding to the opposition's undertaking to supply free ARVs in the province, Mbeki notes that South Africans were being used as 'guinea pigs' and the provincial government's prescription of such dangerous medication could be compared to the biological warfare of the apartheid era.[45]

2001

- In an address to Parliament in March, Mbeki defends his decision not to declare AIDS a national emergency, saying that '[n]o other country has declared a state of emergency on these grounds'.[46]
- In April the Presidential AIDS Panel reports. Not surprisingly, its members fail to reach a consensus about the causes of AIDS or on how the epidemic should be contained. Two parallel sets of recommendations are presented, reflecting the division between mainstream and dissident science.[47] In later media interviews, Mbeki remains adamant that a virus cannot cause a syndrome, and he publicly refuses to take an HIV test, stating that such an act would reflect an embrace on his part of the mainstream view that HIV causes AIDS.[48]
- In an August interview, Mbeki casts doubts on the accuracy of statistics demonstrating that AIDS has become the main killer of adult

South Africans. He tells the BBC's Tim Sebastian that crime is the main killer in the country. Also in August, Mbeki requests his Minister of Health to reassess the government's policy on AIDS, citing seven-year old WHO statistics noting that AIDS is a comparatively minor cause of death in South Africa. In a letter to Tshabalala-Msimang, Mbeki states:

> [n]eedless to say these figures will provoke a howl of displeasure and a concerted propaganda campaign among those who have convinced themselves that HIV and AIDS are the single biggest cause of death in our country. These are the people whose prejudices led them to discover the false reality, among other things, that we are running out of space in our cemeteries as a result of unprecedented deaths caused by HIV and AIDS ... Nevertheless, whatever the intensity of the hostile propaganda that might be provoked by the WHO statistics, we cannot allow that government policy and programmes should be informed by misperceptions, however widespread and well established they may seem to be ... [49]

- In October leaks from an MRC report suggests that the WHO statistics are seriously out of date and that AIDS is, indeed, the main cause of adult mortality in South Africa.[50] The Office of the President delays publication of the MRC report, calling its findings 'not credible'. In a speech at the University of Fort Hare, Mbeki launches a vociferous attack on AIDS activists and the medical establishment, saying:

  > others who consider themselves to be our leaders take to the streets carrying their placards to demand that because [black people] are germ carriers and human beings of a lower order that cannot subject their passions to reason, we must perforce adopt strange opinions to save a depraved and diseased people from perishing from a self-inflicted disease.[51]

- In November the Parliamentary Joint Standing Committee on the Improvement of the Quality of Life and Status of Women (a committee dominated by ANC women members) release a report countering the President's position, requesting the immediate provision of ARVs to rape survivors and to prevent MTCT.[52] Subsequently, the TAC takes the government to court in an effort to force the state to make such provisions. When the court rules in favour of the TAC, the Minister of Health decides to appeal to the Constitutional Court, on the ground that it is not within the authority of the courts to make health policy. Early in 2002 the Court rejects the government's application.

2002

- Early in the year, the government faces increasing opposition to its stance on the provision of ARVs, with Mandela, Archbishop Desmond Tutu, the ANC Gauteng premier, COSATU, the SACP and the Anglican Church all calling for the speedy rollout of ARV programmes. The ANC's spokesman, Smuts Ngonyama, issues a statement criticising the visiting former US president Jimmy Carter for a similar call on the government.
- In March the ANC NEC announces that an ARV rollout programme would follow on a study to determine the drugs' safety and efficacy, and that such a study would only be concluded towards the end of the year.
- News breaks of an extraordinary document entitled 'Castro Hlongwane, Caravans, Cats, Geese, Foot & Mouth, and Statistics: HIV and AIDS and the Struggle for the Humanisation of the African' which circulates among ANC NEC members. The document reiterates fundamentalist dissident rhetoric, and again points to a conspiracy between the media and scientists to sell the idea of an African AIDS epidemic, largely in favour of the consumption of ARVs. It attacks 'Eurocentric science' and 'mental colonisation' and insists that Africa must reject the idea that it is a victim of a self-inflicted disease called HIV and AIDS.
- After its legal defeat, in April the government announces that ARVs will in fact be rolled out at public facilities, but again delay tactics follow – to the extent that the TAC again takes legal action in December to force the Mpumalanga provincial government to start rolling out ARVs. The National Minister of Health states that, were the province's MEC for health to go to prison, 'I'm going with her'.[53]
- At the Barcelona AIDS conference in June, Tshabalala-Msimang responds to the earlier Constitutional Court ruling, saying that the government 'will implement because we are forced to implement … I must give my people poison'.[54]
- In September NEDLAC announces the formation of a task team to negotiate a plan for the rollout of ARVs. TAC and COSATU are partners at the negotiating table. However, the government announces that it will not sign the agreement, leading to a civil disobedience campaign by the TAC.
- Mbeki barely mentions AIDS at the ANC party congress in December.

2003

- Mbeki's state of the nation address at the opening of Parliament in February devotes only two sentences, in a 21-page speech, to AIDS.
- In March the Health Minister advocates that PWAs take garlic and olive oil rather than 'toxic' ARVs to boost their immune systems. Mbeki does not make any public statement on the furore that follows this statement, leading Van der Vliet to ask:

  How does a minister with such a string of gaffes and blunders behind her – and the strong suspicion that she herself is an AIDS 'denialist' – retain her portfolio? ... If she is not censured, disciplined or fired for her sayings and doings, there is a simple explanation. It's because Thabo Mbeki wants it that way. However low a profile Mbeki keeps on the AIDS issue these days, nothing he has done refutes [this].[55]

- Also in March, journalist Samantha Power reports on a conversation between Mbeki and a prominent Cabinet member:

  'I've been to so many AIDS funerals,' the minister said. 'I attend more every month.' The President was irritated by the comment. 'What makes you so sure they died of AIDS?' The official explained that young men in their twenties and thirties don't just die of pneumonia.

  'Yes,' Mbeki said, 'but you don't really know how they died, do you?'[56]

- In response to the TAC's civil disobedience campaign, which enjoys wide support from COSATU, the Minister of Health launches a scathing attack in April on the bona fides of TAC leadership, accusing them of racism. Tshabalala-Msimang also attacks the KwaZulu-Natal province for having submitted – and won – an application to the Global Fund in Geneva for US$72 million, aimed at ARV rollout.[57]
- In a BBC interview in July, Mbeki again questions statistics demonstrating that hundreds of South Africans die every day due to AIDS.
- In an interview with the *Washington Post* in September, Mbeki denies having known anyone in his family or among his associates who had died of AIDS or was infected with HIV.[58]

2004

- At a Kimberley election campaign meeting in March, Mbeki justifies the government's slow implementation of the recently announced ARV rollout programme, saying it would have been 'thoroughly irresponsible' to rush rollout, just as it was irresponsible to build false hopes around ARVs. 'We give people hope that ARVs kill the HI virus. Well, they do not. Why do we tell them that? Why do we do this?'[59]

There have been several attempts by AIDS and policy analysts and commentators to explain Mbeki's stance on HIV and AIDS. Most point to Mbeki's long exile during the apartheid years as the source of a paranoid pathology. This, combined with his evident intelligence, has led to intellectual conceit on his part. When questioned or criticised, the President does not hesitate to play the race card, accusing detractors of being the victims of their own Eurocentrism or internalised colonialism, or just blatantly racist. Any opposition to his own point of view is brushed aside as a conspiracy to unseat him, or to counter his own conception of policy problems and public agenda items in South Africa. In his actions, however, Mbeki has manifested some paradoxical behaviour to back up his controversial views. Crewe highlights some of these, noting that:

- In seeking an African solution and to ensure that Western drugs are not relied upon, he will confer with mainly non-Africans for his answer. Indeed many of the [Presidential AIDS P]anel are already collaborators with local programmes and scientists and could give their input via local expertise.
- His government is committed to the development of an HIV vaccine, a full acknowledgement that HIV is the causal connection with AIDS.
- He is aware of the thousands of people who are infected and dying, but refuses to sanction treatment that could reduce this toll.[60]

It is no coincidence, these commentators note, that Mbeki's disastrous foray into the AIDS discourse commenced with the South African government taking on the global pharmaceutical industry in the late 1990s: this battle raged on throughout Mbeki's flirtation with AIDS dissidence, and his and his spokespeople's repeated reference to the insidious role that these companies play in South Africa have become a key theme of Mbeki's anti-intellectual rhetoric. According to Sparks:

> it was the dissidents' charges against the pharmaceutical companies that first attracted Mbeki's attention. When [South African dissidents] drew his attention to their websites, Mbeki was himself in the throes of a bitter conflict with these companies ... [61]

Crewe notes that '[i]t is possible that there is a senior member of government or the ANC who is living with AIDS at a point where the information could be made public'[62] and yet is so deep in pathological denial that the rest of South Africa has become the victim of irrational thought.

Denial is also cited by Professor William Makgoba, who echoes sentiments raised in the previous chapter, namely that the ANC took so much on when it came to power that the AIDS epidemic became 'one burden too many'[63] – hence the sub-title of this book. The government is faced with such a mammoth challenge in the shape of HIV and AIDS that they have been grasping at quick-fix solutions and explanations and continue to do so. When they come across explanations that threaten to expose their unwillingness to face up to the reality of AIDS, the very tenets of those arguments are attacked. This might serve to explain Mbeki's and some of his ministers' bizarre questioning of science and scientific methodologies: HIV does not cause AIDS; the MRC and UNAIDS get the statistics wrong; ARVs are toxic and black Africans are being manipulated into using them; racist conspiracies are driving domestic and international opposition against Mbeki's positions; the pharmaceutical companies are bribing South Africa's AIDS civil society, who in turn have infiltrated the ANC's alliance partners.

These analysts are of the opinion that the reality of AIDS is such an insult to Mbeki's dream of an African Renaissance that he would do anything and believe anything in an effort to exculpate African culture or modes of behaviour, going so far as to question the science of AIDS itself.[64] As a private individual, Mbeki is free to believe and advocate what he wishes, but as the head of government of a country with the greatest number of HIV-positive citizens in the world, Mbeki is faced with extraordinary responsibilities. His is the responsibility to act swiftly and effectively to counter the spread of HIV and to mitigate the impact of AIDS. Public policy and the rollout of effective AIDS programmes fall within the ambit of government responsibility.

There are few who believe that Mbeki and his government have done a good job. In fact, most members of the South African AIDS community point out that Mbeki has been guilty of gross negligence.[65] This belief is held so strongly that the TAC has even charged his Minister of Health with genocide. According to Schneider, 'the power of political leaders in AIDS lies in three areas: by exerting influence through formal state/government systems, by shaping discourse, and by providing moral authority'.[66] Unfortunately, Mbeki has clearly failed in all three areas.

To make matters worse, Mbeki seems not only to have gone against the mainstream views of science; he has actively sought to redefine the public policy problem of AIDS in South Africa itself and has acted to exclude anyone outside of government from seizing the opportunity to address the AIDS issue at all.[67] In doing so, he has done incredible harm to the efforts of the South African AIDS civil society to keep AIDS on the public agenda. In Mbali's analysis:

> the denialists have overly prolonged a national debate which has undoubtedly diverted government resources and the attention of government officials from the main policy tasks at hand: using the latest mainstream medical and scientific research to prevent new infections and provide the best standards of care for HIV-infected persons and AIDS orphans.[68]

The President and his Minister of Health have acted to delay the implementation of life-saving measures at every possible turn: at the time of writing, AIDS civil society in South Africa are still entangled in legal challenges with the government in an effort to get ARVs and MTCT prevention programmes implemented at public facilities. However, not all in government have adopted Mbeki's position: as noted below, increasingly some provincial governments are gaining the capacity to roll out their own AIDS programmes, and there have been several instances of disquiet from within the ANC itself, as well as its governing alliance partners.[69] Also, South Africa still has what is generally acknowledged to be an excellent AIDS policy in the form of the Strategic Plan. Unfortunately the country's crisis of implementation – conceived during the Mandela administration – continues unabatedly. Reflecting on some sectors within government acting autonomously of the executive in efforts to implement AIDS policy, Walker, Reid and Cornell note that:

> [t]he catapulting of AIDS into the arena of high politics has undoubtedly undermined the ability of the state to mobilise and lead a united response to AIDS in South Africa. However, conflict has tended to occur largely in the political domain and at a national level, involving mainly the Presidency and the health ministry, with the day-to-day bureaucratic realm and provincial governments functioning relatively autonomously and sometimes in contradiction to central political stances.[70]

In terms of the process/stagist public policy approach applied in this study, South Africa does not need a radically altered AIDS policy. However, the country clearly needs to implement its existing policies much more enthusiastically and effectively. Unfortunately, Mbeki's politicisation of AIDS has obfuscated many of the critical messages that his own government's AIDS policy document exemplifies. In doing so, Schlemmer suggests that the government and Mbeki are 'shifting blame onto history. Campaigns today address risk *behaviour*; linking HIV and AIDS with poverty reverts to a risk *group* analysis, once again stereotyping those at risk.'[71]

As will be discussed in the next section, civil society has been and continues to be quite successful in bypassing through litigation central government's reticence to implement MTCT prevention and ARV programmes. Coupled with a capacitated provincial level of AIDS governance, and with radically increased national and provincial AIDS budgets, the policy implementers on the ground might be in a position to ignore the noise and obfuscation coming from Mbeki's office. This is, of course, far from ideal, but the AIDS policy environment seems to have ceased to be as directly influenced by the Office of the President as it has been in the recent past.

MTCT prevention, HAART and the monetarisation of the policy problem

The preceding section demonstrates how Mbeki's anti-intellectual or dissident stance has damaged the public policy process on HIV and AIDS in South Africa by repeatedly obfuscating the conceptualisation of the policy problem itself. This has had the effect of further confusing the public policy agenda, with the government acting on its proclivity to prescribe who has the right to make statements on the epidemic. This has led to the emasculation of the government's own Strategic Plan, rendering it an anachronism in the face of the reality of AIDS. Manning notes that:

> the debate over the causes of AIDS delayed implementation of a MTCT program [*sic*], because of the inherent contradiction between administering drugs to prevent HIV transmission while questioning whether HIV causes AIDS; others believe the delay had more to do with limited health sector capacity than with the dissident debate. In any case, the diversion of energy and attention to debates over the cause of AIDS hurt the formulation and implementation of AIDS policy.[72]

The President and his senior health officials muddied the policy environment by using charges of racism or unfounded conspiracies in an attempt to delegitimise civil society's attempts to create an enabling policy environment for the implementation of (essentially good) policies. The Mbeki administration's actions (and selective inaction) have had three significant consequences: 1) the specific policy problem of treatment has been monetarised; 2) in an effort to bypass the state or force its hand, civil society has responded by using litigation; and 3) the artificial separation of prevention (government) from treatment (civil society) policy response strategies have become increasingly politicised and entrenched.

When the Mandela government drafted the Medicines Bill, which led to the PhrMA court case, it did so for ostensibly financial reasons. As noted, the state's position was that large pharmaceutical companies were abusing intellectual property provisions in an effort to make vast profits from the sale of their ARVs and argued that patent rights should not be applied to such an extent that the majority of PWAs in developing countries would be unable to afford appropriate medical treatment. In other words, when the Medicines Act of 1998 was first conceived, the South African government did not have a problem with the purported toxicity of ARVs. On the contrary, the Mandela government, and then Deputy President Mbeki in particular, were so in favour of these drugs as a solution to the impact of AIDS that they were pushing for their availability. Also, Mbeki was leading the government's effort to register the controversial Virodene. Once the drug had been rejected by the medical community, however, Mbeki and those close to him changed their tune: in 1998 the government announced that AZT would no longer be made available to women who had been raped, citing reasons of toxicity and fiscal conservatism. According to Mbali:

> [t]he long-running dispute between civil society and the Government over the efficacy, affordability and safety of anti-retroviral drugs can be traced back to 1998. This was when the National Association of People Living with HIV and AIDS (NAPWA) began to demand that the anti-retroviral AZT be made available to HIV-positive pregnant women to prevent them passing the virus to their children. It was this campaign that led to the formation of the TAC.[73]

However, as the previous chapter demonstrated, when faced with evidence to the contrary, that ARV drugs or HAART were a safe and essential part of the prevention as well as treatment of AIDS, the Mbeki government increasingly came to use arguments that the drugs were too expensive to provide at public health facilities. To drive their point home, the Mbeki government and his Minister of Health joined forces with the TAC in resisting the PhrMA court action, and when the international public outcry against the pharmaceutical companies rose to a crescendo in 2001, the PhrMA abandoned their legal action, offered significant reductions in the prices charged for ARVs and even volunteered to provide some free of charge. In consequence, the South African government lost the power afforded by their moral high ground. Their response was not the wholesale embrace of these offers, but rather repeated claims that the drugs were unsafe, and again in the face of solid scientific and econometric proof to the contrary, used the fiscal constraint argument. Despite economists' evidence that it would be more expensive for the South African government *not* to treat PWAs with ARVs, the Mbeki administration has remained steadfast in its refusal to purchase and distribute these drugs:

> In March 2000, [presidential spokesman] Parks Mankahlana off-guardedly justified to *Science* magazine why the South African Department of Health refused to provide a relatively inexpensive [ARV] treatment to pregnant, HIV-positive women: 'That mother is going to die and that HIV-negative child will be an orphan. That child must be brought up. Who is going to bring the child up? It's the state, the state. That's resources, you see.'[74]

In response, the TAC in particular has moved towards increasingly using litigation (or the threat thereof) in an effort to compel the government to provide HAART, particularly in the prevention of MTCT.[75] According to Berger:

> [w]hile the distinguishing feature of public interest litigation in the apartheid area was the attempt to control the exercise of public power and thereby limit and reduce human rights violations, TAC's use of the law in securing access to treatment is to ensure – rather than prevent – state action ... [B]y framing political and moral demands in the language of legal rights and constitutional obligations, TAC seeks to use the law without necessarily having to litigate ... Litigation is also used to place issues on the agenda, both before the judge and in the court of public opinion.[76]

When the government was defeated, first in the High Court and then in the Constitutional Court, the Minister of Health warned that a dangerous precedent had been set, namely that civil society was using the courts in an effort to circumvent government's powers to determine and implement public policy. Government acted to delay the implementation of the courts' rulings by calling for further studies on the safety of ARVs, and then by failing to act in provincial governments' rollout of the Strategic Plan.[77] Again, the TAC threatened court action, leading to great animosity between civil society and the state. Van der Vliet notes that:

> [p]rovision of Nevirapine was patchy, to the extent that in December TAC launched an urgent contempt of court application against the worst offender, Mpumalanga's recalcitrant health MEC, Dr Sibongile Manana, for failing to implement the court order. Tshabalala-Msimang was cited as a second respondent for failing to ensure Manana's compliance.[78]

Importantly, cracks started to appear within the different levels of government,[79] with the ANC's main alliance partners becoming vocal in their disregard for the government's delaying tactics: ANC provinces started to rollout HAART and MTCT prevention programmes independently against the wishes of the National Department of Health and the Office of the President. Furthermore, within the ANC there were calls for the President and senior Department of Health officials to cease their meddling. Late in 2002 the TAC and COSATU, its partner in the struggle for the implementation of HAART and MTCT prevention programmes, used NEDLAC as a forum in which to negotiate (with the government) a strategic plan to roll out MTCT prevention and HAART at a national level. The outcome of this clearly corporatist public policy negotiation strategy was successful: a plan was indeed conceptualised, with actuarial scientists noting that the plan could potentially:

- Reduce by nearly three million the number of HIV-related deaths between 2002 and 2015.
- Halve the number of children that will otherwise be orphaned by the HIV epidemic by 2015.
- Produce an average life expectancy in South Africa of approximately 50 years of age as opposed to 40 years in the absence of such interventions.[80]

However, soon after the plan was finalised the government refused to sign it, reneging on their corporatist undertaking. The TAC and COSATU were so incensed by what they perceived as another effort on the part of the government to delay the implementation of a treatment strategy that they started a national campaign of mass action, and continued with legal challenges. In November 2003 the government acquiesced and announced the publication of a strategy, entitled 'Operational Plan for HIV and AIDS Care and Treatment for South Africa', to roll out MTCT prevention and HAART programmes.[81] Despite this, implementation was yet again slow, leading some observers to express their suspicion that the Mbeki government had announced the rollout strategy in an effort to stave off a popular backlash at the national election in April 2004. As Van der Vliet notes:

> [t]he November Cabinet decision, even though it has seen precious few people actually receiving ARVs, did serve to draw the sting from HIV and AIDS as an election issue. Voters challenging the government stance could be reassured that treatment was on the way. In the two provinces where the ANC's grip was least secure, the Western Cape and KwaZulu-Natal, health authority initiatives have pre-empted the minister's glacial rollout delivery.[82]

In the end, AIDS civil society in South Africa succeeded in garnering sufficient political and popular support for the government to announce a treatment strategy – for instance, at the 2003 opening of Parliament, over 10,000 demonstrators marched on Parliament in support of the TAC's civil disobedience campaign.[83] However, Mbeki has never withdrawn his statements casting doubt on the solid scientific evidence that HIV causes AIDS. The TAC has only succeeded in ensuring the drafting of a treatment strategy by using mass action and litigation, and it remains to be seen whether the government will be energetic in implementing the treatment strategy. If the Minister of Health's racist attack on TAC members in April 2003 is anything to go by, the government remains as steadfast as ever in its opposition to any views counter to its own:

> [s]he accused 'a white man' of masterminding the civil disobedience campaign, using Africans, who wait for 'the white man' to deploy them. The attack was obviously directed at TAC's Mark Heywood, who was in the audience. Her repeated reference to 'a white man' eventually led to an angry interchange in which Heywood called the minister a liar.[84]

Unfortunately, then, the civil disobedience campaign has not succeeded in countering the erroneous assumption underpinning the government's policy implementation delay tactics, namely that HAART and MTCT prevention strategies are as much part of AIDS prevention policy as they are of AIDS treatment. The counter-argument is easy to demonstrate, and economists and demographers have provided ample evidence of its accuracy: the bottom line is that MTCT prevention and HAART are cost-effective for two main reasons. First, they prevent the seroconversion of many newborns, which means that the state will later have fewer people to treat for AIDS. Second, HAART lowers morbidity rates among PWAs, which means that there is less of a burden or demand on the fiscus. PWAs thus remain economically productive for longer, which means that MTCT prevention and HAART strategies to a large extent can pay for themselves.

Despite all the national government's rhetoric to the contrary, the National Treasury seems to be in agreement: since 2001 the Minister of Finance has significantly increased the amount of money budgeted for MTCT prevention and HAART. The national government set aside R1.952 billion for HIV and AIDS in 2003/4. In real terms, this was a 75 per cent increase on the sum set aside in the national budget for HIV and AIDS in 2002/3.[85] In 2004, the 2004/5 national budget set aside R1.439 billion – nearly seven times the figure set aside to fight HIV and AIDS in the 2000/1 national budget.[86] Also, provincial governments in particular seem to be increasingly willing to spend money earmarked for AIDS treatments appropriately. This indicates that the tide may be turning – in comparison with earlier years, some provinces are becoming quite adept at responding to the AIDS epidemic. Hickey *et al.* note that '[w]e are beginning to see provinces making special allocations for HIV and AIDS from their own budgets ... However, only a few provinces (primarily KwaZulu-Natal and Gauteng) are taking the lead'.[87]

Tables 6.2 and 6.3 are telling illustrations of the marked increase in the national budget allocation for HIV and AIDS:

> In other words, [the] Budget provides clear evidence that National Treasury is already planning and preparing for a national programme to provide [ARVs] to South Africans ... [In doing so,] National Treasury has essentially done their part, by clearing the spaces and sourcing the necessary resources for implementation of such a national programme. [T]he main challenge for government's response to HIV and AIDS in the foreseeable future is not going to be lack of financial resources, but the capacity to spend.[88]

The challenge now is to make sure the budgeted amount is spent – that it is moved to the provinces quickly, spent transparently and

Table 6.2 HIV and AIDS as a share of total budget[89]

R million	2000/1	2001/2	2002/3	2003/4	2004/5	2005/6	2006/7	Total over MTEF
Total specified for HIV and AIDS in national budget (including conditional grants)	213.7	343.7	646.7	973.5	1,439.0	1,797.2	2,268.6	**5,504.8**
As percentage share of total consolidated expenditure (including interest costs)	0.09	0.13	0.21	0.28	0.37	0.42	0.49	**0.43**
As percentage share of GDP	0.023	0.034	0.056	0.080	0.108	0.123	0.142	**0.126**
Total HIV and AIDS budget including CGs and ES funds	213.7	343.7	1,046.7	2,073.5	3,339.0	4,251.2	4,869.6	**12,459.8**
As percentage share of total consolidated expenditure (including interest costs)	0.09	0.13	0.34	0.59	0.86	1.00	1.06	**0.98**
As percentage share of GDP	0.023	0.034	0.091	0.170	0.251	0.292	0.306	**0.284**

efficiently, and accounted for effectively. There has been a pattern of under-expenditure of money dedicated to HIV and AIDS. For example, in 2000/1 the provinces spent only 35.5 per cent of the total national HIV and AIDS conditional grant allocations. This increased to 85 per cent in 2002/3. Increased monitoring of the provincial government budgets and patterns of expenditure on HIV and AIDS, and in particular HAART, will be needed.

(Re)defining the problem, and implications for policy-making: 1999–2004

In terms of the phase/stage approach applied in this study's context of public policy analysis, the first Mbeki administration's handing of the AIDS epidemic provides a fascinating insight into the interplay between multiple theoretical discourses. At the macro level, the government's purported obfuscation of the public policy environment – particularly

Table 6.3 HIV and AIDS-specific spending in health sector as share of total health expenditure[90]

R million	2000/1	2001/2	2002/3	2003/4	2004/5	2005/6	2006/7	Total over MTEF
HIV and AIDS-specific health spending (including CGs; excluding funds via ES)	181.1	265.8	460.0	766.3	1,212.2	1,545.3	2,008.4	**4,765.9**
As percentage share of consolidated national and provincial health expenditure	0.7	0.9	1.3	1.9	2.8	3.3	4.0	**3.4**
HIV and AIDS health spending (including CGs and funds via IS)	181.1	265.8	860.0	1,866.3	3,112.2	3,999.3	4,609.4	**11,720.9**
As percentage share of consolidated national and provincial health expenditure	0.7	0.9	2.5	4.7	7.3	8.5	9.1	**8.4**
Consolidated national and provincial health expenditure, as percentage share of total consolidated expenditure (including interest costs)	11.4	11.3	11.1	11.3	11.0	11.1	11.0	**11.1**

in terms of the conceptualisation and re-conceptualisation of the AIDS policy problem itself – can be viewed as a continuation of errors made during the Mandela administration. In that sense the policies that were made – and the (in)action that followed in terms of implementation – can be best described by incrementalist public policy theory. As noted in the Introduction, the latter are inherently conservative and thus cautious about overall policy termination, but in this instance that was not a problem, for the NAP of 1994 was an essentially good AIDS policy. Its transformation into the Strategic Plan which was developed in 1999 under the new Mbeki government can therefore not be faulted: the

Strategic Plan incorporated all the positive elements of the NAP, thus providing a natural and appropriate refinement of and add-on to the outcome of the NACOSA process of the early 1990s.

However, incrementalist policy analysis can also assist in explaining the government's subsequent failure to deliver. As was the case with the Mandela government's handling of HIV and AIDS, Mbeki's administration continued the mistakes of the past: the fracture in relations between the state and the South African AIDS civil society that came about as a result of Sarafina II in 1996 was never healed. On the contrary, Mbeki exacerbated this antithetical relationship by refusing to rectify the errors made under Mandela. In fact, he added to these – some analysts would say on account of intellectual conceit – by continuing to question and actively oppose epistemic communities that he was not qualified to second-guess. Mbeki thus continued in his efforts to delegitimise medical science and statisticians who were able to demonstrate valid evidence that the wholesale, national rollout of ARVs is an appropriate response in the prevention of MTCT, as well as in the government's broader treatment strategy.

In doing so, Mbeki essentially emasculated the positive elements of his own government's Strategic Plan: he continually questioned the definition of the public policy problems wrought by HIV and AIDS, and hence attempted to manipulate the public policy agenda. The result has been a paradox: on the one hand, the Mbeki government had a good policy on paper, but on the other, central government itself was acting in a manner inimical to the implementation of that policy. Official policy formulation had gone through without any glitches, but the government's crisis of implementation continued. This rendered an objective, scientific evaluation of such policies very difficult, which reinforced the confusion within the public policy environment surrounding AIDS, and acted to enforce the President and his Minister of Health's delaying tactics in actual AIDS policy implementation.

In this process, three tensions appeared in the government's response to the epidemic. First, the erroneous differentiation between prevention and treatment strategies was reinforced, which in turn exacerbated the frosty relations between government and the South African AIDS civil society. Second, as under Mandela, the Mbeki administration was creating its own policy Frankenstein: in pitting the contents of policy documents against the state's willingness to implement those policies, the government was essentially setting back the entire AIDS public policy environment, and curtailing sections within government's efforts at implementing those policies. Third, and as a direct consequence of the second point, Mbeki was contributing to the weakening and confusion of his own government: central government, driven by the Office of the Presidency and the Ministry of Health, was pitting its own actions and motivations against its own partners (notably the SACP and COSATU), making it difficult for the second (provincial) and third (local) levels of government to react appropriately to the AIDS epidemic. This had the unfortunate effect of government declaring war with itself.

Pluralist public policy theory would underscore this position, noting that government's power to make and implement AIDS policies became increasingly fractured despite Mbeki's efforts to monopolise the right to make statements on, define and determine the road forward in policy conceptualisation. The TAC's increasing, and successful, use of litigation in forcing the state to honour its AIDS treatment policy, as well as the provinces' growing prowess in bypassing central government in implementing the Strategic Plan, demonstrate that central government was being marginalised. In this manner, lower levels of government and the courts were seminal in countering the national government's intransigence on MTCT prevention and HAART in particular.

The central government hit back with claims of racist and other plots to counter its authority, but the effect was an erosion and tacit delegitimisation of Mbeki and his Health Minister's anti-intellectual or denialist stance. Elite and statist theorists would point to the fact that the ANC in Parliament as well as COSATU and the SACP's opposition to the state's position was adding to the increasing isolation of Mbeki *et al*. The Mbeki government's response was a continuing attempt to delegitimise the science and statistics of AIDS in South Africa. In doing so, it unwittingly evoked rational choice rhetoric in claiming that ARVs were either too toxic or too expensive for their wholesale dissemination at public health facilities. In the long run, however, Mbeki's position has become increasingly tenuous, although his rational choice type of rhetoric has done significant harm to the evolution of a concerted effort within and outside of government to combat the epidemic. In the end, the AIDS civil society and other elites turned to a corporatist public policy development response: in using NEDLAC as a forum for issue representation in the negotiation and drafting of an appropriate national treatment strategy, members of the plurality of AIDS actors in South African society came together in an effort to coax the state into action. When the government again reneged on its promises to implement the treatment strategy, AIDS civil society eroded the government's resistance and delay tactics by turning to a populist, pluralist measure: civil disobedience and mass action. Again, the fractured nature of power within the state became apparent.

Ironically, Marxian rhetoric was (unconsciously) used by both government and its detractors: first, the TAC and the Mandela and early Mbeki administrations applied such rhetoric in an effort to inculpate large pharmaceutical companies in putting patent rights above patients' rights to HAART. However, in later years Mbeki in particular would use Marxian analyses of the AIDS industry in an effort to demonstrate that his government was under attack from corporate (and racist) sources. When combined with rational choice assumptions, this had the potential to be quite powerful in government's strategy to cast suspicion on the motives of pro-treatment groups. According to Nattrass:

> [t]he discourse of 'unaffordability' is protected from public scrutiny by what amounts to a technocratic argument on the part of the state that only the government is in a position to evaluate and rank the full spectrum of social objectives/needs/priorities ... [91]

However, pro-treatment groups, and the TAC in particular, were as adept at (unconsciously) using what can be identified as Marxist public policy analysis in an attempt to counter the government's claims: their greatest success has been in moral arguments to force through the passage of the Medicines Act of 1998. As noted above, the monetarisation of issues around AIDS has been a key feature of the first Mbeki administration's response to HIV and AIDS, but civil society's advantage in the use of such analysis of its public policies (as well as litigation) appear to be prevailing.

Conclusion: Looking Back and Looking Forward

Looking back on the book

South Africans are living in an all too visible killing field. If UNAIDS statistics are to be believed, they are dying of AIDS at a rate of around 1,000 people every day – that is currently the equivalent of more than one 11 September 2001 attack on South Africans every three days, all year – and this number is steadily increasing. Yet the South African government has not declared AIDS a national emergency, and – to take the analogy even further – for some years now President Mbeki has been casting doubt on the existence of the terrorist aeroplanes themselves. More than ten years into the South African democratic political dispensation, the government is still prevaricating on the rollout of ARVs to PWAs, despite more than one court action ordering the state to provide these drugs as a basic human right.

Since AIDS first made its appearance in this country in 1982, South Africa's policy response to HIV and AIDS has been ineffectual, despite the formulation and ostensible introduction of several public policy HIV and AIDS interventions by consecutive governments. Analysts are in agreement that national infection rates will only stabilise after 2006 – and this will not be on account of effective policies, but rather as a consequence of the natural saturation point of the epidemic. However, stabilisation does not mean that the impact of HIV and AIDS in South Africa will decrease: at the household level families will have to cope with the ongoing tragedy of losing loved ones, while the economy will continue to suffer under the impact of the epidemic. By 2006, in the absence of effective treatment HIV and AIDS are expected to infect more than 600,000 people every year in South Africa, and since these people will – in the absence of ARVs – die within a few years, the imperative to implement an appropriate public programmatic response effectively is clear.

Some commentators have claimed that AIDS has become 'one burden too many' for the democratic South African government; that its failure to respond to the epidemic is due to the fact that, given the socio-economic and cultural risk environment and the structural variables that need to be addressed in order to turn the situation round, HIV and AIDS have served as cruel indicators of the state's impotence in dealing with a crisis of this scale.

Rather than focusing on the technical contents of AIDS public policy documents (which since 1992 have not been contentious), the main focus of this book has been the *environment* and the *process* of policy-making and implementation itself. It is the aim of this study to identify the reasons for the failure of public HIV and AIDS policies in South Africa. In order to improve the process that is policy-making – identification of the problem, setting the policy agenda, formulating, implementing and evaluating programmatic responses – one should evaluate the instances of public policy-making on AIDS in the past as well as in the present. This should be done in an effort to ascertain which inappropriate or erroneous policies were formulated in the past, and why. Armed with such systematically gathered information, one is better placed to improve the quality of public policy-making on this issue. This has been done to find answers to a number of guiding questions:

- Has the public policy response to HIV and AIDS in South Africa since 1982 been effective?
- What public policies have been formulated to combat the disease?
- What, if any, were the gaps in the policy formulation and implementation process?
- What does public policy theory tell one about successive South African governments' responses to HIV and AIDS?
- What structural impediments were and remain present that might have and continue to sabotage the successful implementation of appropriate policies?
- How should public policy on this issue be conceptualised, formulated, implemented and evaluated differently in an effort to make such policies more effective?

What have we found out?

The phase/stage approach to policy-making

The first key insight of the study is that the *problem identification* phase/stage of the policy-making process on HIV and AIDS in South Africa is at the heart of the current as well as previous governments' difficulties in the appropriate implementation of state responses to the epidemic. *Policy-making and implementation is an iterative process, which means that there is a continual re-evaluation of the appropriateness and accuracy of preceding stages in the policy process. This is the analytical ideal, namely that the policy process remains a generic process, where one stage in the process is not completed and left behind before moving on and exploring the next phase – there is a continual re-conceptualisation and reshaping of the policy response to any public problem. However, the problem identification stage, since it is the motive force for the entire policy process, is a particularly seminal step along the way.

In a society like South Africa, where the policy problem of AIDS first made it onto the public agenda in the early 1980s, the identification of the policy problem was particularly important given the duration of the crisis. The challenge of HIV and AIDS did not appear on the scene more than two decades ago only to be challenged by a single value set or normative policy environment which then drafted a response to that policy problem. Rather, HIV and AIDS remained a feature of the policy environment which continues to exist to this day. This fact has important implications for the manner in which South African society can and has been responding to the epidemic since 1982 – through conflict, ideological strife, value shifts and immense socio-political change. By way of analogy: in the stage production of HIV and AIDS in South Africa the main variable, the epidemic, has remained and even worsened, but at the same time the backdrop against which it operates, the socio-political policy environment, has experienced radical changes. This has had an immense impact on the way in which the state (through different governments) has defined the very policy problem of AIDS itself.

During the NP government's handling of the epidemic (1982–94) HIV and AIDS were first defined as a moral issue. This led to an unwritten policy response steeped in a moralist discourse: in this discourse the real problem that needed to be addressed was not so much a biomedical response combating a virus as the immoral acts of homosexuals, intravenous drug users, commercial sex workers and black migrant workers, who were blamed for the spread of the epidemic. Legal measures were enacted to punish these four groups. As AIDS made its way into 'normal' society, however, the identification of the policy problem shifted: as more and more South Africans became the victims of AIDS, the growing epidemic became increasingly identified with the black sector of society. This served to *racialise* and *politicise* the epidemic, with the apartheid government using AIDS as an excuse to exclude foreign mineworkers, and in some instances blame liberation movements for infecting South African society with AIDS as a new weapon.

As AIDS entered white South African society, the state increasingly made use of biomedical discourse to counter its effects. Rather than dismantle the legal and social infrastructure of apartheid, which compounded the sexual risk factors for all South Africans, the government gradually re-conceptualised AIDS as a biomedical problem, creating medical bodies and legislation to facilitate a biomedical response to the epidemic. As political changes occurred in the late 1980s, this moral-biomedical response policy environment and problem conceptualisation also shifted. By the early 1990s it was clear that radical constitutional changes were imminent, and this led the government to allow greater scope for human rights-based perspectives on the epidemic to enter the policy discourse. As social values changed on the high political level, so too did the response imperatives of the executive branch of government. The latter's status in South African politics had to accommodate previously excluded sectors of society: the liberation movements and AIDS civil society embraced the new human rights approach to politics and economics in the country, and applied this new and evolving value set to the conceptualisation of a response to HIV and AIDS in South Africa. This political evolution culminated in the NACOSA process of 1992–94, which entrenched the view that AIDS was a *developmental* and *human rights* issue or problem in South Africa, and led to the drafting of the democratic NAP of 1994.

The discursive policy environment and problem identification mould thus shifted from blaming and targeting infected carriers of the HI virus, to the conceptualisation of a biomedical response in the late 1980s, to the entrenchment of a human rights-based approach in the 1990s. By the time the Mandela government took office in 1994, this value set was deeply entrenched, not only as the high political value underpinning the manner in which AIDS would be seen by the government, but also in terms of the programmatic response that was drafted in 1994. However, the NAP was morally and programmatically over-ambitious; it assumed the presence of sufficient resources and capacity to rapidly and effectively counter the epidemic. When this did not happen, the Mandela government quickly reverted to a biomedical conceptualisation of the AIDS policy problem. The search was on for a quick fix for AIDS, which was only one policy problem among many. Medical science held the promise for such a rapid solution, and in its haste to resolve the AIDS policy problem, the Mandela government erred, and erred again.

The Virodene debacle, coupled with the obduracy resulting from the government's mishandling of the Sarafina II scandal, effectively has corrupted the AIDS policy environment to this day. In a desperate attempt to embrace the promise of medical science, and in failing to do so, the Mandela government re-conceptualised the AIDS policy problem yet again. This re-conceptualisation was not, however, made explicit: while maintaining the human rights discourse surrounding the epidemic, the government abandoned its intentions of supplying rape survivors with ARVs, clearly backtracking on a human rights orientation in the process. The tension that this created between the government and the South African AIDS civil society soon became a gulf when the state exacerbated the policy problem by reneging on its policy not to declare AIDS a medically notifiable disease. The scale of the AIDS epidemic and the reality of the pragmatism required to respond effectively and appropriately became one burden too many for the new South African government.

This has remained the situation since the Mbeki government took office in 1999. Mbeki has made the situation worse by questioning the fundamental tenets of medical science, forcing politics to enter the biomedical domain and obdurately refusing to make a graceful exit. A feature of Mbeki's handling of the AIDS policy problem has been his re-conceptualisation of the problem as a *monetary* issue. Blaming large pharmaceutical companies and the profit motive, the Mbeki government has used a paranoid discourse in an effort to deflect the responsibility for an appropriate treatment response to the epidemic away from the state. The confusion in the policy environment that this has created is made worse by the fact that Mbeki and his Health Ministry seem to be increasingly isolated within the broader governing alliance: the ANC's own governing partners and the ANC provincial AIDS managers are acting in contravention of the national government's prescriptions. A tacit alliance has been developing from below, with members of South Africa's AIDS civil society working with sub-national (provincial) governments in an effort to ensure the rollout of treatment strategies.

Within this context, HIV and AIDS have become probably the most politicised issue in South African society. What should be a relatively simple response, namely the definition of the policy problem in biomedical terms, and the response emanating from a human rights perspective, the public sector in this country remains to all intents and purposes at war with itself. Mbeki and his senior health technocrats continue to phrase the AIDS policy problem in a discourse that runs counter to the rest of South African and international society. The very policy problem remains an area of contention.

The continuing controversy surrounding the conceptualisation of the AIDS policy problem has rendered the other stages of the policy-making environment a quagmire of indecision and ineffective as well as inconsistent policy implementation. If there is no certainty as to what the policy problem is, then it becomes impossible for the public sector to respond coherently and consistently. Answers to the questions 'Who or what is the enemy?' 'Who should take responsibility to respond?' 'What should this response look like?' 'Who is accountable?' and so on remain unanswerable – and undiscussable. Rather, the AIDS policy environment degenerates into an arena for blame and efforts at auto-exculpation.

Significantly, the public gaps that this situation creates have been filled by actors who for the most part come from outside of government. Under the NP government the absence of a coherent and appropriately conceptualised policy response led to the mobilisation of three key sets of other policy actors: the private sector (the mining industry in particular); the biomedical community; and the legal fraternity, who all became important actors and agents in the policy environment. Even within the public sector, segments of the health institutions responded to redress the erroneous or ineffective responses of the national government. Under the successive ANC governments, this situation has continued: most recently provincial ANC governments have been mobilising in an effort to get localised treatment responses off the ground, whereas the South African AIDS civil society increasingly has been making use of legal strategies to force the government into action. This has led to a situation where the government has even been bypassed: civil society has taken the AIDS fight straight to the courts, which use constitutional measures to get the government to fulfil its constitutional obligations in terms of the provision of health measures.

Gradually, the policy environment seems to be shifting towards the operationalisation of the NAP and the Strategic Plan, which remain couched in the human rights approach established in the early 1990s. Although this is creating greater effectiveness in securing the rights of PWAs, there is still no rapprochement between the high levels of national government on the one hand, and the broader AIDS civil society on the other. The result has been some successes in the rollout of treatment for PWAs, but the reality remains one where these advances come only slowly and intermittently. Although the South African government has now been forced by the courts to implement the terms of the Strategic Plan for the rollout of ARV drugs, the policy agenda regarding HIV and AIDS remains as contested as ever. The TAC has entered the policy environment as a key policy entrepreneur, but the gulf between TAC and the government remains as wide as ever.

Ironically, actual policy formulation has gone relatively smoothly since the NACOSA process of 1992–94, which led to the formulation of the NAP of 1994. The iterative process of such formulation and reformulation has been successful on more than one occasion – first with the National Health Review in 1997, which established the GAAP, and again with the drafting of the Strategic Plan in 1999–2000. Key to the success of these processes of reformulation has been the fact that they were so inclusive of all sectors of the South African AIDS community. However, the inclusiveness of the policy formulation and adoption phases has never been followed through at the level of policy implementation. Time and again the South African government acts on a proclivity to want to monopolise such implementation, and when this fails, it reverts to blaming on extra-governmental forces. Instead of allowing the explicit bottom-up implementation of these appropriate policy documents, the government has insisted on a top-down approach. This creates a situation where the rest of the South African AIDS community is not only virtually excluded from implementation; it also excuses these potential policy agents from accountability of the policies' contents.

The result is inevitable failure on the part of the government, which leaves it open it to attack from AIDS civil society. And soon this context recreates the patterns of the past: counter-attack, blame, the invocation of racist politics and a total breakdown in any possible constructive engagement in the policy environment. This also means that the policy evaluation phase becomes deeply flawed, with the government refusing to acknowledge regular benchmarks for policy success or failure, such as biomedical peer review, statistical measures, and so on. In embracing the latter, the South African AIDS civil society effectively places itself in a different evaluatory paradigm from that of the government, which then defensively accuses civil society of Eurocentrism or blatant racism. Again, it is worth noting that this environment of strong policy contestation does not reflect the content of the actual policies; rather, the manner in which these policies are implemented (or not) becomes the arena for contestation – and all of this is the result of antagonistic definitions of the actual AIDS policy problem itself.

What does the theory tell us? And what does AIDS teach the theory of policy-making?

The use in this book of an eclectic, synthetic approach to the public policy process on HIV and AIDS in South Africa has been remarkably useful and constructive in assisting the analyst to identify the manner in which AIDS policy issues and problems were and are identified and policy agendas set. It has also enabled one to cut through the various theoretical perspectives of public policy-making – steering clear of theoretical exclusivity or inductive reasoning. Instead, the study has been able to highlight the critical descriptive as well as prescriptive functions as the theoretical positions were synthesised in both their conjectural and practical application to this specific policy problem. The particular value of this study lies in the fact that such an analysis has never been done – there has been no analysis of any segment of the 23-year history of public policy-making on HIV and AIDS in South Africa by systematically applying either the phase/stage approach or the theories of public policy-making.

In using these theories as a device to reflect on the phase/stage approach in this case, several important implications of as well as for public policy theory are highlighted.

Pluralism succeeds in emphasising the fractured nature of political power. Despite its efforts to dominate the definition of the AIDS policy problem since 1982, the state did not succeed in excluding a multiplicity of AIDS policy actors and entrepreneurs from conceptualising the policy problems associated with the epidemic, or placing these alternative conceptions on the public agenda. This description of actors external to the state should not, however, be overemphasised in terms of their power to implement essentially good AIDS policies: public choice theory is useful in demonstrating that the state remained a very important policy agent throughout the history of the South African epidemic. For example, the Mbeki government's ability to delay the formulation and implementation of an AIDS treatment strategy indicates just how influential the national government is in affecting such a strategy.

Successive South African governments retained this influential position (with varying degrees of success) by invoking rational choice theory: Mbeki and his sycophants in particular repeatedly attempted to monopolise the right to define the AIDS policy problem and a response strategy by emphasising the use of rationality. By questioning science and the use of statistics, they attempted to delegitimise the mainstream view of HIV and AIDS, creating their own exclusive epistemic community in the process. Clearly, national government was acting out of self-interest in doing so, but the strategy has largely backfired: human rights and biomedical elites inside and outside government increasingly opposed this strategy, and elite theory and statism, by focusing on elites within the public sector itself, can be used quite effectively to demonstrate how these other key sectors of the South African AIDS community were successful at wresting the agenda-setting capacity away from the national government.

On the other hand, incrementalism is useful in the accuracy with which it describes the actual formulation of AIDS policy since 1982. Once a human rights-centred approach won the high political discursive battle in the early 1990s, South African AIDS policy formulation became quite predictable. After the successful NACOSA process in the early to mid-1990s, policy formulation on HIV and AIDS became a matter of adjusting existing policy scripts. Although such an approach is inherently conservative, this did not detract from the fact that the contents of these policies themselves could not be faulted – from the NAP of 1994 through the GAAP of 1998 to the Strategic Plan of 2000. Even the most recent Treatment Plan (announced in November 2003) can be seen as a natural follow-on of such an incrementalist approach. However, incrementalism cannot explain the growing dissonance between the content of these policies on the one hand, and the government's reticence to implement them on the other: there was a real breakdown between lofty formulations of policy ideals and the pragmatic implementation of these policies in the field.

Both the government and civil society have unconsciously used Marxist public policy analysis in an effort to score points and explain the real problems associated with HIV and AIDS in South Africa. In the late 1990s, as the government legislated to force pharmaceutical companies to provide ARVs at less cost to PWAs in the developing world, the state and AIDS civil society both emphasised the disastrous consequences of a profit motive with regards to essential drugs. However, whereas the TAC and other members of AIDS civil society had ceased using this argument by the first years of the new millennium, the Mbeki government has continued in its invective against what it views as Western, capitalist interests. The government has done so by couching their arguments in the language of rational choice theory, but this should come as no surprise given the emphasis of both Marxian and rational choice analyses on the political consequences of economic dynamics. However, as demonstrated in the previous chapter, the government has been obfuscating the policy environment by combining these different strategies and in insisting on a rational 'choice-ist' mode of policy implementation (or rather the lack thereof).

Quite a significant development – one that will be interesting to watch in the second Mbeki administration – has been the appearance of a subtle corporatist approach to AIDS public policy-making. After the success of the CODESA process on the South African political playing field in the early 1990s, as well as the achievements of the NACOSA process of the same era, it is surprising that a stronger culture of corporatist policy interaction among policy networks has not developed in South Africa – particularly in the AIDS policy environment. However, most recently the government, business, AIDS civil society and labour have interfaced through the NEDLAC process and thrashed out a treatment strategy in 2002. Despite the acrimony that followed this development, the public announcement of the strategy in November 2003 means that the corporatist approach has proved to be successful – certainly in terms of its recent application in terms of the HIV and AIDS environment. It will be interesting to see how and whether this 'AIDS caucus' approach will continue to bear fruit during the second Mbeki administration, particularly in policy areas of great contention.

What do we still need to find out?

Three clusters of issues can be identified that require further research in the context of HIV and AIDS in South Africa as well as in the context of other policy issues.

First, in terms of policy implementation specifically, the problem identification phase has been shown to be an essential and undervalued step in the process of AIDS policy-making. Further enquiry should explore the different ways in which policy actors can and should attain sufficient consensus on the conceptualisation of HIV and AIDS as a policy issue. Only in identifying a common conception of a policy problem is the appropriate and effective formulation, adoption, implementation and evaluation of policies assured.

HIV and AIDS have become emblematic in South Africa as an area of contention in the specific case of bringing policies to fruition through implementation. The breakdown between policy and implementation needs further exploration. The book has shown that a bottom-up approach to policy implementation has led to the greater effectiveness of policies – in spite of opposition from central government. Further research needs to be done on how policy actors inside and outside government can co-operate in an effort to make policy implementation more effective. This is the case especially when evaluating the role of provincial and local governments, as well as members of civil society – NGOs and CBOs in particular.

The second cluster of issues relate to the relationship between the government and other policy actors and agents. Since the mid-1990s a chasm has appeared between the government's and AIDS civil society's respective perspectives on the best way forward for AIDS policy design. The government has been pushing for the continual drafting of AIDS *prevention* strategies, whereas the TAC in particular has been emphasising the importance of *treatment* strategies. Increasingly, analysts are in agreement that these two strategies – AIDS prevention and AIDS treatment – should be seen not in zero-sum, but in complementary terms. This is an under-researched area in terms of the literature on AIDS policy formulation in South Africa.

The use of *litigation* and *legislation* strategies to combat AIDS has proved to be extremely successful in operationalising the principles underpinning appropriate AIDS policies. This study concludes that litigation in particular will continue to be used as a vector to implement AIDS policies. This strategy is profoundly under-researched. Successive South African governments have used anti-intellectual discourses in an effort to shield themselves from blame within the high political environment of public policy-making on HIV and AIDS. Research needs to be conducted into the socio-political structures which enable the political application of this as a delay strategy in the implementation of policies.

The third cluster of issues refers to the broadly identified discursive environment that needs to be further researched. Paradoxically, the state has used anti-intellectual arguments by applying highly technical discourses in an effort to exclude non-state policy actors from exercising the right to make statements on and define the very problem of AIDS policies themselves. Research should be conducted to explore how technical knowledge and discourses can be democratised in an effort to preclude such abuse of certain epistemologies.

AIDS has become a metaphor for all the societal ills South Africa is currently facing. There is significant scope for exploring these metaphors in an effort to enable social learning or insight from HIV and AIDS. In this way the epidemic might lead to national introspection about the deeper structural or systemic issues that plague South African society. Sex and morality are at the centre of the South African AIDS epidemic. Research on the interplay and ostensible tensions between sexual relations and the context of morality should continue.

AIDS has been demonstrated to be the result of social patterns of sexual and political interaction. Politically, apartheid has created a context of risk for all South Africans. Socially, however, politicians and other policy actors and agents appear steadfast in their reticence to address the structural variables upon which these patterns of interaction rest: the impact of culture, and the history of racism and exploitative gender relations. Research should be conducted to explore how South Africa as a society can overcome shying away from these issues.

Recent developments – and the road ahead

Although this book formally covers the period from when the AIDS epidemic appeared in South Africa in 1982 until the end of the first Mbeki administration on 14 April 2004, there have been a number of developments since April 2004 that can be included as a postscript. After the April 2004 elections, President Mbeki reappointed Dr Manto Tshabalala-Msimang for a second term as the Minister of Health. This explicit approval of the Minister's record from the Office of the Presidency was immediate slammed by the official opposition in the South African Parliament as a 'slap in the face' of PWAs.[1] The TAC also expressed disappointment with the President's decision, citing the Minister's record of tardy implementation of HIV and AIDS policies.

If newspaper reports are to be believed, such opposition to Mbeki's decision to reappoint Tshabalala-Msimang came from within the National Department of Health itself, with the Head of the government's AIDS Directorate, Dr Nono Similela, resigning within weeks of Mbeki's announcement.[2] Within the first month of the Minister's reappointment, her historical difficulties in relating to South Africa's AIDS civil society and the broader medical community continued: her Department had to face two legal challenges from medical bodies representing South African health care workers, who were unhappy with the directives coming from the Health Department regarding job specifications with regards to the distribution of drugs.

Any hope of a rapprochement between the Minister and AIDS civil society were dashed during the 15th International AIDS Conference, held in Bangkok, in July 2004. Tshabalala-Msimang reacted badly to suggestions from UN Secretary-General Kofi Annan's Special Envoy on HIV and AIDS in Africa, Dr Stephen Lewis, that the South African government was 'dragging its feet' on the rollout of ARVs.[3] The Minister accused Lewis – despite his numerous visits to South Africa – of being ignorant about the epidemic there.[4]

This context of animosity at the Bangkok conference was made worse by the Minister's continued questioning of the efficacy and safety of the use of the ARV Nevirapine for the purpose of preventing MTCT. Despite evidence to the contrary, the Minister repeated her oft-stated claims that the drug was toxic and that its application for MTCT prevention was irresponsible.[5] The public spat between the Minister and the TAC dominated the rest of the conference. The situation was exacerbated when the Minister – citing official obligations in South Africa – left Bangkok after attending the conference for only one day. This led to members of South Africa's AIDS civil society again questioning Tshabalala-Msimang's commitment to the fight against the epidemic.

Since the Bangkok conference, the battle between the Health Department and the TAC has heated up. The latter has – since the announcement of the government's Treatment Plan in November 2003 – been struggling to get access to the government's timetable for the implementation of this latest policy venture. Citing the government's failure to implement its stated intentions to have 53,000 HIV-positive South Africans on ARV treatment by March 2004 (the government had by October 2004 succeeded in rolling out the treatment to only 15,000 PWAs),[6] the TAC in November 2004 once again turned to the courts to force the government to make public its proposed treatment schedule, invokng the Promotion of Access to Information Act. The High Court ruled on 14 December. Citing a legal technicality, the judge found that the particular amendments that the TAC wanted access to were drafts, and were thus beyond the remit of the Act. However, the state had to pay the costs of the case. To this day the government has not made public its treatment schedule.[7]

President Mbeki has also come under fire for his continued silence on the AIDS epidemic. In October 2004 the official opposition's spokesperson on health, Ryan Coetzee, during official question time in Parliament, asked Mbeki whether the government was not concerned that the high incidence of rape in South Africa is fuelling the AIDS epidemic. Mbeki refused to answer, instead attacking Coetzee and the official opposition in a thinly veiled attempt (once again) to emphasise the fact that racism was a bigger problem for South Africans. Mbeki has since come under criticism from the media and other policy actors, who accuse him of attempting to monopolise the right to determine the public policy agenda.[8]

In addition, in late November 2004 Archbishop Desmond Tutu was involved in a public spat with the President after Tutu questioned what he saw as a culture of sycophancy within the ruling party and Mbeki's reticence in answering questions on AIDS, among other issues. This has led to some acrimonious exchanges between Tutu and ANC spokespeople, as well as directly with the President.[9] Mbeki has also been criticised for not owing up to South Africa's bad record on sexual violence – in October the President launched a scathing attack on a journalist, Charlene Smith, and UNAIDS's Deputy Director, Dr Kathleen Cravero, for emphasising the need to address the issue of rape. Such emphases were, in Mbeki's analysis, really racist attempts to discredit the new South Africa.

In December 2004 elements within the ANC repeated their earlier attacks on the TAC, namely that the organisation is cahoots with large pharmaceutical companies, using poor South Africans as guinea pigs in a ploy to distribute toxic drugs to the indigent.[10] The TAC hit back by pointing out that the government is trying to deflect attention from the fact that, by the end of 2004, fewer than 20,000 people in the public sector were on ARV therapy while more than 45,000 people in the private sector have access to ARVs: 'Those of us who can afford it have the chance to live, while poor and mainly black people die because of bureaucratic neglect. A section of the ANC leadership frequently misuses the allegation of racism to cover up mistakes or lies.'[11]

To drive their point home, the government around the same time pointed out that the South African National Blood Service (SANBS) was still applying outdated racist criteria in deciding which blood donations to accept.[12] The SANBS until early 2005 was excluding the serum of black people, since this group's blood had been found to contain high levels of HIV. The vitriol that resulted from this revelation of racial profiling in the health services eventually led to the institution of a more expensive but racially blind system to make the South African blood supply safer. This positive outcome was, however, clouded by the re-racialising of the issue of the national blood supply, providing the government with an opportunity to deflect attention from their slack roll-out of ARV treatment. Ironically – despite the fact that the South African epidemic is chiefly heterosexually established – in January 2006 the SANBS announced that blood from gays would (again) be excluded.

In January 2005 this context of contestation became even more political when the head of the Catholic Bishops Conference in Southern Africa, Cardinal Wilfred Napier, criticised the government for promoting the use of condoms in the fight against HIV and AIDS 'when it's clearly not working'.[13] Confusing theology with sociology, the Catholic Church used the most recent AIDS fracas in an attempt to drive their own anachronistic and moralistic agenda – at the expense of tried-and-tested methods for preventing the spread of HIV.

By the end of January 2005 the Health Department admitted that their ARV rollout programme was running late. The National Department of Health's new Director for HIV and AIDS, Dr Nomonde Xundu, reported that only 33,000 people with full-blown AIDS were receiving free drugs by the end of January. Xundu noted that the Department's biggest challenge was to get the human resources up to capacity – the Health Department had set a goal of hiring 220 doctors by March 2005, but only 111 had been employed. Also, out of the 271 pharmacists needed to help roll out the ARV treatment programme, only 90 were hired, and 64 of the 136 dieticians required were hired. Members of AIDS civil society reacted to this by saying that missed targets were rooted in a lack of political will from a government whose leader has in the past openly shown his scepticism over the need to make the fight against the AIDS epidemic a priority.[14] Responding to the 2005–6 national budget allocation to health, these activists also criticised the government for not keeping up with inflation or with health practitioners' salaries, and for focusing so exclusively on the expansion of health infrastructure that inadequate planning goes into expanding the actual delivery of services where they are needed.[15]

Perhaps the most significant recent development in the world of HIV and AIDS in South Africa occurred in February 2005, when the South African Medical Research Council announced national mortality figures. The data showed that deaths among adults had risen by around 60 per cent between 1997 and 2003. The researchers concluded that the underreporting of deaths related to AIDS was the greatest cause for this increase.[16] An editorial in the medical journal *Lancet* used this information to lambaste the Mbeki government for its continued denial and foot-dragging on the rollout of ARV drugs:

> Social stigma associated with HIV/AIDS, tacitly perpetuated by the government's reluctance to bring the crisis out in the open and face it head on, prevents many from speaking out about causes of illness and deaths of loved ones and leads doctors to record uncontroversial diagnoses on death certificates ... The South African government needs to stop being defensive and show backbone and courage to acknowledge and seriously tackle the HIV/AIDS crisis of its people. The progress in provision of [ARV] treatment to all people with advanced HIV has been painfully slow since the Government's first report of a planned programme in August, 2003.[17]

Despite this potentially explosive information, the government seems to be continuing its intransigent position on ARVs, and continues to prevaricate on the rollout of ARV treatments. In fact, if recent media reports are to be believed, the government, with the blessing of Mbeki himself, has been acting surreptitiously to establish a dissident AIDS activist organisation to serve as a counterweight to the TAC.[18]

Reviewing these events since the second Mbeki administration came to power in April 2004, it is clear that the negative patterns of public rhetoric and actions on HIV and AIDS established during 1999–2004 seem to be continuing. Negative aspects centre on the fact that Mbeki and his Minister of Health seem to be continuing their policy of neglect and foot-dragging on ARV rollout. The approach from the top continues to include the questioning of medical science, casting doubt on any data demonstrating the affordability and imperative of life-saving drugs, or the negative impact that AIDS is having on national mortality and morbidity levels.

However, not all is lost. There are clear signals in and around government that forces are at work to undo some of the damage done under the Mbeki government. These include:

- A greater willingness by the Ministry of Finance to provide the capital to improve the rollout of ARV treatment.
- Some provinces and local authorities have demonstrated an increase in their capacity to provide essential services.
- AIDS civil society in South Africa seems to be succeeding in bypassing those at the very top of government, using the courts to force through legal sanctions to create the programmatic infrastructure for future success.
- Inside the National Department of Health a number of newly appointed officials seem to have a genuine desire to speed up the delivery of essential services to combat AIDS: Dr Nomonde Xundu and Deputy Minister of Health Nozizwe Madlala-Routledge are driving real efforts to integrate HIV into the areas of healthcare and AIDS treatment. Importantly, Madlala-Routledge seems more amenable than her Minister to see the TAC and other members of AIDS civil society as allies, rather than as foes.[19]

One can only hope that these developments will create an institutional tipping point to change the AIDS policy landscape. For unless the government (particularly at the provincial and local levels) and civil society work together and stop viewing prevention and treatment strategies as mutually exclusive, all of South Africa will lose in the long run. But in order to get there, it is imperative a way is found to address the real vectors underpinning the spread of HIV in this country: perversely unequal and violent gender relations, cultural practices that facilitate the spread of the virus in our society, and government denial about the impact – indeed, very existence – of the horror that is AIDS. The bottom line is that we should learn to take *individual* responsibility for our sex lives and not defer that questionable privilege to the state. In order to achieve all this, we need to become a society that is not afraid to speak the truth to power, wherever it may lurk. *A luta continua.*

Appendix
AIDS Timeline (1982–2004)

	1981	**1982**
Headlines	Acquired Immune Deficiency Syndrome (AIDS) identified by Centre for Disease Control (CDC) in the United States	First two AIDS related deaths recorded in South Africa
Institutions		
Legal context		
	1983	**1984**
Headlines	Tricameral Parliamentary system instituted in South Africa	HI virus isolated and photographed by scientists in France and the United States Civil 'unrest' rife in South Africa
Institutions		
Legal context	Human Tissues Act restricts homosexuals' and other groups' freedom to donate blood and blood products	
	1985	**1986**
Headlines	Blood test to identify HIV-antibodies becomes available	
Institutions	Government establishes the AIDS Advisory Group (AAG)	
Legal context	HIV tests mandatory for all blood donations in South Africa	Compulsory HIV testing of foreigners wishing to work on South African mines
	1987	**1988**
Headlines		HIV found to have made the jump from gay to the heterosexual South African community

Continued

Institutions	AIDS Virus Research Unit (AVRU) established in the Medical Research Council (MRC)	SAIMR establishes the AIDS Centre (focus on education) AIDS Unit established in the National Department of Health Health Ministry establishes a number of AIDS Training, Information and Counselling Centres (ATICCs)
Legal context	Public Health Act amended to give medical officers of Health special powers regarding AIDS Admission of Persons to the Republic Regulation Act introduced to restrict entrance into South Africa of HIV+ individuals	Immorality Amendment Act introduced (drives HIV deeper underground)
	1989	**1990**
Headlines	Chamber of Mines and the National Union of Mine workers (NUM) start negotiations on a common strategy against AIDS COSATU congress in Maputo calls for a more holistic, human rights based approach to AIDS Metropolitan Life introduces the first South African demographic AIDS model (the Doyle model)	2 February: De Klerk government announces far-reaching political changes First annual national ante-natal HIV survey Heterosexual AIDS cases exceed homosexual AIDS cases for the first time ANC AIDS conference in Maputo NP government and ANC jointly request WHO assistance in combating AIDS
Institutions	Government dismantles the AAG and reconstitutes it more democratically	The NP government establishes an Interdepartmental Committee for AIDS prevention (ICA), aimed at mainstreaming and greater policy co-ordination

Continued

Legal context		
	1991	**1992**
Headlines	AIDS Consortium adopts a Charter of Rights on AIDS and HIV ANC AIDS policy conference in Lusaka COSATU conference devoted to AIDS strategy	'South Africa United Against AIDS' conference held; launch of the National AIDS Co-ordinating Committee of South Africa (NACOSA)
Institutions	AIDS Unit and ICA work towards the establishment of a comprehensive AIDS information & prevention strategy	MRC launches the National AIDS Research Programme (NARP) AIDS Unit dismantled due to its limited efficacy NACOSA established
Legal context	1997 Legal context revoked McGeary case entrenches rights of HIV+ individuals	Hansen case further underscores rights of HIV+ individuals
	1993	**1994**
Headlines		First democratic elections in South Africa The ANC comes to power
Institutions		National AIDS Plan (NAP) adopted by new government
Legal context		
	1994	**1995**
Headlines	First democratic elections in South Africa The ANC comes to power Nelson Mandela sworn in as first democratically elected South African Head of State	
Institutions	National AIDS Plan (NAP) adopted by new government The RDP is introduced as the government's blueprint for socio-economic and macroeconomic change An HIV and AIDS and STD Directorate is established inside the National Department of Health	

Continued

Legal context		The Labour Relations Act is passed, providing PWAs with some protection against unfair dismissal
	1996	**1997**
Headlines	The National Party leaves the GNU The Sarafina II scandal erupts	The Virodene debacle makes headlines
Institutions	The RDP is abandoned and *de facto* replaced with the GEAR macroeconomic strategy	Government publishes a review of the NAP Cabinet approves the establishment of an Inter-Departmental Committee on AIDS (IDC), chaired by the deputy president
Legal context	The constitution of democratic South Africa is finalised and passed in Parliament – it is written broadly enough for potential use in protecting rights to equality and privacy of PWAs in the workplace The National Education Policy Act is passed, making provision for AIDS education in schools The Mines Health and Safety Act is passed, compelling employers to implement work safety measures relating specifically to HIV The department of correctional services adopts an HIV and AIDS Management Policy focusing on AIDS education, the distribution of condoms in prisons, the desegregation of all HIV-positive prisoners, and the recognition of confidentiality	The Law Commission publishes its First Interim Report on Aspects of the Law Relating to AIDS, containing proposals to forbid pre-employment HIV testing except in limited situations The Criminal Law Amendment Act is passed, providing for a higher minimum sentence (life) for an HIV-positive first offender who is convicted of rape The Criminal Procedures Second Amendment Act is adopted, denying bail to a defendant with HIV accused of rape unless exceptional circumstances are established Parliament passes the Medicines and Related Substances Control Amendment Act, enabling the state to parallel import AIDS drugs, as well as to apply compulsory licensing in manufacturing

Continued

		The Basic Conditions of Employment Act formalises workers' rights to sick leave
	1998	**1999**
Headlines	The government announces that AZT will not be provided to prevent the vertical transmission of HIV Deputy President Mbeki addresses the nation in a live TV broadcast, announcing a 'new partnership against AIDS' AIDS activist Gugu Dlamini reveals her HIV-positive status and is killed by her community The Treatment Action Campaign is founded	The NP controlled Western Cape provincial government announces that it will provide ARVs at selected public health sites – against the wishes of the central government The ANC wins the second democratic elections by an even greater electoral margin, and Thabo Mbeki is elected as state president
Institutions	In light of the Virodene scandal,government disbands and reconstitutes the MCC The NAP of 1994 is renamed the Government AIDS Action Plan (GAAP)	Government disbands the AIDS Advisory Group (AAG)
Legal context	The Employment Equity Act is passed, making it illegal to discriminate against PWAs in the workplace The Medical Schemes Act categorises AIDS under the 'prescribed minimum benefits' which provides for the compulsory cover of medical and surgical management for opportunistic infections or localised malignancies	The government gazettes its intention to make AIDS a notifiable medical condition
	1999	**2000**
Headlines	The NP controlled Western Cape provincial government that it will provide ARVs at selected public health sites – against the wishes of the central government	Mbeki casts doubt on the causal link between HIV and AIDS Mbeki sends a letter to world leaders, questioning the causal link between HIV and AIDS

Continued

	The ANC wins the second democratic elections by an even greater electoral margin, and Thabo Mbeki is sworn in as state president Mbeki questions the efficacy and toxicity of ARVs A research study in Uganda shows that Nevirapine is effective when used for MTCT prevention	The 13th International AIDS Conference is held in Durban Five major drug companies announce that they will reduce AIDS drug prices for countries in Africa Resistance surfaces against Mbeki's stance – from within the ANC itself
Institutions	Government disbands the AIDS Advisory Group (AAG) The government announces the 'HIV and AIDS/STD Strategic Plan for South Africa (2000–2005)' as its main AIDS policy document	The South African National AIDS Commission (SANAC) is created to replace the AAG, with the deputy president as its chairman Mbeki appoints his controversial Presidential AIDS Panel to investigate the aetiology of AIDS
Legal context	The government gazettes its intention to make AIDS a notifiable medical condition	The TAC uses legal action in an effort to coax the government into providing MTCT prevention and HAART
	2001	**2002**
Headlines	The WHO endorses the use of nevirapine for MTCT prevention Mbeki and his health minister continue their invective against ARVs and MTCT prevention The Mbeki government attempts to stall release of an MCC report that finds that AIDS is the leading cause of death for South African adults	Mbeki and his health minister continue their invective against ARVs and MTCT prevention In April the government announces that it will no longer oppose providing ARVs to rape survivors The TAC and COSATU convene an AIDS treatment congress to begin outlining a proposed national plan on treatment
Institutions	The Presidential AIDS Panel reports: no consensus is reached between mainstream and dissident scientists	NEDLAC is used as a corporatist forum for policy negotiations between TAC, COSATU and the government

Continued

	The South African MCC endorse the use of nevirapine for MTCT prevention The government announces that it will rollout ARVs for MTCT prevention and rape survivors at two public facilities	
Legal context	PhrMA withdraw their legal challenge to the government's Medicines Act of 1998; government does not use this as a motivation to provide ARVs at all public facilities The TAC uses legal action in an effort to coax the government into expanding MTCT and prevention HAART – the Pretoria High Court rules that limiting the provision of Nevirapine only to pilot sites is a violation of the right to healthcare as enshrined in the Constitution; the government appeals the decision and lodges a case with the Constitutional Court	The Constitutional Court upholds the tenets of the earlier Pretoria High Court and calls for an end to the government's policy of limiting the provision of Nevirapine to pilot-test sites The TAC uses legal action in an effort to coax the government into providing MTCT prevention and HAART
	2003	**2004 (to 14 April)**
Headlines	Mbeki and his health minister continue their invective against ARVs and MTCT prevention In March and April TAC and COSATU use a campaign of civil disobedience to force the government to accept their NEPAD agreement The TAC and its chairman, Zackie Achmat, are nominated for the 2004 Nobel Peace Prize	Mbeki and his health minister continue their invective against ARVs and MTCT prevention The ANC wins the third democratic elections, widening their support to 70 per cent nationally; Mbeki is sworn in as state president for a second term; Tshabalala-Msimang is reappointed Minister of Health
Institutions	In November the 'Operational Plan for HIV and AIDS Care and Treatment for South Africa' is announced as the government's main policy document regarding treatment	

Continued

Legal context	The TAC uses legal action in an effort to coax the government into providing MTCT prevention and HAART – following litigation via the Competition Commission, unprecedented agreements are signed with pharmaceutical companies for the provision of cheaper ARVs for sub-Saharan Africa	The TAC warns that, should the health ministry continue to delay the release of details of the implementation timetable contained in the operational plan they would use the provision of the Access to Information Act to compel her to make it available

Notes

Foreword

1. E. Gouws and Q. Karim, 'HIV Infection in South Africa: An Evolving Epidemic', in S. Karim and Q. Karim (eds), *HIV/ AIDS in South Africa* (New York: Cambridge University Press, 2005), pp. 48–66.
2. K. Edelstone, *AIDS: Countdown to Doomsday* (Johannesburg: Media House Publications, 1988).
3. A. Whiteside, *AIDS in Southern Africa: A Position Paper* (Development Bank of Southern Africa and Economic Research Unit, University of Natal Durban, Halfway House, 1990), p. 38.
4. D. Adams, *The Hitchhiker's Guide to the Galaxy* (London: Pan Macmillan, 1979).
5. W. M. Gumede, *Thabo Mbeki and the Battle for the Soul of the ANC* (Cape Town: Zebra Press, 2005).
6. S. Lewis, *Race against Time* (Toronto: House of Anansi Press, 2005).
7. Department of Health, *National HIV and Syphilis Antenatal Sero-prevalence Survey in South Africa: 2005* (Pretoria: Department of Health, 2005).

Introduction

1. UNAIDS, *Report on the Global AIDS Epidemic* (Switzerland: UNAIDS, 2004), pp. 190–3.
2. UNAIDS, *HIV and AIDS and Human Development South Africa* (New York: UNAIDS, 1998), p. 66.
3. ING Barings, *Economic Impact of AIDS in South Africa – a Dark Cloud on the Horizon* (South Africa: ING Barings, 2000), p. 16.
4. R. Loewenon and A. Whiteside, 'HIV and AIDS in Southern Africa', in A. Whiteside (ed.), *Implications of AIDS for Demography and Policy in Southern Africa* (Pietermaritzburg: University of Natal Press, 1998), p. 13.
5. M. Crewe, *HIV and AIDS and Policy in South Africa Today.* Address to diplomats at a meeting of political and economic research officers at the Dutch Embassy (Pretoria, 19 April 2000).
6. Y. Sadie and M. Schoeman, 'Vigs-Politiek in Suid Afrika: 1987–1992', *Politikon* 19, no. 3 (1992): 85–9.
7. H. Marais, *To the Edge: AIDS Review 2000* (Pretoria: Centre for the Study of AIDS, 2000), pp. 1–68.
8. Crewe, *HIV and AIDS and Policy in South Africa Today.*
9. See chapter 5.
10. Marais, *To the Edge*, p. 28.
11. *Ibid.*, p. 47.
12. *Ibid.*, p. 47; Crewe, *HIV and AIDS and Policy in South Africa Today.*
13. Marais, *To the Edge*, p. 48.

14. Crewe, *HIV and AIDS and Policy in South Africa Today*; L. Thomas and J. Howard, 'AIDS and Development Planning', in A. Whiteside (ed.), *Implications of AIDS for Demography and Policy in Southern Africa* (Pietermaritzburg: University of Natal Press, 1998); A. Whiteside, 'Policymakers' and Planners' Needs in Projecting the Epidemic', in A. Whiteside (ed.), *Implications of AIDS for Demography and Policy in Southern Africa* (Pietermaritzburg: University of Natal Press, 1998).
15. J. Anderson, *Public Policymaking* (Boston: Houghton Mifflin, 2000), p. 4.
16. *Ibid.*, p. 4.
17. *Ibid.*, pp. 4–7; M. Hill, *The Policy Process in the Modern State* (New York, Prentice-Hall Harvester Wheatsheaf, 1997), pp. 7–8; G. Van der Waldt, 'Public Policy and Policy Analysis', in D. Van Niekerk, G. Van der Waldt and A. Jonker (eds), *Governance, Politics, and Policy in South Africa* (Cape Town: Oxford University Press Southern Africa, 2001), pp. 90–1.
18. Van der Waldt, 'Public Policy and Policy Analysis', p. 91.
19. Anderson, *Public Policymaking*, p. 7.
20. B. Hogwood and L. Gunn, *Policy Analysis for the Real World* (London: Oxford University Press, 1984).
21. Van der Waldt, 'Public Policy and Policy Analysis', p. 91.
22. P. John, *Analysing Public Policy* (London and New York: Continuum, 2000), p. 1.
23. R. Heineman, W. Bluhm, S. Peterson and E. Kearny, *The World of the Policy Analyst – Rationality, Values and Politics* (New York and London: Chatham House Publishers, 2002), p. 48.
24. Anderson, *Public Policymaking*, p. 44.
25. W. Parsons, *Public Policy: an Introduction to the Theory and Practice of Policy Analysis* (Cheltenham: Edward Elgar, 1997), p. 87.
26. T. Dye, *Understanding Public Policy* (Englewood Cliffs, NJ: Prentice-Hall, 1995), p. 13.
27. B. Hogwood and L. Gunn, *Policy Analysis for the Real World* (London: Oxford University Press, 1989), p. 267.
28. R. Cobb and C. Elder, *The Political Uses of Symbols* (New York: Longman, 1983), p. 85.
29. Parsons, *Public Policy*, pp. 128–9.
30. Anderson, *Public Policymaking*, p. 98.
31. *Ibid.*, p. 101.
32. W. Dunn, *Public Policy Analysis: an Introduction* (Englewood Cliffs, NJ: Prentice-Hall, 1994), pp. 282–9.
33. Dye, *Understanding Public Policy*, pp. 320–1.
34. *Ibid.*, p. 331.
35. *Ibid.*, p. 332.
36. *Ibid.*, p. 15.
37. *Ibid.*, p. 24.
38. G. McLennan, 'The Evolution of Pluralist Theory', in M. Hill (ed.), *The Policy Process. A Reader* (London and New York: Prentice-Hall Harvester Wheatsheaf, 1997), p. 53.
39. John, *Analysing Public Policy*, p. 76.
40. M. Hill, *The Policy Process in the Modern State* (New York: Prentice-Hall Harvester Wheatsheaf, 1997), p. 34.

41. G. Tullock, 'The Economic Theory of Bureaucracy', in M. Hill (ed.), *The Policy Process. A Reader* (London and New York: Prentice-Hall Harvester Wheatsheaf, 1997), pp. 87–9.
42. Anderson, *Public Policymaking.*
43. *Ibid.*, p. 25.
44. R. Gregory, 'Political Rationality or Incrementalism?' in M. Hill (ed.), *The Policy Process. A Reader* (London and New York: Prentice-Hall Harvester Wheatsheaf, 1997), p. 175.
45. Dye, *Understanding Public Policy*, pp. 30–2.
46. *Ibid.*, p. 25.
47. J. March and J. Olsen, 'Institutional Perspectives on Political Institutions', in M. Hill (ed.), *The Policy Process. A Reader* (London and New York: Prentice-Hall Harvester Wheatsheaf, 1997), p. 139.
48. Dye, *Understanding Public Policy*, p. 19.
49. John, *Analysing Public Policy*, pp. 49, 52, 53–5.
50. M. Smith, 'Policy Networks', in M. Hill (ed.), *The Policy Process. A Reader* (London and New York: Prentice-Hall Harvester Wheatsheaf, 1997), p. 78.
51. Milliband, in M. Hill, *The Policy Process. A Reader* (London and New York: Prentice-Hall Harvester Wheatsheaf, 1997), p. 46.
52. John, *Analysing Public Policy*, pp. 92–5.
53. Hill, *The Policy Process*, p. 54.
54. John, *Analysing Public Policy*, p. 97.
55. Anderson, *Public Policymaking*, p. 27.
56. Dye, *Understanding Public Policy*, pp. 40–1.
57. Heineman *et al.*, *The World of the Policy Analyst*, p. 180.

1 AIDS, Poverty and Development in Southern Africa

1. Of course, the human security issue of HIV and AIDS is not self-evident. It depends on a set of prior judgements about what is of value. Some might attribute to AIDS the beneficial effect of curtailing population growth. What this study assumes *a priori* is an ethic which accords value to individual human life.
2. It is important to insert the caveat that all the predictions and projections offered in this chapter are based on a set of *ceteris paribus* clauses. This is what will happen if nothing is done, if no coherent social policy is introduced, no new drugs are discovered, no new sexual practices are adopted, and so on.
3. G. MacLean, *The Changing Perceptions of Human Security: Coordinating National and Multinational Response* (Manitoba: UNAC, 1998), p. 2. R. Bedeski, *Defining Human Security* (Victoria: Centre for Global Studies, 1991), p. 1.
4. J. Hadingham, 'Human Security and Africa: Polemic Opposites', *South African Journal of International Affairs* 7, no. 2 (2000): 113.
5. L. Axworthy, *Human Security: Safety for People in a Changing World* (Ottawa: Canadian Department of Foreign Affairs and Trade, 1999), p. 2.
6. D. Hubert, *Human Security: Safety for People in a Changing World*, paper presented at a regional conference on the Management of African Security in the 21st Century (Lagos: Nigerian Institute of International Affairs, 1999), p. 39.

7. Hadingham, 'Human Security and Africa', p. 120.
8. UN Press Release, 'Security Council Holds Debate on Impact of AIDS on Peace and Security in Africa', SC/6781, 4086 Meeting.
9. *Ibid.*
10. *The Star*, 12 January 2000.
11. *Washington Post*, 5 July 2000.
12. NIC, 'The Global Infectious Threat and its Implications for the United States', *National Intelligence Council, US Government, NIE 99-17D* (Washington DC, NIC, 2000), p. 2.
13. UN, 'Global Crisis–Global Action', *United Nations Special Session on HIV and AIDS* (2001): 9.
14. M. Malan, 'The Influence of HIV and AIDS on National Security for South Africa: The Concerns and Implications from a Human Resources Perspective', *Forum* 5 (2001): 53.
15. H. Holzhausen, 'The Main Challenges to Security in the Southern African Region', *Forum* 5 (2001): 17.
16. UNECA, 'Human Security and Africa: Polemic Opposites: Operationalising the Millennium Partnership for the Africa Recovery Programme', http://www.uneca.org/coference ofministers/compact_for_african_recovery.htm.
17. L. Brown, 'HIV-Epidemic Restructuring Africa's Population', *Worldwatch Issue Alert* (2000): 1.
18. UNAIDS, *Report on the Global AIDS Epidemic* (Switzerland: UNAIDS, 2004), p. 190.
19. SAIRR, *South Africa Survey 2000/2001* (Johannesburg: SA Institute of Race Relations, 2001), p. 226.
20. UNECA, 'Human Security and Africa'.
21. NIC, 'The Global Infectious Threat and its Implications for the United States'.
22. J. Decosas, 'Preventing HIV Transmission through Social Policy', *AIDS Analysis Africa* 9, no. 4 (1999): 2.
23. Decosas explains social cohesion by way of analogy: Fascist Germany was a highly cohesive society and the state actively increased cohesion by murdering those who did not conform to the Aryan ideal. Cohesion may refer to the cultural homogeneity of a society, the product of good governance and a strong civil society, related to a prescriptive religious culture, or the result of a controlling authoritarian political system or military dictatorship. Cohesion may thus be a deciding factor in determining a society's susceptibility to HIV infection.
24. *Ibid.*, p. 3.
25. These questions are of critical importance for the analysis of public policy interventions in chapters 2–6, since it is at this vector level that problem identification and initial policy interventions could occur.
26. J. Decosas, 'Labour Migration and HIV Epidemics in Africa', *AIDS Analysis Africa* 9, no. 2 (1998): 167. R. Shell, 'Halfway to the Holocaust: the Economic, Demographic and Social Implications of the AIDS Pandemic to the year 2010 in the Southern African Region', *HIV and AIDS: A Threat to the African Renaissance?* (Konrad Adenauer Stifting Occasional Paper, 2000), pp. 12–15.
27. Decosas, 'Labour Migration and HIV Epidemics in Africa', p. 167.

28. See chapters 2–5 for an exposition of how the respective National Party and the Mandela governments developed policies aimed specifically at the curbing or alleviating the movement of people regionally as a vector for viral spread.
29. P. Chalk, *Non-military Security and the Global Order: The Impact of Extremism, Violence and Chaos on National and International Security* (London, Macmillan, 2000), p. 103.
30. M. Fleshman, 'AIDS Prevention in the Ranks – UN Targets Peacekeepers. Combatants in War against Disease', *Africa Recovery* 15, nos. 1–2 (2001): 16.
31. S. Matthews, 'Women in Conflict', *Conflict Trends* 4 (2000): 2.
32. R. Gardiner, 'AIDS – the Undeclared War', *HIV and AIDS Briefing Paper*, social briefing no. 1, UNED (2001): 2.
33. UNAIDS, 'Refugees and AIDS', *UNAIDS Point of View* (1997): 4–5.
34. Shell, Halfway to the Holocaust', p. 13.
35. *Ibid.*, p. 13.
36. *Ibid.*, p. 13.
37. *Ibid.*, p. 14.
38. K. Quattek, 'The Economic Impact of AIDS in South Africa: A Dark Cloud on the Horizon', *HIV and AIDS: A Threat to the African Renaissance?* (Konrad Adenauer Stifting Occasional Paper, 2000), pp. 33–4.
39. *African Eye News Service*, 7 February 2000.
40. Quattek, 'The Economic Impact of AIDS in South Africa', p. 49.
41. *Ibid.*, p. 52.
42. *The Financial Times*, 19 June 2001.
43. S. Forsythe and M. Roberts, 'Measuring the Impact of HIV and AIDS on Africa's Commercial Sector', *AIDS Analysis Africa* 4, no. 5 (1994).
44. SAIRR, *South Africa Survey 2000/2001*, p. 355.
45. *Ibid.*, p. 405.
46. N. Wilkins, 'HIV and AIDS in the Informal Sector', *AIDS Analysis Africa* 10, no. 1 (1999): 223.
47. *Ibid.*, p. 223.
48. *Mail & Guardian*, 16 August 1999.
49. *IRIN*, 27 July 2001.
50. D. Norse, 'Impact of AIDS on Food Production in East Africa', *AIDS Analysis Africa* 1, no. 5 (1991).
51. FAO, 'The Impact of HIV and AIDS on Food Security', *Committee on World Food Security, Rome, 28 May–1 June* (2001).
52. *Mail & Guardian*, 16 August 1999.
53. Shell, Halfway to the Holocaust', p. 17.
54. J. Du Guerny, 'AIDS and Agriculture in Africa: Can Agricultural Policy Make a Difference?' *Food, Nutrition & Agriculture* 25 (1999): 15.
55. FAO, 'The Impact of HIV and AIDS on Food Security'.
56. Du Guerny, 'AIDS and Agriculture in Africa', p. 16.
57. Norse, 'Impact of AIDS on Food Production in East Africa', p. 39.
58. *Mail & Guardian*, 16 August 1999.
59. FAO, 'The Impact of HIV and AIDS on Food Security'.
60. M. Raubenheimer, 'AIDS Activist Murdered', *Women's Health Project Newsletter* 29 (1999): 1–2.

61. Note that 'gender' refers to the socially defined identities and roles assigned to men and women, whereas 'sex' refers to the biological differences between men and women. V. Tallis, 'Gendering the Response to HIV and AIDS: Challenging Gender Inequality', Agenda 44 (2000): 58.
62. Shell, 'Halfway to the Holocaust', p. 19.
63. S. Leclerk-Madlala, 'Crime in an Epidemic: the Case of Rape and AIDS', *Acta Criminalogica* 9, no. 2 (1996): 35.
64. *Ibid.*, pp. 35–6.
65. *Ibid.*, p. 32.
66. *Ibid.*, pp. 33–4.
67. S. Maman *et al., HIV and Partner Violence: Implications for HIV Voluntary Counselling and Testing Programs in Dar-es-Salaam, Tanzania* (New York: The Population Council Inc., 2001).
68. J. Bujra, 'Targeting Men for a Change: AIDS Discourse and Activism in Africa', *Agenda* 44 (2000): 7.
69. S. O'Sullivan, 'Uniting across Global Boundaries – HIV Positive Women in Global Perspective', *Agenda* 44 (2000): 26.
70. *Ibid.*, p. 29.
71. M. Gottemoeller, 'Empowering Women to Prevent HIV: The Microbicide Advocacy Agenda', *Agenda* 44 (2000): 39.
72. C. F. Ndiaye, 'Women and AIDS in Africa: The Experience of the Society for Women and AIDS in Africa', *South African Journal of International Affairs* 7, no. 2 (2000): 61.
73. S. Willan, 'Will HIV and AIDS Undermine Democracy in South Africa?' *AIDS Analysis Africa* 11, no. 1 (2000): 14.
74. A. Whiteside *et al.*, 'Examining HIV and AIDS in Southern Africa through the Eyes of Ordinary Southern Africans', *Afrobarometer Paper* 21 (2002): 22–3.
75. Willan, 'Will HIV and AIDS Undermine Democracy in South Africa?' p. 14.
76. K. Goyer, 'HIV and Political Instability in sub-Saharan Africa', *AIDS Analysis Africa* 12, no. 1 (2001): 13.
77. *Ibid.*, p. 13.
78. NIC, 'The Global Infectious Threat and its Implications for the United States', p. 39.
79. World Bank, *Confronting AIDS: Public Priorities in a Global Epidemic* (New York: Oxford University Press, 1999), pp. 221–3.
80. *Ibid.*, p. 207.
81. J. Young, *The Exclusive Society* (London: Sage, 1999), p. 8.
82. H. Marais, *To the Edge: AIDS Review 2000* (Pretoria: Centre for the Study of AIDS, 2000), p. 55.

2 The HIV and AIDS Policy Environment in Apartheid South Africa (1982–1994)

1. E. Serpa, 'AIDS in Africa: The Social-Cultural Roots of a Disease'. *Africa Insight* 32 no. 3 (2002): 43.
2. L. Fransen, 'HIV in Developing Countries', in A. Whiteside (ed.) *Implications of AIDS for Demography and Policy in Southern Africa* (Pietermaritzburg: University of Natal Press, 1998), p. 10.

3. *Ibid.*, p. 10.
4. R. Dorrington and L. Johnson, 'Epidemiological and Demographic', in J. Gow and C. Desmond (eds), *Impacts and Interventions: The HIV and AIDS Epidemic and the Children of South Africa* (Pietermaritzburg: University of Natal Press, 2002), p. 14.
5. Q. A. Karim, 'Trends in HIV and AIDS Infection: Beyond Current Statistics', *South African Journal of International Affairs* 7 no. 2 (2000): 11.
6. R. Shell, 'Halfway to the Holocaust: the Economic, Demographic and Social Implications of the AIDS Pandemic to the Year 2010 in the Southern African Region', in *HIV and AIDS: A Threat to the African Renaissance?* (Konrad Adenauer Stifting Occasional Paper, June 2000): 14.
7. Dorrington and Johnson, 'Epidemiological and Demographic', pp. 14–16.
8. *Ibid.*, p. 21.
9. S. Terreblanche, *A History of Inequality in South Africa 1652–2002.* (Pietermaritzburg: University of Natal Press, 2002), p. 44.
10. C. Evian, 'AIDS and the Cycle of Poverty', *AIDS Scan* 4 no. 4 (1992): 4.
11. N. Mboi, 'Women and AIDS in South and South-East Asia: the challenge and the response', in *World Health Statistics Quarterly* 49(2). (1996): 97.
12. Dorrington and Johnson, 'Epidemiological and Demographic', p. 18.
13. Anon., 'War, Armies and the Spread of HIV', *AIDS Analysis Africa* 2 no. 1 (1991): 4.
14. J. Marais, *To the Edge: AIDS Review 2000* (Pretoria: Centre for the Study of AIDS, 2000), p. 6.
15. Dorrington and Johnson, 'Epideniological and Demographic', p. 19.
16. *Ibid.*, p. 51.
17. D. Fassin, 'Embodied History. Uniqueness and Exemplarity of South African AIDS', *African Journal of AIDS Research* 1 no. 1 (2002): 64.
18. *Ibid.*, pp. 64–5.
19. T. Barnett and A. Whiteside, *AIDS in the Twenty First Century: Disease and Globalisation* (Basingstoke: Palgrave Macmillan, 2002), p. 130.
20. D. Elazar, *American Federalism: A View from the State* (New York, Harper & Row, 1984).
21. K. Jochelson, 'HIV and Syphilis in the Republic of South Africa', *African Urban Quarterly* 6 No. 1/2 (1991): 20.
22. J. Metz and J. M. Malan, 'The Impact of AIDS on Society', *South African Journal of Continuing Medical Education* 6 no. 3 (1988): 26.
23. L. Grundlingh, 'Early Attitudes and Responses to HIV and AIDS in Southern Africa as Reflected in Newspapers, 1983–1988', *Journal for Contemporary History* 26 no. 1 (2001): 94.
24. P. Strasheim, 'When Prescience Might be Better than Cure: The Media's Reporting of AIDS', *Responsa Meridiana* 5 no. 1 (1986): 144.
25. *Ibid.*, p. 144.
26. *Ibid.*, p. 146.
27. L. Grundlingh, 'HIV and AIDS in South Africa: A Case of Failed Responses Because of Stigmatisation, Discrimination and Morality, 1983–1994', *New Contree* 46 (1999): 59.
28. Strasheim, 'When Prescience Might be Better than Cure', p. 154.
29. J. Van Niftrik, 'Opinion: Finally, the Courage of Cutting the Crap', *AIDS Analysis Africa* 3 no.6 (1993): 4.

30. A. Coetzee, 'The Role of Censorship in Defeating HIV and AIDS in South Africa', *Positive Outlook* 1 no. 3 (1994): 10.
31. Strasheim, 'When Prescience Might be Better than Cure', 156.
32. Grundlingh, 'HIV and AIDS in South Africa', p. 61.
33. *Ibid.*, p. 60.
34. *Ibid.*, p. 66.
35. *Ibid.*, p. 68.
36. G. G. Miller, 'AIDS: A Theological and Pastoral Response', *Koers: Bulletin for Christian Scholarship* 55 no. 2 (1990).
37. Metz and Malan, 'The Impact of AIDS on Society', p. 26.
38. D. Louw, 'Ministering and Counselling the Person with AIDS', *Journal of Theology for Southern Africa* no. 71 (1990): 37.
39. King, in Anglican Newsletter, 1987, p. 48.
40. M. Tiba, 'AIDS – Some Socio-Cultural Considerations', *Social Work Practice* (1990): 19.
41. A. T. Viljoen, 'VIGS in Afrika, Met Spesiale Verwysing na Suid-Afrika', *Koers: Bulletin for Christian Scholarship* 55 no. 3 (1990): 340.
42. 'Ethics: Where African Traditions Differ', *AIDS Analysis Africa* 2 no. 5 (1992b): 5.
43. Viljoen, 'VIGS in Afrika, Met Spesiale Verwysing na Suid-Afrika', p. 336.
44. P. Winsbury, 'Where the AIDS War Can Be Won', *AIDS Analysis Africa* 2 no. 5 (1992): 3.
45. Viljoen, 'VIGS in Afrika, Met Spesiale Verwysing na Suid-Afrika', p. 336.
46. A. Ashford, *AIDS, Witchcraft and the Problem of Power in Post-Apartheid South Africa* (Durban: University of Natal Press, 2001), p. 39.
47. M. Zazayokwe, 'Some Barriers to Education about AIDS in the Black Community', *Social/Work Practice* (1990): 8.

3 Biomedical and Workplace Responses in Apartheid South Africa (1982–1994)

1. L. Grundlingh, 'HIV and AIDS in South Africa: A Case of Failed Responses Because of Stigmatisation, Discrimination and Morality, 1983–1994', *New Contree* 46 (1999): 91.
2. *Ibid.*, 93.
3. MRC News, 'VIGS: Tot Hiertoe en Verder: Algemeen', *MRC News* 18 no. 3 (1987): 19.
4. N. O'Farrell, 'South African AIDS', *South African Medical Journal* 72 (1987): 436.
5. R. Dorrington and L. Johnson, 'Epidemiological and Demographic', in J. Gow and C. Desmond (eds), *Impacts and Interventions: The HIV and AIDS Epidemic and the Children of South Africa* (Pietermaritzburg: University of Natal Press, 2002), p. 23.
6. Q. A. Karim, 'Trends in HIV and AIDS Infection: Beyond Current Statistics', *South African Journal of International Affairs* 7 no. 2 (2000): 11.
7. Dorrington and Johnson, 'Epidemiological and Demographic', p. 51.
8. D. Webb, 'The Geographical Progression of HIV in South Africa, 1990–1993', *AIDS Analysis Africa* 5 no. 2 (1994): 39.

9. Karim, 'Trends in HIV and AIDS Infection', p. 11.
10. Grundlingh, 'HIV and AIDS in South Africa', p. 95.
11. *Ibid.*, p. 97.
12. P. Brain, 'Blood Transfusion and AIDS', *SA Journal of Continuing Medical Education* 6 no. 3 (1988): 47.
13. S. Sello, 'A Strange Mating', *Drum* 98 (February 1987): 12.
14. K. Coleman and S. Naidoo, 'AIDS Community Awareness: Aspects for an Evolving Campaign', *Nursing RSA* 5 no. 10 (1990): 32.
15. *Ibid.*, p. 33.
16. J. Kriel, 'VIGS (En die Grense van die Mediese Wetenskap)', *Die Suid Afrikaan* 29 (1990): 31.
17. M. Heyns, 'Hurdles and Voids Encountered in the Battle against AIDS', *Rehabilitation in South Africa* 36 no. 2 (1992): 62.
18. M. Heydt, 'Reporting AIDS to Dental Practitioners', *South African Medical Journal* 71 (1987): 332.
19. B. D. Schoub, 'Progress and Problems in the Development of an AIDS Virus Vaccine', *South African Journal of Continuing Medical Education* 6 no. 3 (1988): 51.
20. R. J. Van Rooyen, 'Moet 'n Pasient Uitdruklik Toestemming Verleen Voordat vir AIDS Getoets kan Word?' *Geneeskunde* 32 no. 11 (1990): 22.
21. S. A. Strauss, 'Testing for AIDS', *AIDS Analysis Africa* 1 no. 3 (1990): 7.
22. A. Spier, 'Industry Analysis: AIDS and the Hospital Industry'. *AIDS Analysis Africa* 1 no. 2 (1990a): 3.
23. H. Kustner, 'The Truth about AIDS', *Epidemiological Comments*, 17(3) (1990): 32.
24. Heyns, 'Hurdles and Voids Encountered in the Battle against AIDS', p. 64.
25. P. E. Hilsenrath and H. Joseph, 'Health Economics: Issues for South Africa', *The South African Journal of Economics* 59 (1991): 146.
26. J. W. Moodie, 'Serology of AIDS', *South African Journal of Continuing Medical Education* 6 no. 3 (1988): 58.
27. Editorial, 'AIDS Virus Research Unit Established', *MRC News* 18 no. 1 (1987): 1.
28. *Ibid.*, p. 15.
29. S. F. Lyons and B. D. Schoub, 'AIDS-Related Research in South Africa', *South African Journal of Science* 83 (1987): 184.
30. MRC Press Statement, 'MRC Commitment to AIDS Research', *AIDS Scan* 2 (1) 1989.
31. AIDS Scan, 'MRC Launches AIDS Bulletin', *AIDS Scan* 4 no. 3 (1992): 15.
32. M. Steinberg, 'The National AIDS Research Programme of the MRC', *AIDS Analysis Africa* 4 no. 2 (1993): 3.
33. L. Sherr, G. Christie, R. Sher and J. Mets, 'Evaluation of the Effectiveness of AIDS Training and Information Courses in South Africa', *AIDS Scan* 2 (1989).
34. P. M. Van Ammers, 'Human Immunodeficiency Virus in Obstetrics', *South African Journal of Continuing Medical Education* 8 no. 3 (1990): 39.
35. N. McKerrow, *The South African Response to the HIV and AIDS Epidemic: An Input Paper to the Report on the Elimination of Poverty and Inequality in South Africa* (South Africa, 2003), p. 2.
36. Kustner 'The Truth about AIDS', p. 32.

37. G. Taylor, 'AIDS and Medical Aid – Ten Years' Experience', *AIDS Analysis Africa* 4 no. 2 (1993): 8.
38. *Ibid.*, p. 8.
39. *Ibid.*, p. 8.
40. *Ibid.*, p. 8.
41. *Financial Mail*, 2 June 1989.
42. C. Booth, 'The Insurance Industry and AIDS – an Insider's Perspective', *South African Journal on Human Rights* 9 (1993): 151–2.
43. *Geneeskunde* 31 no. 6 (1989): 36. 'Sanlam Borg Opvoeding Oor VIGS'.
44. N. G. Atkins, 'AIDS and Insurance – II: Further Classes of Short-Term Business', *Businessman's Law* 19 (1990): 118.
45. G. Wood, 'AIDS and the Insurance Industry', *AIDS Analysis Africa* 4 no. 4 (1993/94): 1.
46. A. Spier, 'Medical Aid', *AIDS Analysis Africa* 1, no. 1 (1990b): 5.
47. *Ibid.*, p. 5.
48. Taylor, 'AIDS and Medical Aid', p. 8.
49. *Ibid.*, p. 39.
50. Terreblanche, *A History of Inequality in South Africa 1652–2002*, p. 12.
51. P. Lurie, 'AIDS and Labour Policy', *South African Labour Bulletin* 12 no. 8 (1987): 83.
52. R. Rafel, 'The Politics of Disease', *Finance Week* 34 no.3 (1987): 116.
53. *Ibid.*, p. 116.
54. *Ibid.*, p. 120.
55. C. Raphaely, 'Frightening Figures', *Finance Week* 42 no. 5 (1989): 14.
56. *Ibid.*, p. 14.
57. M. Hermanus, 'AIDS – Whose Responsibility?' *IPM Journal* 9 no. 1 (1990): 29.
58. IPM Journal (1988): 20.
59. M. Van der Merwe, 'Het Jy al Ernstig Gedink Oor', *Entrepreneur* 8 no. 6 (1989): 13.
60. SA Construction World, *Guidelines on AIDS in the Work Place* 8 no. 3 (1989): 65.
61. *Finance Week*, 6–12 April 1989.
62. L. Dancaster and E. Jamieson, 'Company Policies on AIDS – The Answer?' *AIDS Analysis Africa* 1 no. 4 (1990): 39.
63. M. Finnemore, 'Pre-Employment Screening for AIDS', *IPM Journal* 9 no. 3 (1990).
64. D. Holding, 'AIDS, a Corporate Reaction', *Boardroom* 4 (1991).
65. *Finance Week*, 24–30 October 1991.
66. C. Russel, 'The AIDS Crisis: a Mining Industry Perspective', *Mining Survey* 2 (1991): 28.
67. G. Christie, 'AIDS Issues in the Workplace', *People* 30 (1991): 13.
68. P. Boulle, 'An Organisational Response to AIDS', *AIDS Analysis Africa* 2 no. 5 (1992): 10.
69. D. Mokhobo, 'AIDS: Balancing Individual Rights With Business Imperatives', *South African Journal on Human Rights* 9 (1993): 111.
70. M. Hermanus, 'HIV and AIDS Policy in the Mining Industry', *South African Journal on Human Rights* 9 no. 1 (1993): 113.
71. *Ibid.*, p. 115.
72. Q. A. Karim, N. Morar, N. Zuma, Z. Stein and E. Preston-Whyte, 'Women and AIDS in Natal/KwaZulu: Determinants of the Adoption of HIV-Protective Behaviour', *Urbanisation and Health Newsletter* 20 (1994): 8.

4 Public Sector Responses to HIV and AIDS in Apartheid South Africa (1982–1994)

1. M. Kirby, 'AIDS & the Law', *South African Journal on Human Rights* 9 (1993): 1.
2. C. W. Van Wyk, 'South African Thesis on Legal Questions Concerning AIDS Recommends ...', *AIDS Scan* 4 no. 1 (1992).
3. J. Burchell, 'AIDS and the Law: Discrimination Against the AIDS Sufferer', *Businessman's Law* 20 (1990/91): 195.
4. S. A. Strauss, 'Legal Issues Concerning AIDS: An Outline'. *South African Practice Management* 9 (1) (1988): 14.
5. E. Cameron, 'AIDS in Employment. Facts, Fantasies and Fairness', *Employment Law* 7 no. 5 (1991): 195.
6. Burchell, 'AIDS and the Law', p. 196.
7. J. L. Beckmann and J. G. Prinsloo, 'Some Legal Aspects of AIDS in Schools and Other Educational Institutions', *South African Journal of Education* 13 no. 2 (1993): 52; *Southern African Practice Management* (1988): 5; *Southern African Practice Management* 13 no. 1 (1992). 'First SA Court Ruling on Doctor's Duty of Confidentiality Towards Patient with AIDS'.
8. E. Cameron, 'AIDS in Employment. Facts, Fantasies and Fairness', *Employment Law* 7 no. 5 (1991): 197.
9. E. Cameron and E. Swanson, 'Public Health and Human Rights – the AIDS Crisis in South Africa', *South African Journal on Human Rights* 8 (1992): 498.
10. *Ibid.*, p. 499.
11. E. Cameron, 'Human Rights, Racism and AIDS: The New Discrimination', *South African Journal on Human Rights* 9 (1993): 23.
12. Cameron and Swanson, 'Public Health and Human Rights', p. 499.
13. F. J. De Jager, 'VIGS: Die Rol Van die Strafeg', *Journal of South African Law* 2 (1991): 214.
14. *Ibid.*, pp. 216–17.
15. E. Cameron, 'Overview of McGeary Decision', *AIDS Analysis Africa* 4 no. 5 (1994).
16. M. Chetty, 'Human Rights, Access to Health Care and AIDS', *South African Journal on Human Rights* 9 (1993): 76.
17. Cameron, 'Human Rights, Racism and AIDS', p. 22.
18. Ibid., p. 26.
19. COSATU, 'Key Policy Issue Papers and Major Resolutions from 4th National Congress July 1991', *History in the Making* 2 no. 1 (1991).
20. F. Viljoen, 'Verligting of Verlustiging: Regshervorming in 'n Tyd van VIGS', *The South African Law Journal* 110 (1993): 114.
21. R. Sher, 'Women and HIV and AIDS', *AIDS Scan* 2 no. 4 (1990): 3.
22. D. Yach, 'Development and Health: The Need for Integrated Approaches in South Africa', *Development Southern Africa* 9 no. 1 (1992): 39.
23. AIDS Consortium, 'The AIDS Consortium Charter of Rights on AIDS and HIV', *South African Journal on Human Rights* 9 (1993).
24. V. Van der Vliet, 'Dealing with AIDS: a Work in Progress', *Focus* 34 (2004): 50.
25. *Ibid.*, p. 50.
26. C. Ngwena and A. Pelser, *Strengthening Local Government and Civic Responses to the HIV/AIDS Epidemic – a Study for the Ford Foundation.* Working

Paper: Centre for Health Systems Research and Development, University of the Free State (2001), p. 2.

27. N. Nattrass, *The Moral Economy of AIDS in South Africa* (Cambridge, Cambridge University Press, 2004), p. 42.
28. T. Barnett and A. Whiteside, *AIDS in the Twenty First Century: Disease and Globalisation* (Basingstoke: Palgrave Macmillan, 2002), p. 335.
29. Anderson, *Public Policymaking*, p. 7.
30. Dunn, *Public Policy Analysis: an Introduction*, p. 299.
31. Cobb and Elder, *The Political Uses of Symbols*, p. 85.
32. Anderson, *Public Policymaking*, 101.
33. Parsons, *Policy: an Introduction to the Theory and Practice of Policy Analysis*, 463.
34. J. Stover and A. Johnston, *The Art of Policy Formulation: Experiences from Africa in Developing National HIV/AIDS Policies* (Washington, DC, 1999), p. 12.
35. Ibid., pp., 11–12.

5 AIDS Policy-making during the Mandela Administration (1994–1999)

1. N. Nattrass, *The Moral Economy of AIDS in South Africa* (Cambridge: Cambridge University Press), p. 189.
2. *Ibid.*, p. 42.
3. A. Jaffe, 'South Africans Divided Against AIDS', *AIDS Bulletin* 8 no. 43 (1999): 17.
4. R. Dorrington and L. Johnson, 'Epidemiological and Demographic', in J. Gow and C. desmond (eds), *Impacts and Interventions: The HIV and AIDS Epidemic and the Children of South Africa* (Pietermaritzburg: University of Natal Press, 2002), p. 34.
5. H. Marais, *South Africa: Limits to Change: The Political Economy of Transformation* (Cape Town: University of Cape Town Press, 1998), p. 180.
6. D. Blaauw and L. Gilson, 'Voices of National and Provincial Managers'. Available at: legacy.hst.org.za/sahr/2001/chapter14.htm.
7. M. Mbali, 'HIV and AIDS Policy-Making in Post-Apartheid South Africa', in J. Daniel, A. Habib and R. Southall (eds), *State of the Nation: South Africa 2003–2004* (Cape Town: HSRC Press, 2003), p. 313.
8. Marais, *South Africa*, p. 180.
9. M. Price and A. Van den Heever, 'The Reconstruction and Development Programme and Health', *Southern African Journal of Epidemiology and Infection* 9 no. 2 (1994): 34.
10. C. Evian, 'AIDS, Reconstruction and Development, and Corporate Response', *AIDS Analysis Africa* 5 no. 6 (1995): 3.
11. ANC, *National Health Plan for South Africa* (May 1994): 1.
12. H. Schneider, *The AIDS Impasse in South Africa as a Struggle for Symbolic Power* (Johannesburg, Centre for Health Policy, WITS, 2001), p. 3; H. Schneider, 'On the Fault-Line: the Politics of AIDS Policy in Contemporary South Africa', *African Studies* 61 no. 1 (2002): 145.
13. R. Smart, 'Preventing Transmission of HIV', in J. Gow and C. Desmond (eds), *Impacts and Interventions: The HIV and AIDS Epidemic and the Children of South Africa* (Pietermaritzburg: University of Natal Press, 2002), pp. 190–2.

14. Marais, *South Africa*, pp. 12–13.
15. *Ibid.*, pp. 6, 8.
16. *Ibid.*, p. 15.
17. H. Schneider in *ibid.*, p. 32.
18. 'Africa Veers between Inertia and Coercion', *AIDS Analysis Africa* 6 no. 1 (1995): 1.
19. M. Ainsworth, 'Government Priorities for Preventing HIV and AIDS', *AIDS Analysis Africa* 9 no. 4 (1999): 107.
20. Marais, *South Africa*, p. 87.
21. H. Marais, *To the Edge: AIDS Review 2000* (Pretoria: Centre for the Study of AIDS, 2000), p. 16.
22. Dorrington and Johnson, 'Epidemiological and Demographic', p. 22.
23. V. Van der Vliet, 'South Africa Divided against AIDS: a Crisis of Leadership' in K. D. Kauffman and D. L. Lindauer, *AIDS and South Africa: The Social Expression of a Pandemic* (Basingstoke: Macmillan, 2004), p. 49; C. Joseph, 'HIV and AIDS and Local Government', *Occasional Paper* 12 (2002): 30–1.
24. R. E. Manning, 'Noble Intentions, Harsh Realities: The Politics of AIDS Policy in South Africa', PhD Thesis (Woodrow Wilson School of Public and International Affairs, 2001), p. 62.
25. P. Badcock-Walters, 'Education', in J. Gow and C. Desmond (eds), *Impacts and Interventions: The HIV and AIDS Epidemic and the Children of South Africa* (Pietermaritzburg: University of Natal Press, 2002), p. 108.
26. H. Schenider and J. McIntyre, 'Is the 1993/94 AIDS Programme Budget Adequate?' *AIDS Scan* 6 no. 2 (1994): 14; K. Strachan, 'The Month in Review', *HST Update* 5 (1995): 2; K. Strachan, 'The Current Health Budget: Who Gets What?' *South African Family Practice* 17 no. 7 (1996): 322.
27. Marais, *To the Edge*, p. 17.
28. *Ibid.*, pp. 10, 11.
29. *Ibid.*, p. 15.
30. Nattrass, *The Moral Economy of AIDS in South Africa*, p. 44.
31. H. Schneider, *The Politics Behind AIDS: The Case of South Africa* (Johannesburg: Centre for Health Policy, WITS, 1998), pp. 7–8.
32. J. McIntyre, 'The Government Strategy on Combating AIDS', *HST Update* 13 (1996): 20.
33. Schneider, 'On the Fault-Line', p. 163.
34. A. Whiteside and C. Sunter, *AIDS: The Challenge for South Africa* (Cape Town: Human & Rousseau/Tafelberg, 2000), p. 122; Ngwena and Pelser *Strengthening Local Government and Civic Responses to the HIV/AIDS Epidemic*, p. 4.
35. Marais, *To the Edge*, p. 22.
36. *Ibid.*, pp. 24, 28.
37. W. Parker, 'A National Media Campaign – Who Makes the Decisions and What is Really Needed?', *AIDS Bulletin* 5 no. 2 (1996): 15.
38. B. Zuma, 'Cross-Cultural Counselling', *Positive Outlook* 3 no. 4 (1996): 2.
39. G. Kitching, 'Sal "Sarafina" VIGS Oorleef?', *Insig* (April 1996): 40.
40. J. Eichbaum, 'AIDS Education: But Who is Being Aided?', *Scenaria* 182 (1996): 3.
41. M. Crewe, 'South Africa: Touched by the Vengeance of AIDS Responses to the South African Epidemic', *South Africa Journal of International Affairs* 7(2) (2000): 30.

42. L. Walker, G. Reid and M. Cornell, *Waiting to Happen: HIV and AIDS in South Africa* (Colorado: Lynne Rienner, 2004), p. 107.
43. Marais, *To the Edge*, p. 36.
44. Nattrass, *The Moral Economy of AIDS in South Africa*, p. 45.
45. Phila, 'The Sarafina II Controversy', *Phila Legislative Update* 3 (1996): 4.
46. Schneider, 'On the Fault-Line', p. 158.
47. M. R. Galloway, 'South African National AIDS Council (SANAC) Launched', *AIDS Bulletin* 9 no. 1 (2000): 21.
48. 'AZT on Trial to Stop Mother-to-Child Transmission', *AIDS Analysis Africa* 5 no. 5 (1995b): 8.
49. *Finansies & Tegniek*, 13 September 1996.
50. P. Busse, 'Response of People with HIV and AIDS to Representations of Themselves', *AIDS Bulletin* 4 no. 1 (1995): 22.
51. M. Crewe, 'South Africa: Touched by the Vengeance of AIDS Responses to the South African Epidemic', *South Africa Journal of International Affairs* 7(2) (2000): 31.
52. A. Coetzee, 'The Role of Censorship in Defeating HIV and AIDS in South Africa', *Positive Outlook* 1 (3) (1994); I. Van der Linde, 'The Costing of HIV and AIDS – Without a Clue?' *AIDS Scan* 11 no. 1 (1999): 16.
53. J. Cowlin, 'Cheaper to Manage HIV than to Treat AIDS – the Medscheme Experience', *South African Medical Journal* 89 no. 1 (1999): 17.
54. Marais, *To the Edge*, p. 39.
55. D. Wilkinson, K. Floyd and C. F. Gilks, 'A National Programme to Reduce Mother-to-Child HIV Transmission is Potentially Cost Saving', *AIDS Bulletin* 8 no. 1 (1999): 15.
56. Nattrass, *The Moral Economy of AIDS in South Africa*, pp. 47–8.
57. P. Bond, *Against Global Apartheid: South Africa Meets the World Bank, IMF and International Finance* (Lansdowne: UCT Press, 2001), p. 156.
58. S. Ekambaram, 'Health before Profits', *Women's Health Project Newsletter* 31 (1999): 11.
59. Nattrass, *The Moral Economy of AIDS in South Africa*, p. 49.
60. T. Mbeki, 'The South African Declaration on AIDS', *The South African Dental Journal* 54 no. 12 (1999): 576.
61. V. Van der Vliet, 'AIDS: Losing the New Struggle?', *Daedalus* 130 no. 1 (2001): 151.
62. ALQ, '1999 Legislative Review', *AIDS Legal Quarterly* no.1 (February 1999): 17–18.
63. A. S. S. Karim, 'Making AIDS a Notifiable Disease – Is it an Appropriate Policy for South Africa?' *South African Medical Journal* 89 no. 6 (1999): 18.
64. 'Information, Ignorance and the Politicisation of AIDS', *AIDS Analysis Africa* 9 no. 5 (1999): 2.
65. M. Heywood, 'SADC Moves towards Making AIDS and HIV Notifiable', *AIDS Analysis Africa* 10 no. 1 (1999): 3; A. N. Smith, 'Notification of HIV and AIDS', *AIDS Bulletin* (July 1999): 6; M. Colvin, 'AIDS Notification – Not a Viable Method of Data Gathering', *AIDS Bulletin* 8 no. 2 (1999): 4–5.
66. *Washington Post*, 14 July 2000.
67. Nattrass, *The Moral Economy of AIDS in South Africa*, p. 47.
68. *Financial Mail*, 14 June 1996.

6 AIDS Policy-making during the First Mbeki Administration (1999–2004)

1. UNAIDS, *Report on the Global AIDS Epidemic*, pp. 190–3.
2. M. Crewe, 'Face of the Future', *Siyaya* 6 (Summer 1999): 31.
3. *National Health Review* (2001): 11–15. '1997 Strategic Plan'.
4. M. Heywood, 'From Rhetoric to Action – An Evaluation of Progress in Relation to Priority Area 4: Human Legal Rights, HIV and AIDS National Plan', *AIDS Law Project* (2002): 2.
5. *Ibid.*, p. 3.
6. A. Hickey, N. Ndlovu and T. Guthrie, *Budgeting for HIV and AIDS in South Africa: Report on Intergovernmental Funding Flows for an Integrated Response in the Social Sector* (Cape Town: IDASA, 2003), p. 11.
7. *Ibid.*, p. 13.
8. A. Hickey, *Budgets and Funding Flows in the National Integrated Plan for HIV and AIDS* (Cape Town: IDASA, 2001), p. 1; 'The Department of Education's Life Skills, Sexuality and HIV and AIDS Programme', *Agenda* 53 (2002): 96.
9. *SAPA*, 14 November 2001.
10. A. Strode and K. B. Grant, *Understanding the Institutional Dynamics of South Africa's Response to HIV and AIDS Pandemic* (Pretoria: IDASA, 2004), p. 14.
11. R. Smart, 'Preventing Transmission of HIV', in J. Gow and C. Desmond (eds), *Impacts and Interventions: The HIV and AIDS Epidemic and the Children of South Africa*, p. 193; '1997 Strategic Plan', *National Health Review* (2001): 11–15.
12. M. R. Galloway, 'South African National AIDS Council (SANAC) Launched', *AIDS Bulletin* 9 no. 1 (2000): 15.
13. T. Trengove-Jones, *Who Cares? AIDS Review 2001* (Pretoria: University of Pretoria, 2001), p. 31.
14. Strode and Grant, *Understanding the Institutional Dynamics of South Africa's Response to HIV and AIDS Pandemic*, pp. 24–36.
15. *Ibid.*, p. 23.
16. *Ibid.*, pp. 16–17.
17. L. Forman et al., 'Health Legislation 1994–2003', in P. Ijumba (ed.), *South African Health Review 2003/04* (Johannesburg: Health Systems Trust, 2003): 13.
18. The Super 301 watch list is a legal mechanism resulting from American trade legislation implemented in 1988. It enables the US government unilaterally to punish states suspected of transgressing trade agreements or forms of international law pertaining to commerce.
19. SAPA-Associated Press, 14 November 2001.
20. V. Van der Vliet, 'South Africa Divided against AIDS: a Crisis of Leadership', in K. D. Kauffman and D. L. Lindauer (eds), *AIDS and South Africa: The Social Expression of a Pandemic* (Basingstoke: Macmillan, 2004), p. 63.
21. T. Kasper, 'Patents, Pills and Public Policy: the Pharmaceutical Industry and International Trade', in K. Kelly, W. Parker and S. Gelby (eds), *HIV and AIDS, Economics and Governance in South Africa: Key Issues in Understanding Response* (Johannesburg: The Centre for AIDS Development, Research and Education, 2002), p. 157.

22. E. Buch, 'Equity in Health Care: Is the Jury Still Out?' in C Manganyi (ed.), *On Becoming a Democracy: Transition and Transformation in South African Society* (Pretoria: University of South Africa Press, 2004), p. 95.
23. C. Ngwena, 'HIV and AIDS and Equal Opportunities in the Workplace: The Implications of the Employment Equity Act', *The Comparative and International Law Journal of Southern Africa* 33(1) (2000): 112.
24. M. Du Plessis, 'The South African Employment Equity Act and HIV', *AIDS Analysis Africa* 10 no. 4 (2000): 3.
25. '1999 Legislative Review', *AIDS Legal Quarterly* 1 (February 1999): 4.
26. J. Joni and M. Heywood, 'Error in Judgement or Failure by the Judiciary to Give Clarity on the Interpretation of the Law?', *AIDS Analysis Africa* 12 no. 3 (2001): 11.
27. K. Goyer, 'Compulsory HIV Testing for Alleged Sex Offenders: Victim Empowerment or Violation of Rights?', *AIDS Analysis Africa* 11 no. 6 (2001): 8.
28. *SAPA*, 4 April 2001.
29. Forman et al., 'Health Legislation 1994–2003', p. 19.
30. T. Motebele and M. Heywood, 'South Africa's Constitutional Court Declares Pre-employment Testing a Human Rights Violation', *AIDS Analysis Africa* 11 no. 4 (2001): 10.
31. M. Figueira, ' "A" Versus South African Airways', *AIDS Legal Quarterly* (September 2000): 12.
32. M. Du Plessis, 'The Constitutional Court Sets the Matter Straight: Applicants for Employment Who are HIV Positive', *AIDS Analysis Africa* 11 no. 5 (2001): 13.
33. Barnett and Whiteside, *AIDS in the Twenty-First Century*, p. 335.
34. M. Crewe, 'How Do We Make Sense of President Mbeki?' *AIDS Analysis Africa* 11 no. 1 (June/July 2000): 123.
35. *SAPA*, 2 October 2000.
36. T. Lodge, *Politics in South Africa: From Mandela to Mbeki* (Indiana: Indiana University Press, 2002), p. 257.
37. *SAPA*, 2 October 2000.
38. *Sunday Times*, 23 April 2000.
39. *Sunday Times*, 9 July 2000.
40. *Business Day*, 6 October 2000.
41. *AFP*, 4 July 2000.
42. A. Sparks, *Beyond the Miracle: Inside the New South Africa* (London: Profile Books, 2003), p. 295.
43. *Mail and Guardian*, 28 September 2000.
44. SAPA-Associated Press, 12 March 2000.
45. *Mail and Guardian*, 26 October 2000.
46. *Washington Post*, 15 March 2001.
47. *SAPA*, 4 April 2001.
48. *Associated Press*, 24 April 2001.
49. *Business Day*, 10 September 2001.
50. *SAPA*, 17 September 2001.
51. Mbeki inaugural ZK Matthews Memorial Lecture 2001.
52. SAPA-Associated Press, 14 November 2001.
53. V. Van der Vliet, 'Dealing with AIDS: a Work in Progress', *Focus* 34 (2004): 75.
54. *Ibid.*, p. 76.
55. *Ibid.*, p. 77.

56. S. Power, 'The AIDS Rebel Letter from South Africa', *The New Yorker* 79 no. 12 (2003): 67.
57. C. Bisseker, 'AIDS Fracas in Natal', *Financial Mail* (8 February 2002), p. 19.
58. *SAPA*, 28 September 2003.
59. Van der Vliet, 'Dealing with AIDS'.
60. Crewe, 'How Do We Make Sense of President Mbeki?' p. 124.
61. Sparks, *Beyond the Miracle*, p. 292.
62. Crewe, 'How Do We Make Sense of President Mbeki?' p. 125.
63. Sparks, *Beyond the Miracle*, 285.
64. T. Trengove-Jones, *Who Cares? AIDS Review 2001* (Pretoria: University of Pretoria, 2001), p. 6.
65. Makgoba 2001. Internet source.
66. H. Schneider, 'On the Fault-line: the Politics of AIDS Policy in Contemporary South Africa', *African Studies* 61 (2002): 161.
67. Van der Vliet, 'Dealing with AIDS', 80–1.
68. Mbali, *State of the Nation*, p. 322.
69. Schneider, 'On the Fault-line', pp. 153–4.
70. L. Walker, G. Reid and M. Cornell, *Waiting to Happen: HIV and AIDS in South Africa* (Colorado: Lynne Riener, 2004), p. 125.
71. Van der Vliet, 'Dealing with AIDS', p. 81.
72. R. E. Manning, 'Noble Intentions, Harsh Realities: the Politics of AIDS Policy in South Africa', PhD thesis, Woodrow Wilsob School of Public and International Affairs (2001), p. 106.
73. Mbali, *State of the Nation: South Africa 2003–2004*, p. 317.
74. P. Bond, *Against Global Apartheid: South Africa Meets the World Bank, IMF and International Finance* (Lansdwone: UCT Press, 2001), p. 177.
75. J. Kromberg, 'Time to Act', *Leadership* (May 2004): 15.
76. J. Berger, "Litigation Strategies to Gain Access to Treatment for HIV/AIDS: the Case of South Africa's Treatment Action Campaign', in *Global Treatment Access: Legal Developments and Strategies*. Papers prepared for Putting Third First: Vaccines, Access to Treatment and the Law – A satellite meeting of the 14th International AIDS Conference (Barcelona), pp. 598, 599.
77. Van der Vliet, *The Social Expression of a Pandemic*, p. 63.
78. *Ibid.*, p. 75.
79. *Ibid.*, p. 69.
80. Mbali, *State of the Nation*, p. 325.
81. Cabinet statement 2003, internet source.
82. Van der Vliet, *AIDS and South Africa*, p. 23.
83. Mbali, *State of the Nation: South Africa 2003–2004*, p. 326.
84. Van der Vliet, *AIDS and South Africa*, p. 79.
85. A. Hickey, N. Ndlovu and T. Guthrie, *Budgeting for HIV and AIDS in South Africa: Report on Intergovernmental Funding Flows for an Integrated Response in the Social Sector* (Cape Town: IDASA, 2003), p. 1.
86. A. Hickey, *Budgets and Funding Flows in the National Integrated Plan for HIV and AIDS* (Cape Town: IDASA, 2001), p. 1.
87. Hickey et al., *Budgeting for HIV and AIDS in South Africa*, p. 87.
88. *Ibid.*, p. 2.
89. Hickey, *Budgets and Funding Flows in the National Integrated Plan for HIV and AIDS*, p. 36.

90. Hickey, *Budgets and Funding Flows in the National Integrated Plan for HIV and AIDS*, p. 38.
91. Nattrass, *The Moral Economy of AIDS in South Africa*, 59.

Conclusion Looking Back and Looking Forward

1. *Washington Post*, 29 April 2004.
2. *Mail and Guardian*, 4 June 2004.
3. *Reuters NewMedia*, 16 July 2004.
4. *Sunday Times*, 18 July 2004.
5. *Sunday Herald*, 18 July 2004.
6. TAC, "Why the TAC is Going to Court Tomorrow and Holding Country-wide Demonstrations', Internet source (2004). www.tac.org.za.
7. *News24.com*, 14 December 2004.
8. *Cape Times*, 22 October 2004.
9. J. Michael, 'Tutu Praises Whites and Lashes Black Elite', *The Star*, 24 November 2004, p. 9.
10. *ANC Today*, 17 December 2004.
11. *News24.com*, 18 January 2005.
12. *Sunday Independent*, 12 December 2004; *Mail and Guardian*, 10–16 December.
13. *News24.com*, 24 January 2005.
14. *News24.com*, 14 March 2005.
15. *Mail and Guardian*, 25 February–3 March 2005.
16. *News24.com*, 18 February 2005; *Sunday Independent*, 20 February 2005.
17. *Lancet*, 12 February 2005.
18. *Mail and Guardian*, 24–31 March 2005.
19. *Sunday Times*, 13 March 2005.

Bibliography

Books and journal articles

AFP, *AIDS Declaration Fit for Dustbin*. Mbeki's spokesman (4 July 2000).

Agenda 53 'The Department of Education's Life Skills, Sexuality and HIV and AIDS Programme' (2002).

AIDS Analysis Africa 2 (2), 'ANC to Test its Exiles for AIDS' (1991).

AIDS Analysis Africa 3 (1), 'AIDS and Behaviour Change: A Statement of Belief' (1992a).

AIDS Analysis Africa 2 (5), 'Ethics: Where African Traditions Differ' (1992b).

AIDS Analysis Africa 4 (6), 'Editorial' (1994).

AIDS Analysis Africa 6 (1), 'Africa Veers Between Inertia and Coercion' (1995a).

AIDS Analysis Africa 5 (5), 'AZT on Trial to Stop Mother-to-Child Transmission' (1995b).

AIDS Analysis Africa 9 (1), 'Government's Mixed Messages are not Helping' (1998).

AIDS Analysis Africa 9 (5), 'Information, Ignorance and the Politicisation of AIDS' (1999).

AIDS Consortium, 'The AIDS Consortium Charter of Rights on AIDS and HIV', *South African Journal on Human Rights* 9 (1993).

AIDS Scan, 'International Conference on Health in Southern Africa Releases Draft Statement on HIV and AIDS in Southern Africa', *AIDS Scan* 2 (2) (1990).

AIDS Scan, 'MRC Launches AIDS Bulletin', *AIDS Scan* 4 (3) (1992).

Ainsworth, M., 'Government Priorities for Preventing HIV and AIDS'. *AIDS Analysis Africa* 9 (4) 1999.

Albertyn, S. and Rosengarten, D., 'HIV and AIDS: Some Critical Issues in Employment Law'. *South African Journal on Human Rights* 9 (1) (1993).

Allison, G., *The Essence of Decision: Explaining the Cuban Missile Crisis*. Boston: Little, Brown, 1971.

Almond, G. and Verba, S., *The Civic Culture*. Boston: Little, Brown, 1965.

ALQ, '1999 Legislative Review', *AIDS Legal Quarterly* (1) (February 1999).

ANC Today 2 (14), 'Beginning of Health Month' (5–11 April 2002).

ANC Today 4 (50), 'Nevirapine, Drugs and African Guinea Pigs' (17–23 December 2004).

Anderson, J., *Public Policymaking*. New York: Holt, Rinehardt & Winston, 1984.

Anderson, J., *Public Policymaking*. Boston: Houghton Mifflin Company, 2000.

Anderson, J., *Public Policymaking*. Boston: Houghton Mifflin Company, 2001.

Annual Survey of South African Law, Johannesburg: Juta & Co, Limited, 1993.

Anon., 'War, Armies and the Spread of HIV'. *AIDS Analysis Africa* 2 (1) (1991).

Anthony, J. Coetzee, E. J. Kent, A. P. *et al.*, 'Need for SA Policy on HIV in Pregnancy', *South African Medical Journal* 85 (9) (1995).

Arendse, N., 'HIV and AIDS Infected Employees: Some Legal Implications for the Work-Place'. *Industrial Law Journal* 12 (1991).

Arya, S., 'Antiretroviral Therapy in Countries with Low Health Expenditure'. *Lancet* 351 (9113) (1998).
Ashford, A., *AIDS, Witchcraft and the Problem of Power in Post-Apartheid South Africa*. Durban: University of Natal Press, 2001.
Atkins, N. G., 'AIDS and Insurance – II: Further Classes of Short-Term Business', *Businessman's Law* 19 (1990).
Axworthy, L., *Human Security: Safety for People in a Changing World*. Ottawa: Canadian Department of Foreign Affairs and Trade, 1999.
Badcock-Walters, P., 'Education', In *Impacts and Interventions: The HIV and AIDS Epidemic and the Children of South Africa*, ed. J. Gow and C. Desmond. Pietermaritzburg: University of Natal Press, 2002.
Baker, R. Michaels, R. and Preston, E., *Public Policy Development: Linking the Technical and Political Processes*. New York: John Wiley, 1975.
Barnett, T., *The Effects of HIV and AIDS on Farming Systems and Rural Livelihoods in Uganda, Tanzania and Zambia, a Summary Analysis of Case Studies from Research Carried out in the Period July–September 1993*. Norwich: Overseas Development Group, 1994.
Barnett, T. and Whiteside, A., *AIDS in the Twenty First Century: Disease and Globalisation*. Basingstoke: Palgrave Macmillan, 2002.
Beckmann, J. L. and Prinsloo, J. G., 'Some Legal Aspects of AIDS in Schools and Other Educational Institutions'. *South African Journal of Education* 13 (2) (1993).
Bedeski, R., *Defining Human Security*. Victoria: Centre for Global Studies, 1999.
Bell, P., 'Double Trouble'. *Leadership South Africa* 9 (9) (1990).
Berger, J., 'Tripping over Patents: AIDS, Access to Treatment and the Manufacturing of Scarcity'. Unpublished Master's thesis: University of Toronto, 2001.
Berger, J. 'Litigation Strategies to Gain Access to Treatment for HIV/AIDS: the Case of South Africa's Treatment Action Campaign', in *Global Treatment Access: Legal Developments and Strategies*. Papers prepared for Putting Third First: Vaccines, Access to Treatment and the Law – A satellite meeting of the 14th International AIDS Conference (Barcelona, 2002).
Bernstein, A. (ed.), 'Political Institutions and Policy-Making'. In *Policy Making in a New Democracy – South Africa's Challenges for the 21st Century*. Johannesburg: Centre for Development and Enterprise, 1999.
Bisseker, C., 'AIDS Fracas in Natal', *Financial Mail*, 8 February 2002.
Bond, G., *AIDS in Africa and the Caribbean*. Boulder: Westview Press, 1997.
Bond, P., *Against Global Apartheid: South Africa Meets the World Bank, IMF and International Finance*. Lansdowne: UCT Press, 2001.
Bond, P., 'Thabo Mbeki and NEPAD: Breaking or Shining the Chains of Global Apartheid?' In *Thabo Mbeki's World: The Politics and Ideology of the South African President*, ed. S. Jacobs and R. Calland. Pietermaritzburg: University of Natal Press, 2002.
Booth, C., 'The Insurance Industry and AIDS – an Insider's Perspective', *South African Journal on Human Rights* 9 (1993).
Booysen, S. and Erasmus, E., 'Public Policy-Making'. In *Government and Politics in the New South Africa*, ed. A. Venter. Pretoria: Van Schaik, 2001.
Boulle, P., 'An Organisational Response to AIDS'. *AIDS Analysis Africa* 2 (5) (1992).
Bracks, R. and Van Wyk, M. W., 'The Position of HIV and AIDS Employees in South African Companies: A Legal and Empirical Survey'. *South African Journal of Labour Relations* 18 (4) (1994).

Brain, P., 'Blood Transfusion and AIDS'. *SA Journal of Continuing Medical Education* 6 (3) (1988).

Brewer, T. and Heymann, S., 'Two-Tiered Health Care: the Root of Ethical Problems in Recent Clinical Trials', *International Journal of Infectious Diseases* 2 (3) (1998).

Brown, L., 'HIV-Epidemic Restructuring Africa's Population'. *Worldwatch Issue Alert* (31 October 2000).

Brynard, P., 'Policy Implementation'. In *Improving Public Policy*, ed. F. Cloete and H. Wissink. Pretoria: Van Schaik, 2000.

Buch, E., 'Equity in Health Care: Is the Jury Still Out?' In *On Becoming a Democracy: Transition and Transformation in South African Society*, ed. C. Manganyi. Pretoria: University of South Africa Press, 2004.

Bujra, J., 'Targeting Men for a Change: AIDS Discourse and Activism in Africa'. *Agenda* 44 (2000).

Burchell, J., 'AIDS and the Law: Discrimination against the AIDS Sufferer', *Businessman's Law* 20 (1990/1).

Busse, P., 'Response of People with HIV and AIDS to Representations of Themselves'. *AIDS Bulletin* 4 (1) (1995).

Cameron, E., 'Screening Recruits for AIDS: Yes or No?' *Employment Law* 7 (6) (1991a).

Cameron, E., 'AIDS in Employment. Facts, Fantasies and Fairness'. *Employment Law* 7 (5) (1991b).

Cameron, E., 'AIDS – Some Problems in Employment Law', *Industrial Law Journal* 12 (1991c).

Cameron, E., 'Registrations on Migrant Workers, Immigrants and Travellers with HIV and AIDS: South Africa's Step Forward', *Industrial Law Journal* 13 (1992).

Cameron, E., 'Human Rights, Racism and AIDS: The New Discrimination', *South African Journal on Human Rights* 9 (1993a).

Cameron, E., 'Legal Rights, Human Rights, and AIDS: the First Decade', *AIDS Analysis Africa* 4 (3) (1993b).

Cameron, E., 'Overview of McGeary Decision', *AIDS Analysis Africa* 4 (5) (1994).

Cameron, E. and Swanson, E., 'Public Health and Human Rights – the AIDS Crisis in South Africa', *South African Journal on Human Rights* 8 (1992).

Chalk, P., *Non-Military Security and the Global Order – The Impact of Extremism, Violence and Chaos on National and International Security*. London: Macmillan, 2000.

Cheru, F., 'Debt, Adjustment and the Politics of Effective Response to HIV and AIDS in Africa', *Third World Quarterly* 23 (2) (2002).

Chetty, M., 'Human Rights, Access to Health Care and AIDS'. *South African Journal on Human Rights* 9 (1993).

Christie, G., 'AIDS Issues in the Workplace', *People* 30 (1991).

Cobb, R. and Elder, C., *The Political Uses of Symbols*. New York: Longman, 1983.

Coetzee, A., 'The Role of Censorship in Defeating HIV and AIDS in South Africa', *Positive Outlook* 1 (3) (1994).

Coleman, K. and Naidoo, S., 'AIDS Community Awareness: Aspects for an Evolving Campaign', *Nursing RSA* 5 (10) (1990).

Colvin, M., 'AIDS Notification – Not a Viable Method of Data Gathering', *AIDS Bulletin* 8 (2) (1999).

COSATU, 'Key Policy Issue Papers and Major Resolutions from 4th National Congress July 1991'. *History in the Making* 2 (1) (1991).

Cowlin, J., 'Cheaper to Manage HIV than to Treat AIDS – the Medscheme Experience', *South African Medical Journal* 89 (1) (1999).
Crafford, G., *AIDS Policy Formulation in the Workplace and the Economic Cost of AIDS: a Western Cape Survey*. University of Stellenbosch: Department of Economics, 1992.
Crewe, M., 'Learning Aids', *Work in Progress* 94 (1993).
Crewe, M., 'An Interdepartmental Response to HIV and AIDS', *AIDS Bulletin* 5 (2) (1996a).
Crewe, M., 'How Far Has NACOSA Plan Been Implemented?' *AIDS Bulletin* 5 (2) (1996b).
Crewe, M., 'Life Skills and AIDS Education in Schools'. *AIDS Bulletin* 5 (2) (1996c).
Crewe, M., 'Face of the Future', *Siyaya* 6 (Summer 1999).
Crewe, M., *HIV and AIDS and Policy in South Africa Today*. Address to diplomats at a meeting political and economic research officers at the Dutch Embassy, Pretoria, 19 April 2000a.
Crewe, M., 'How Do We Make Sense of President Mbeki?' *AIDS Analysis Africa* 11 (1) (June/July 2000b).
Crewe, M., 'South Africa: Touched by the Vengeance of AIDS Responses to the South African Epidemic', *South Africa Journal of International Affairs* 7 (2) (2000c).
Croy, B. B., 'Personalia' *Community Health in SA* (November/December 1989).
Dahl, R., *Who Governs? Democracy and Power in an American City*. New Haven, CT: Yale University Press, 1961.
Dancaster, L. and Jamieson, E., 'Company Policies on AIDS – The Answer?' *AIDS Analysis Africa* 1 (4) (1990).
Dancaster, L., 'AIDS and Employment'. *Journal of the University of Stellenbosch Business School* 11 (2) 1991.
Dancaster, L., 'Doctor/Patient Confidentiality', *Supreme Court Decision* 2 (5) (1992).
De Bruyn, P. J., 'VIGS en Menslike Gedrag: 'n Teologies-Etiese Beooredeling', *Koers: Bulletin for Christian Scholarship* 55 (3) (1990).
De Coning, C. and Cloete, F., 'Theories and Models for Analysing Public Policy'. In *Improving Public Policy*, ed. F. Cloete and H. Wissink. Pretoria: Van Schaik, 2000.
De Jager, F .J., 'VIGS: Die Rol Van die Strafeg'. *Journal of South African Law* 2 (1991).
Decosas, J., 'Labour Migration and HIV Epidemics in Africa', *AIDS Analysis Africa* 9 (2) (August/September 1998).
Decosas, J., 'Preventing HIV Transmission through Social Policy', *AIDS Analysis Africa* 9 (4) (1999).
Delate, R., 'HIV and AIDS: Developing a National Strategy with a Human Rights Approach', *South African Journal of International Affairs* 7 (2) (2000).
Desmond, C. Michael, K. and Gow, J., 'The Hidden Battle: HIV and AIDS in the Household and Community', *South African Journal of International Affairs* 7 (2) 2000.
Devine, D., *The Political Culture of the United States*. Boston: Little, Brown, 1972.
Dorrington, R. and Johnson, L., 'Epidemiological and Demographic'. In *Impacts and Interventions: The HIV and AIDS Epidemic and the Children of South Africa*, ed. J. Gow and C. Desmond. Pietermaritzburg: University of Natal Press, 2002.

Draft Maputo Statement, 'Draft Maputo Statement on HIV and AIDS in Southern Africa', *History in the Making* 1 (5) (1991).

Du Guerny, J., 'AIDS and Agriculture in Africa: Can Agricultural Policy Make a Difference?' *Food, Nutrition & Agriculture* 25 (1999).

Du Plessis, M., 'The South African Employment Equity Act and HIV', *AIDS Analysis Africa* 10 (4) (2000).

Du Plessis, M., 'The Constitutional Court Sets the Matter Straight: Applicants for Employment Who are HIV Positive', *AIDS Analysis Africa* 11 (5) (2001).

Dunleavy, P. and O'Leary, B., 'The Evolution of Marxist Approaches to State Organization'. In *The Policy Process. A Reader*, ed. M. Hill. London and New York: Prentice-Hall Harvester Wheatsheaf, 1997.

Dunn, W., *Public Policy Analysis: an Introduction*. Englewood Cliffs: Prentice-Hall, 1994.

Durrheim, D. N. and Ogunbanjo. G. A., 'Statistics for General Practitioners. "Does HIV Cause AIDS?" ' *SA Family Practice* 23 (5) (2001).

Dye, T., *Understanding Public Policy*. Englewood Cliffs, NJ: Prentice Hall, 1978.

Dye, T., *Understanding Public Policy*. Englewood Cliffs, NJ: Prentice Hall, 1995.

Easton, D., *The Political System*. New York: Alfred A. Knopf, 1953.

Easton, D., *A Framework for Political Analysis*. Englewood Cliffs, NJ: Prentice-Hall, 1965.

Editorial, 'AIDS Virus Research Unit Established', *MRC News* 18 (1) (1987).

Eichbaum, J., 'AIDS Education: But Who is Being Aided?' *Scenaria* 182 (1996).

Ekambaram, S., 'Health before Profits', *Women's Health Project Newsletter* 31 (1999).

Elazar, D., *American Federalism: A View from the State*. New York: Harper & Row, 1984.

Elmore, R., 'Backward Mapping', *Political Science Quarterly* 94 (1979).

Evian, C., 'AIDS and the Cycle of Poverty'. *AIDS Scan* 4 (4) (1992).

Evian, C., 'AIDS, Reconstruction and Development, and Corporate Response', *AIDS Analysis Africa* 5 (6) (1995).

FAO, *The Impact of HIV and AIDS on Food Security*. Committee on World Food Security: Rome, 28 May–1 June 2001.

Fassin, D., 'Embodied History. Uniqueness and Exemplarity of South African AIDS', *African Journal of AIDS Research* 1 (1) (2002).

Figueira, M. ' "A" Versus South African Airways', *AIDS Legal Quarterly* (September 2000).

Finnemore, M., 'Pre-Employment Screening for AIDS', *IPM Journal* 9 (3) (1990).

FitzSimons, D., 'AIDS and Human Rights', *AIDS Analysis Africa* 2 (4) (1990/1).

Fleming, A., 'A National AIDS Plan for South Africa', *AIDS Analysis Africa* 5 (2) (1994).

Fleshman, M., 'AIDS Prevention in the Ranks – UN Targets Peacekeepers, Combatants in War against Disease', *Africa Recovery* 15 (1–2) June 2001.

Forman, L., 'Health Legislation 1994–2003', in P. Ijumba (ed.), *South African Health Review 2003/04*. Johannesburg: Health Systems Trust, 2003.

Forsythe, S. and Roberts, M., 'Measuring the Impact of HIV and AIDS on Africa's Commercial Sector', *AIDS Analysis Africa* 4 (5) (September/October 1994).

Fourie, P. and Vickers, B., 'Pharmaceuticals, Patents, Polemics and Pretoria', *South African Journal of International Affairs* 9 (2) (2002).

Fransen, L., 'HIV in Developing Countries'. In *Implications of AIDS for Demography and Policy in Southern Africa*, ed. A. Whiteside. Pietermaritzburg: University of Natal Press, 1998.

Friedman, S., 'The Revenge of the Intellectuals: Policy Research and Dialogue in the New South Africa'. *AIDS Bulletin* 6 (1/2) (1997).

Galloway, M. R., 'Views From the Regions', *AIDS Bulletin* 5 (2) (1996).

Galloway, M. R., 'Bringing together Scientific Rigour and Public Health Needs', *AIDS Bulletin* 8 (1) (1999).

Galloway, M. R., 'South African National AIDS Council (SANAC) Launched', *AIDS Bulletin* 9 (1) (2000).

Gardiner, R., 'AIDS – The Undeclared War', *HIV and AIDS Briefing Paper, Social Briefing No. 1 UNED* (February 2001).

Geneeskunde 31 (6), 'Sanlam Borg Opvoeding Oor VIGS' (1989).

Gordon, I., Lewis, J. and Young, K., 'Perspectives on Policy Analysis'. In *The Policy Process.A Reader*, ed. M. Hill. London and New York: Prentice-Hall Harvester Wheatsheaf, 1997.

Gottemoeller, M., 'Empowering Women to Prevent HIV: The Microbicide Advocacy Agenda', *Agenda* 44 (2000).

Goyer, K., 'HIV and Political Instability in Sub-Saharan Africa', *AIDS Analysis Africa* 12 (1) (June/July 2001a).

Goyer, K., 'Compulsory HIV Testing for Alleged Sex Offenders: Victim Empowerment or Violation of Rights?' *AIDS Analysis Africa* 11 (6) (2001b).

Gregory, R., 'Political Rationality or Incrementalism?' In *The Policy Process. A Reader*, ed. M. Hill. London and New York: Prentice-Hall Harvester Wheatsheaf, 1997.

Gresak, G., 'The Urgent Need for an HIV and AIDS Benefit on Medical Schemes', *AIDS Analysis Africa* 7 (4) (1997).

Gresak, G. A., 'AIDS in the Workplace – HIV and AIDS and the Law', *AIDS Bulletin* 7 (1) (1998).

Grundlingh, L., 'HIV and AIDS in South Africa: A Case of Failed Responses Because of Stigmatisation, Discrimination and Morality, 1983–1994', *New Contree* 46 (1999).

Grundlingh, L., *A Critical Historical Analysis of Government Responses to HIV and AIDS in South Africa as Reported in the Media, 1983–1994*. Paper presented to the AIDS in Context Conference: University of Witwatersrand, 4–7April 2001a.

Grundlingh, L., 'Early Attitudes and Responses to HIV and AIDS in Southern Africa as Reflected in Newspapers, 1983–1988', *Journal for Contemporary History* 26 (1) (2001b).

Hadingham, J., 'Human Security and Africa: Polemic Opposites', *South African Journal of International Affairs* 7 (2) (2000).

Haldenwang, B., *AIDS in South Africa: Its Impact on Society*. Bellville: Institute for Futures Research, 1993.

Hambridge, M., 'Migrant Labour and its Impact on AIDS/HIV', *AIDS Analysis Africa* 1 (4) (1990).

Harber, M., 'Social Policy Implications for the Care and Welfare of Children Affected by HIV and AIDS in KwaZulu-Natal'. Master's dissertation: University of Natal, 1999.

Hatane, L., 'Ensuring Political Commitment and an Expanded Response to the HIV and AIDS Epidemic', *AIDS Bulletin* 8 (2) (1999).

Heclo, H., 'Review Article: Policy Analysis', *British Journal of Political Science* 2 (1972).

Heineman, R. Bluhm, W. Peterson, S. and Kearny, E., *The World of the Policy Analyst – Rationality, Values and Politics*. New York and London: Chatham House, 2002.

Hermanus, M., 'AIDS – Whose Responsibility?' *IPM Journal* 9 (1) (1990).

Hermanus, M., 'HIV and AIDS Policy in the Mining Industry', *South African Journal on Human Rights* 9 (1) (1993).

Heydt, H., 'Dentistry in Relation to the Global HIV Epidemic – A Draft Policy Statement', *Journal of the Dental Association of South Africa* 45 (1) (1990).

Heydt, H., 'HIV and AIDS Policy Statement: Practitioners Corner', *The Journal of the Dental Association of South Africa* 47 (8) (1992).

Heydt, M., 'Reporting AIDS to Dental Practitioners', *South African Medical Journal* 71 (1987).

Heyns, M., 'Hurdles and Voids Encountered in the Battle against AIDS', *Rehabilitation in South Africa* 36 (2) (1992).

Heywood, M., 'SADC Moves towards Making AIDS and HIV Notifiable', *AIDS Analysis Africa* 10 (1) (1999).

Heywood, M., 'From Rhetoric to Action – An Evaluation of Progress in Relation to Priority Area 4: Human Legal Rights, HIV and AIDS National Plan', *AIDS Law Project* (2002).

Hickey, A., *Budgets and Funding Flows in the National Integrated Plan for HIV and AIDS*. Cape Town: IDASA, 2001.

Hickey, A., Ndlovu, N. and Guthrie, T., *Budgeting for HIV and AIDS in South Africa: Report on Intergovernmental Funding Flows for an Integrated Response in the Social Sector*. Cape Town: IDASA, 2003.

Hill, M., *The Policy Process in the Modern State*. New York: Prentice-Hall Harvester Wheatsheaf, 1997.

Hilsenrath, P. E. and Joseph, H., 'Health Economics: Issues for South Africa', *The South African Journal of Economics* 59 (1991).

Hogwood, B. and Gunn, L., *Policy Analysis for the Real World*. London: Oxford University Press, 1984.

Hogwood, B. and Gunn, L., *Policy Analysis for the Real World*. London: Oxford University Press, 1989.

Hogwood, B. and Gunn, L., 'Why "Perfect Implementation" is Unattainable'. In *The Policy Process. A Reader*, ed. M. Hill. London and New York: Prentice-Hall Harvester Wheatsheaf, 1997.

Holding, D., 'AIDS, a Corporate Reaction', *Boardroom* 4 (1991).

Holmshaw, M., 'When Will They Ever Learn?' *Current AIDS Literature* 5 (5) (1992).

Holzhausen, H., 'The Main Challenges to Security in the Southern African Region', *Forum 5 SA Defence College* (2001).

Hubert, D., 'Human Security: Safety for People in a Changing World'. Paper presented at a regional conference on *The Management of African Security in the 21st Century*. Nigerian Institute of International Affairs, Lagos, 23–24 June 1999.

Hyde, S., 'AIDS Education: Proactive Planning', *People Dynamics* (August 1992a).

Hyde, S., 'Planning AIDS Education for the Workplace', *AIDS Analysis Africa* 3 (2) (1992b).

ING Barings, *Economic Impact of AIDS in South Africa – a Dark Cloud on the Horizon*. South African Research: ING Barings, 2000.

Jacobs, S. and Calland, R., 'Thabo Mbeki: Myth and Context'. In *Thabo Mbeki's World: The Politics and Ideology of the South African President*, ed. S. Jacobs and R. Calland. Pietermaritzburg: University of Natal Press, 2002.

Jaffe, A., 'South Africans Divided against AIDS', *AIDS Bulletin* 8 (43) (1999).

Jenkins, B., 'Policy Analysis: Models and Approaches'. In *The Policy Process. A Reader*, ed. M. Hill. London and New York: Prentice-Hall Harvester Wheatsheaf, 1997.

Jochelson, K., 'HIV and Syphilis in the Republic of South Africa'. *African Urban Quarterly* 6 (1/2) (1991).

John, P., *Analysing Public Policy*. London and New York: Continuum, 2000.

Joni, J. and Heywood, M., 'Error in Judgement or Failure by the Judiciary to Give Clarity on the Interpretation of the Law?' *AIDS Analysis Africa* 12 (3) (2001).

Joseph, C., 'HIV and AIDS and Local Government'. *Occasional Paper* 12 (2002).

Joseph, P., 'AIDS and the Strategic Balance: The African Connection. Is There a Need for a "Medical Curtain?" ' *African Armed Forces* (September 2000).

Journal of Contemporary Roman-Dutch Law, 'Vonnisse. Vigs, Boni Mores en Vertroulikheid'. Johannesburg: Digma, 1992.

Journal of the Dental Association of South Africa 48 (7) (1993). 'FDI Policy Statement on the Human Immunodeficiency Virus (HIV), The Acquired Immune Deficiency Syndrome (AIDS), and Dentistry'.

Karim, A. S. S., 'Making AIDS a Notifiable Disease – Is It an Appropriate Policy for South Africa?' *South African Medical Journal* 89 (6) (1999).

Karim, Q. A., 'Government Role in AIDS Prevention and Relationship with Private Sector', *AIDS Scan* 7 (3) (1995).

Karim, Q. A., 'Trends in HIV and AIDS Infection: Beyond Current Statistics', *South African Journal of International Affairs* 7 (2) (2000).

Karim, Q. A., Morar, N., Zuma, N., Stein, Z. and Preston-Whyte, E., 'Women and AIDS in Natal/KwaZulu: Determinants of the Adoption of HIV-Protective Behaviour', *Urbanisation and Health Newsletter* 20 (1994).

Kasper, T., 'Patents, Pills and Public Policy: the Pharmaceutical Industry and International Trade'. In *HIV and AIDS, Economics and Governance in South Africa: Key Issues in Understanding Response*, ed. K. Kelly, W. Parker, and S. Gelby. Johannesburg: The Centre for AIDS Development, Research and Education, 2002.

Keir, D., 'AIDS and Group Insurance', *AIDS Analysis Africa* 1 (3) (1990).

Kenis, P. and Marin, B., *Managing AIDS: Organizational Responses in Six European Countries*. Brookfield: Aldershot, 1997.

Kirby, M., 'AIDS & the Law', *South African Journal on Human Rights* 9 (1993a).

Kirby, M., 'Life's Dominion – Closing Reflections', *South African Journal on Human Rights* 9 (1993b).

Kistner, U., 'Necessity and Sufficiency in the Aetiology of HIV and AIDS: The Science, History and Politics of the Causal Link', *African Journal of AIDS Research* 1 (1) (2002).

Kitching, G., 'Sal "Sarafina" VIGS Oorleef?', *Insig* (April 1996).

Klouda, T., 'It's Called "Fiddling While Rome Burns" ', *AIDS Analysis Africa* 5 (2) (1994).

Kotze, M. and Van Wyk, J., 'South African Opinion-Leaders' Perspectives on HIV and AIDS', *AIDS Analysis Africa* 6 (2) (1995).

Kriel, J., 'VIGS (En die Grense van die Mediese Wetenskap)', *Die Suid Afrikaan* 29 (1990).

Kromberg, J., 'Time to Act'. *Leadership* (May 2004).

Kustner, H., 'The Truth about AIDS', *Epidemiological Comments* 17(3) (1990).

Labour Bulletin 14 (4) (1989). 'Briefings: Mineworkers Tackle Health and Safety'.

Lancet (12 February 2005). 'South Africa Needs to Face the Truth About HIV Mortality 365 (9459)'.

Lane, J., 'Implementation Accountability and Trust'. *European Journal of Political Research*, 15 (5) (1987).

Lasswell, H., *Politics: Who Gets What, When, How*. Meridian Books: Cleveland, [1936] 1958.

Leclerk-Madlala, S., 'Crime in an Epidemic: the Case of Rape and AIDS', *Acta Criminalogica* 9 (2) (1996).

Leech, B. E., 'The Right of the HIV-Positive Patient to Medical Care: An Analysis of the Costs of Providing Medical Treatment', *South African Journal on Human Rights* 9 (1993).

Leech, B. E., 'The Charter of Rights on Aids and HIV: Panacea or Chimera', *South African Public Law* 9 (2) (1994).

Levy, A. D., 'Employer Considerations in Determining a Policy on AIDS', *South African Journal of Human Rights* 9 (1) (1993).

Lindblom, C., 'The Science of Muddling Through'. *Public Administration Review* 19 (1959).

Lindblom, C., 'Still Muddling Through'. *Public Administration Review* 39 (6) (1979).

Lodge, T., *Politics in South Africa: From Mandela to Mbeki*. Indiana: Indiana University Press, 2002.

Loewenon, R. and Whiteside, A., 'HIV and AIDS in Southern Africa'. In *Implications of AIDS for Demography and Policy in Southern Africa*, ed. A. Whiteside. Pietermaritzburg: University of Natal Press, 1998.

Louw, D., 'Ministering and Counselling the Person with AIDS. *Journal of Theology for Southern Africa* no. 71 (1990).

Lurie, P., 'AIDS and Labour Policy'. *South African Labour Bulletin* 12 (8) (1987).

Lush, L. and Makoala, S., 'Implementing Policies to Integrate HIV/STD Services with Primary Health Care in Northern Province, South Africa', *Women's Health Project Newsletter* 31 (1999).

Lyons, S. F. and Schoub, B. D., 'AIDS-Related Research in South Africa', *South African Journal of Science* 83 (1987).

MacLean, G., *The Changing Perceptions of Human Security: Co-ordinating National and Multilateral Responses*. Manitoba: UNAC, 1998.

Makgoba, M., 'HIV: The Greatest Threat to the African Renaissance'. *MRC News* 32 (4) (2001).

Malan, M., 'The Influence of HIV and AIDS on National Security for South Africa: The Concerns and Implications from a Human Resources Perspective'. *Forum 5 SA Defence College* (2001).

Maman, S. *et al., HIV and Partner Violence: Implications for HIV Voluntary Counselling and Testing Programs in Dar es Salaam, Tanzania*. New York: The Population Council Inc., 2001.

Mann, J. and Tarantola, D., *AIDS in the World II: Global Dimensions, Social Roots, and Responses*. New York: Oxford University Press, 1996.

Manning, R. E., 'Noble Intentions, Harsh Realities: The Politics of AIDS Policy in South Africa'. PhD Thesis: Woodrow Wilson School of Public and International Affairs, 2001.

Marais, H., *To the Edge: AIDS Review 2000*. Pretoria: Centre for the Study of AIDS, 2000.

Marais, H., *South Africa: Limits to Change: The Political Economy of Transformation.* Cape Town: University of Cape Town Press, 1998.

March, J. and Olsen, J., 'Institutional Perspectives on Political Institutions'. In *The Policy Process. A Reader*, ed. M. Hill. London and New York: Prentice-Hall Harvester Wheatsheaf, 1997.

Martin, D. J., Tilley, J. F. G., Smith, A. N. and Schoub, B. D., 'AIDS Clinic – A Year On', *South African Medical Journal* 75 (1) (1989).

Matthews, S., 'Women in Conflict'. *Conflict Trends* 4 (2000).

Mbali, M., 'HIV and AIDS Policy-Making in Post-Apartheid South Africa'. In *State of the Nation: South Africa 2003–2004*, ed. J. Daniel, A. Habib and R. Southall. Cape Town: HSRC Press, 2003.

Mbeki, T., 'The South African Declaration on AIDS', *The South African Dental Journal* 54 (12) (1999).

Mboi, N., 'Women and AIDS in South and South-East Asia: the Challenge and the Response', *World Health Statistics Quarterly* 49(2) (1996).

McIntyre, J., 'The Government Strategy on Combating AIDS', *HST Update* 13 (1996).

McKerrow, N., 'Treatment of HIV and AIDS and Related Illnesses'. In *Impacts and Interventions: The HIV and AIDS Epidemic and the Children of South Africa*, ed. J. Gow and C. Desmond. Pietermaritzburg: University of Natal Press, 2002.

McKerrow, N., *The South African Response to the HIV and AIDS Epidemic: An Input Paper to the Report on the Elimination of Poverty and Inequality in South Africa.* South Africa, 2003.

McLennan, G., 'The Evolution of Pluralist Theory'. In *The Policy Process. A Reader*, ed. M. Hill. London and New York: Prentice Hall Harvester Wheatsheaf, 1997.

Metz, J. and Malan, J. M., 'The Impact of AIDS on Society', *South African Journal of Continuing Medical Education* 6 (3) (1988).

Meyer, I. and Cloete, F., 'Policy Agenda-Setting'. In *Improving Public Policy*, ed. F. Cloete and H. Wissink. Pretoria: Van Schaik, 2000.

Michael, J., 'Tutu Praises Whites and Lashes Black Elite', *The Star*, 24 November 2004.

Miller, G. G., 'AIDS: A Theological and Pastoral Response', *Koers: Bulletin for Christian Scholarship* 55 (2) (1990).

Milton, V. C., 'Times Picturing of HIV and AIDS'. In *Tydskrif vir Letterkunde*, ed. H. Willemse. Pretoria: University of Pretoria, 2004.

Minogue, M., 'Theory and Practice in Public Policy and Administration. In *The Policy Process. A Reader*, ed. M. Hill. London and New York: Prentice Hall Harvester Wheatsheaf, 1997.

Mokhobo, D., 'AIDS: Balancing Individual Rights with Business Imperatives', *South African Journal on Human Rights* 9 (1993).

Moodie, J. W., 'Serology of AIDS', *South African Journal of Continuing Medical Education* 6 (3) (1988).

Motobele, T. and Heywood, M., 'South Africa's Constitutional Court Declares Pre-employment Testing a Human Rights Violation', *AIDS Analysis Africa* 11 (4) (2001).

MRC News, 'VIGS: Tot Hiertoe en Verder: Algemeen'. *MRC News* 18 (3) (1987).

MRC Press Statement, 'MRC Commitment to AIDS Research'. *AIDS Scan* 2 (1) (1989).

Nattrass, N., *The Moral Economy of AIDS in South Africa*. Cambridge: Cambridge University Press, 2004.

Ndiaye, C. F., 'Women and AIDS in Africa: The Experience of the Society for Women and AIDS in Africa', *South African Journal of International Affairs* 7 (2) (2000).

New South African Outlook 3 (4) (2001). 'HIV and AIDS: The Current Reality, the MRC Report'.

Ngwena, C., 'HIV and AIDS and Equal Opportunities in the Workplace: The Implications of the Employment Equity Act', *The Comparative and International Law Journal of Southern Africa* 33 (1) (2000a).

Ngwena, C., 'HIV and AIDS and Equal Opportunities in the Workplace: The Implications of the Employment Equity Act', *The Comparative and International Law Journal of Southern Africa* 33 (1) (2000b).

Ngwena, C. and Pelser, A., *Strengthening local government and civic responses to the HIV/AIDS epidemic – a study for the Ford Foundation*, Working Paper: Centre for Health Systems Research and Development, University of the Free State (2001).

NIC, *The Global Infectious Threat and its Implications for the United States*. National Intelligence Council, US Government, NIE 99-17D: Washington DC, 2000.

Norse, D., 'Impact of AIDS on Food Production in East Africa', *AIDS Analysis Africa* 1 (5) (November/December 1991).

NUE Comment 2 (1) (1999). 'HIV and AIDS and Schools'.

O'Farrell, N., 'South African AIDS', *South African Medical Journal* 72 (1987).

O'Sullivan, S., 'Uniting across Global Boundaries – HIV Positive Women in Global Perspective', *Agenda* 44 (2000).

Oosthuizen, I., 'The Management of AIDS in South African Schools', *Koers: Bulletin for Christian Scholarship* 59 (2) (1994).

Parker, W., 'A National Media Campaign – Who Makes the Decisions and What is Really Needed?' *AIDS Bulletin* 5 (2) (1996).

Parsons, W., *Public Policy: an Introduction to the Theory and Practice of Policy Analysis*. Cheltenham: Edward Elgar, 1997.

Phila, 'The Sarafina II Controversy', *Phila Legislative Update* 3 (1996).

Porter, R., *Presidential Decision Making: the Economic Policy Board*. New York: Cambridge University Press, 1980.

Power, S., 'The AIDS Rebel Letter From South Africa', *The New Yorker* 79 (12) (2003).

Price, M. and Van den Heever, A., 'The Reconstruction and Development Programme and Health', *Southern African Journal of Epidemiology and Infection* 9 (2) (1994).

Quattek, K., 'The Economic Impact of AIDS in South Africa: A Dark Cloud on the Horizon'. In *HIV and AIDS: A Threat to the African Renaissance?*. Konrad Adenauer Stifting Occasional Paper (June 2000).

Race Relations Survey, 1986. Johannesburg: South African Institute of Race Relations, 1986.

Race Relations Survey, 1987–1988. Johannesburg: South African Institute of Race Relations, 1988.

Race Relations Survey, 1988–1989. Johannesburg: South African Institute of Race Relations, 1989.

Race Relations Survey, 1989–1990. Johannesburg: South African Institute of Race Relations, 1990.

Race Relations Survey, 1991–1992. Johannesburg: South African Institute of Race Relations, 1992.

Race Relations Survey, 1992–1993. Johannesburg: South African Institute of Race Relations, 1993.
Race Relations Survey, 1993–1994. Johannesburg: South African Institute of Race Relations, 1994.
Race Relations Survey, 1994–1995. Johannesburg: South African Institute of Race Relations, 1995.
Race Relations Survey, 1995–1996. Johannesburg: South African Institute of Race Relations, 1996.
Race Relations Survey, 1996–1997. Johannesburg: South African Institute of Race Relations, 1997.
Race Relations Survey, 1997–1998. Johannesburg: South African Institute of Race Relations, 1998.
Race Relations Survey, 1998–1999. Johannesburg: South African Institute of Race Relations, 1999.
Race Relations Survey, 1999–2000. Johannesburg: South African Institute of Race Relations, 2000.
Race Relations Survey, 2000–2001. Johannesburg: South African Institute of Race Relations, 2001.
Race Relations Survey, 2001–2002. Johannesburg: South African Institute of Race Relations, 2002.
Race Relations Survey, 2002–2003. Johannesburg: South African Institute of Race Relations, 2003.
Race Relations Survey, 2003–2004. Johannesburg: South African Institute of Race Relations, 2004.
Radipati, B., 'HIV and AIDS and Employment Law: A Comparative Synopsis', *Comparative and International Law Journal of Southern Africa* 13 (1993).
Rafel, R., 'The Politics of Disease', *Finance Week* 34 (3) (1987).
Ranney, A. (ed.), *Political Science and Public Policy*. Chicago: Markham, 1968.
Raphaely, C., 'Frightening Figures', *Finance Week* 42 (5) (1989).
Raubenheimer, M., 'AIDS Activist Murdered'. *Women's Health Project Newsletter* 29 (1999).
Roux, N., 'Policy Design'. In *Improving Public Policy*, ed. F. Cloete and H. Wissink. Pretoria: Van Schaik, 2000.
Russel, C., 'The AIDS Crisis: a Mining Industry Perspective'. *Mining Survey* 2 (1991).
SA Construction World, *Guidelines on AIDS in the Work Place* 8 (3) (1989).
SA Survey, 1986–1987. Johannesburg: South African Institute of Race Relations, 1987.
SA Survey, 1987–1988. Johannesburg: South African Institute of Race Relations, 1988.
SA Survey, 1988–1989. Johannesburg: South African Institute of Race Relations, 1989.
SA Survey, 1989–1990. Johannesburg: South African Institute of Race Relations, 1990.
SA Survey, 1990–1991. Johannesburg: South African Institute of Race Relations, 1991.
SA Survey, 1991–1992. Johannesburg: South African Institute of Race Relations, 1992.
SA Survey, 1992–1993. Johannesburg: South African Institute of Race Relations, 1993.

SA Survey, 1993–1994. Johannesburg: South African Institute of Race Relations, 1994.
SA Survey, 1994–1995. Johannesburg: South African Institute of Race Relations, 1995.
SA Survey, 1995–1996. Johannesburg: South African Institute of Race Relations, 1996.
SA Survey, 1996–1997. Johannesburg: South African Institute of Race Relations, 1997.
SA Survey, 1997–1998. Johannesburg: South African Institute of Race Relations, 1998.
SA Survey, 1999–2000. Johannesburg: South African Institute of Race Relations, 1999.
SA Survey, 2000–2001. Johannesburg: South African Institute of Race Relations, 2000.
SA Survey, 2001–2002. Johannesburg: South African Institute of Race Relations, 2001.
SA Survey, 2002–2003. Johannesburg: South African Institute of Race Relations, 2002.
SA Survey, 2003–2004. Johannesburg: South African Institute of Race Relations, 2003.
Sabatier, P., 'Top-down and Bottom-up Approaches to Implementation Research: A Critical Analysis and Suggested Synthesis', *Journal of Public Policy* 6 (1) (1986).
Sadie, Y. and Schoeman, M., 'Vigs-Politiek in Suid Afrika: 1987–1992'. *Politikon* 19 (3) (1992).
Sadie, Y. and Schoeman, M., 'The Virus of Mistrust', *Leadership* 2 (1993).
Sadie, Y., Schoeman, M. and Verwey, S., 'Public Policy Formulation and Implementation as Political Communication: The Case of AIDS in South Africa', *Communitas: Journal for Community Communication* 1 (1994).
SAIRR, *South Africa Survey 2000/2001*. Johannesburg: SA Institute of Race Relations, 2001.
Sanlam, 'AIDS Major Cause for Concern in South Africa', *AIDS Scan* 2 (3) (1990).
Sarkin, J., 'Health', *South African Human Rights Yearbook 1994* 5 (1993).
Schneider, H. and Stein, J., *From Policy on Paper to Action on the Ground: Contextual Issues Affected Implementation of the National AIDS Plan in South Africa*. Johannesburg: Centre for Health Policy, WITS, 1997.
Schneider, H. and McIntyre, J., 'Is the 1993/94 AIDS Programme Budget Adequate?' *AIDS Scan* 6 (2) (1994).
Schneider, H., *The Politics behind AIDS: The Case of South Africa*. Johannesburg: Centre for Health Policy, WITS, 1998.
Schneider, H., *The AIDS Impasse in South Africa as a Struggle for Symbolic Power*. Johannesburg: Centre for Health Policy, WITS, 2001.
Schneider, H., 'On the Fault-Line: the Politics of AIDS Policy in Contemporary South Africa', *African Studies* 61 (1) (2002).
Schneider, H. and Stein, J., 'Implementing AIDS Policy in Post-Apartheid South Africa', *Social Science and Medicine* 52 (2001).
Schönteich, M., 'Age and AIDS: South Africa's Crime Timebomb?' *African Security Review* 8 (4) (1999).
Schoub, B. D., 'Progress and Problems in the Development of an AIDS Virus Vaccine', *South African Journal of Continuing Medical Education* 6 (3) (1988).

Schoub, B. D., Smith, A. N., Johnson, S., Martin, D. J., Lyons, S. F., Padayachee, G. N. and Hurwitz, H. S., 'Considerations on the Further Expansion of the AIDS Epidemic in South Africa – 1990'. *AIDS Scan* 2 (3) (1990).

Schrire, R., 'The Realities of Opposition in South Africa: Legitimacy, Strategies and Consequences'. *Democratization* 8 (1) (2001).

Sello, S., 'A Strange Mating', *Drum* 98 (February 1987).

Serpa, E., 'AIDS in Africa: The Social-Cultural Roots of a Disease', *Africa Insight* 32 (3) (2002).

Setiloane, M., 'AIDS in South Africa: Some Issues and Considerations', *Social Work Practice* (1991).

Shell, R., 'The Silent Revolution: the AIDS Pandemic and the Military in South Africa', *Consolidating Democracy in South Africa* (1999).

Shell, R., 'Halfway to the Holocaust: the Economic, Demographic and Social Implications of the AIDS Pandemic to the Year 2010 in the Southern African Region'. In *HIV and AIDS: A Threat to the African Renaissance?* Konrad Adenauer Stifting Occasional Paper (June 2000).

Sher, R., 'Women and HIV and AIDS', *AIDS Scan* 2 (4) (1990).

Sherr, L., Christie, G., Sher, R. and Mets, J., 'Evaluation of the Effectiveness of AIDS Training and Information Courses in South Africa, *AIDS Scan* 2 (1989).

Simelala, N., 'South Africans Need to Wake up to the Realities of this Epidemic', *AIDS Bulletin* 8 (3) (1999).

Sing, D., 'An Industrial Relations Perspective of AIDS in the Public Sector', *Journal of the University of Stellenbosch Business School* 11 (2) (1991).

Smart, R., 'Preventing Transmission of HIV'. In *Impacts and Interventions: The HIV and AIDS Epidemic and the Children of South Africa*, ed. J. Gow and C. Desmond. Pietermaritzburg: University of Natal Press, 2002.

Smart, R. and Strode, A., 'South African Labour Law and HIV and AIDS', *AIDS Analysis Africa* 10 (3) (1999).

Smit, T., 'A Human Rights Approach to the Protection of HIV Vaccine Trial Participants', *AIDS Legal Quarterly* (December 2000).

Smith, A. N., 'Notification of HIV and AIDS'. *AIDS Bulletin* (July 1999).

Smith, M., 'Policy Networks'. In *The Policy Process. A Reader*, ed. M. Hill. London and New York: Prentice-Hall Harvester Wheatsheaf, 1997.

Sontag, S., *Illness as Metaphor and AIDS and its Metaphors*. London: Penguin Group, 2002.

South African Medical Journal 79 (1991). 'Management of HIV Patients – Policy Statement from the College of Medicine of South Africa'.

Southern African Practice Management 13 (1) 1992. 'First SA Court Ruling on Doctor's Duty of Confidentiality towards Patient with AIDS'.

Sparks, A., *Beyond the Miracle: Inside the New South Africa*. London: Profile Books, 2003.

Spencer, D. C., 'The Management of South Africa's HIV Infected. What are the Challenges?' *South African Journal of Epidemiology and Infection* 10 (2) (1995).

Spier, A., 'Industry Analysis: AIDS and the Hospital Industry'. *AIDS Analysis Africa* 1 (2) (1990a).

Spier, A., 'Medical Aid', *AIDS Analysis Africa* 1 (1) (1990b).

Starling, G., *The Politics and Economics of Public Policy: An Introductory Analysis with Cases*. Homewood, IL: Dorsey, 1979.

Stein, J., 'Policy Analysis – Understanding How Things Happen', *AIDS Bulletin* 5 (2) (1996).

Steinberg, M., 'The National AIDS Research Programme of the MRC', *AIDS Analysis Africa* 4 (2) (1993).

Steytler, N., 'Federal Homogeneity From the Bottom Up: Provincial Shaping of National HIV and AIDS Policy in South Africa', *Publias* 33 (1) (2003).

Stipp, E. *Government Responses to HIV and AIDS. Still Everybody's Business: The Enlightening Truth About AIDS*. Ed. C. Desmond, L. Karam and M. Steinberg. Belville: Metropolitan Group, 2003.

Stone, K. and Barrett, C., 'HIV and AIDS in Prisons: New Developments', *Positive Outlook* 3 (4) (1996).

Stover, J. and Johnston, A., *The Art of Policy Formulation: Experiences from Africa in Developing National HIV/AIDS Policies*, Washington, DC, 1999.

Strachan, K., 'The Month in Review'. *HST Update* 5 (1995).

Strachan, K., 'The Current Health Budget: Who Gets What?' *South African Family Practice* 17 (7) (1996).

Strange, S., *States and Markets: an Introduction to International Political Economy*. London: Pinter Publishers, 1988.

Strasheim, P., 'When Prescience Might Be Better than Cure: The Media's Reporting of AIDS', *Responsa Meridiana* 5 (1) (1986).

Strauss, S. A. 'Legal Issues Concerning AIDS: An Outline'. *South African Practice Management* 9 (1) (1988a).

Strauss, S. A., 'Oordraagbare Siektes en Aanmelding van Aanmeldbare Mediese Toestande', *Southern African Practice Management* 9 (4) (1988b).

Strauss, S. A., 'AIDS and Employment: Some Key Issues', *AIDS Analysis Africa* 1 (1) (1990).

Strauss, S. A., 'Testing for AIDS'. *AIDS Analysis Africa* 1 (3) 1990.

Strode, A. 'Patients are People with Rights', *Positive Outlook* 1 (3) (1994).

Strode, A. 'Pre-employment Testing Bill'. *Positive Outlook* 3 (1) 1995.

Strode, A. and Grant, K.B., *Understanding the Institutional Dynamics of South Africa's Response to HIV and AIDS Pandemic*. Pretoria: IDASA, 2004.

Strode, A. and Smart, R., 'The National HIV and AIDS and STD Directorate's Progress in Setting upon Inter-Departmental Committee on HIV and AIDS', *AIDS Bulletin* 5 (2) (1996).

Tallis, V., 'Gendering the Response to HIV and AIDS Challenging Gender Inequality', *Agenda* 44 (2000).

Taylor, G., 'The Medical Aid Response', *AIDS Analysis Africa* 2 (2) (1991).

Taylor, G., 'AIDS and Medical Aid – Ten Years' Experience'. *AIDS Analysis Africa* 4 (2) (1993).

Taylor, G., 'Employers Still Cautious'. *AIDS Analysis Africa* 5 (1) (1994).

Terreblanche, S., *A History of Inequality in South Africa 1652–2002*. Pietermaritzburg: University of Natal Press, 2002.

The National Institute of Allergy and Infectious Diseases. Maryland: National Institutes of Health, 1995.

Thomas, C., 'Trade Policy and the Politics of Access to Drugs'. *Third World Quarterly* 23 (2) (2002).

Thomas, L. and Howard, J., 'AIDS and Development Planning'. In *Implications of AIDS for Demography and Policy in Southern Africa*, ed. A. Whiteside. Pietermaritzburg: University of Natal Press, 1998.

Tiba, M., 'AIDS – Some Socio-Cultural Considerations', *Social Work Practice* (1990).
Treichler, P., *How to Have Theory in an Epidemic: Cultural Chronicles of AIDS*. London: Duke University Press, 1999.
Trengove-Jones, T., *'Who Cares?' AIDS Review 2001*. Pretoria: University of Pretoria, 2001.
Tullock, G., 'The Economic Theory of Bureaucracy'. In *The Policy Process. A Reader*, ed. M. Hill. London and New York: Prentice Hall Harvester Wheatsheaf, 1997.
Ulin, P. R., 'African Women and AIDS: Negotiating Behavioural Change', *AIDS Scan* 4 (3) (1992).
UN, *Global Crisis – Global Action*. United Nations Special Session on HIV and AIDS, 25–27 June: New York, 2001.
UNAIDS, *Refugees and AIDS*. UNAIDS Point of View: May 1997.
UNAIDS, *AIDS and the Military*. UNAIDS Point of View: May 1998.
UNAIDS, *HIV and AIDS and Human Development South Africa*. New York: UNAIDS, 1998.
UNAIDS, *Report on the Global AIDS Epidemic*. Switzerland: UNAIDS, 2004.
United Nations Press Release, *Security Council Holds Debate on Impact of AIDS on Peace and Security in Africa*. SC/6781, 4086 meeting, 10 January 2000.
Van Ammers, P. M., 'Human Immunodeficiency Virus in Obstetrics', *South African Journal of Continuing Medical Education* 8 (3) (1990).
Van der Linde, I., 'The Costing of HIV and AIDS – Without a Clue?' *AIDS Scan* 11 (1) (1999).
Van der Merwe, M., 'Het Jy al Ernstig Gedink Oor'. *Entrepreneur* 8 (6) (1989).
Van der Schyf, C. J., 'Die Behandeling van VIGS – Geneesmiddels en Vaksiene – Wat Hou die Toekoms in?' *Koers: Bulletin for Christian Scholarship* 55 (3) (1990).
Van der Vliet, V., 'AIDS: Losing "the New Struggle?" ' *Daedalus* 130 (1) (2001).
Van der Vliet, V., 'Dealing with AIDS: a Work in Progress'. *Focus* 34 (2004a).
Van der Vliet, V., 'South Africa Divided against AIDS: a Crisis of Leadership'. In *AIDS and South Africa: The Social Expression of a Pandemic*, ed. K. D. Kauffman and D. L. Lindauer. Basingstoke: Macmillan, 2004b.
Van der Waldt, G., 'Public Policy and Policy Analysis'. In *Governance, Politics, and Policy in South Africa*, ed. D. Van Niekerk, G. Van der Waldt and A. Jonker. Cape Town: Oxford University Press Southern Africa, 2001.
Van Dyk, A. C., 'AIDS: To Care or not to Care'. *Unisa Psychologia* 18 (1) (1991).
Van Niftrik, J., 'Industry and AIDS – Closing the Credibility Gap', *AIDS Analysis Africa* 1 (3) (1990).
Van Niftrik, J., 'The Pandemic and the Press', *AIDS Analysis Africa* 1 (4) (1991).
Van Niftrik, J., 'SAMDC Rules on HIV and Doctor's Ethics', *AIDS Analysis Africa* 2 (5) (1992).
Van Niftrik, J. 'Opinion: Finally, the Courage of Cutting the Crap'. *AIDS Analysis Africa* 3 (6) (1993).
Van Rooyen, C. A. J. and Bernstein, A. J., 'AIDS Education for Student Social Workers in South Africa: Are Social Workers Being Educated to Meet the Needs of the Society in Which They Function?'. *Social Week* 28 (4) (1992).
Van Rooyen, R. J., 'Moet 'n Pasient Uitdruklik Toestemming Verleen Voordat vir AIDS Getoets kan Word?' *Geneeskunde* 32 (11) 1990.
Van Wyk, C., 'May a Company Terminate an Employee's Service Once He/She Has Been Diagnosed as Being HIV-Positive?' *AIDS Scan* 2 (2) (1990).

Van Wyk, C., 'Legal Consequences of AIDS in the Workplace', *Codicillus* 31 (1991).
Van Wyk, C., 'Vigs en Bloedoortrappings: Enkele Regaspekte'. *De Jure* 1 (1992b).
Van Wyk, C. W., 'Deceased AIDS Patient's Challenge to Medical Ethics Fails in South African Supreme Court', *AIDS Scan* 4 (2) (1992a).
Van Wyk, C. W., 'South African Thesis on Legal Questions Concerning AIDS Recommends ...' *AIDS Scan* 4 (1) (1992b).
Viljoen, A. T., 'VIGS in Afrika, Met Spesiale Verwysing na Suid-Afrika', *Koers: Bulletin for Christian Scholarship* 55 (3) (1990).
Viljoen, F., 'Verligting of Verlustiging: Regshervorming in 'n Tyd van VIGS', *The South African Law Journal* 110 (1993).
Walker, L., Reid, G., and Cornell, M., *Waiting to Happen: HIV and AIDS in South Africa*. Colorado: Lynne Rienner, 2004.
Webb, D., 'The Geographical Progression of HIV in South Africa, 1990–1993', *AIDS Analysis Africa* 5 (2) (1994).
Whiteside, A., 'Lessons from Africa', *AIDS Analysis Africa* 1 (5) (1991).
Whiteside, A., 'AIDS in South Africa: The First Ten Years'. *AIDS Bulletin* 4 (2) (1993).
Whiteside, A., 'Policymakers' and Planners' Needs in Projecting the Epidemic'. In *Implications of AIDS for Demography and Policy in Southern Africa*, ed. A. Whiteside. Pietermaritzburg: University of Natal Press, 1998.
Whiteside, A., 'Drugs: the Solution?' *AIDS Analysis Africa* 11 (6) (April/May 2001a).
Whiteside, A., 'There is None so Blind'. *AIDS Analysis Africa* 12 (3) (October/November 2001b).
Whiteside, A. and Sunter, C., *AIDS: The Challenge for South Africa*. Cape Town: Human & Rousseau/Tafelberg, 2000.
Whiteside, A. *et al.*, 'Examining HIV and AIDS in Southern Africa through the Eyes of Ordinary Southern Africans', *Afrobarometer Paper No. 21*. IDASA, 2002.
Wilkins, N., 'HIV and AIDS and the Informal Sector', *AIDS Analysis Africa* 10 (1) (June/July 1999).
Wilkinson, D., Floyd, K. and Gilks, C. F., 'A National Programme to Reduce Mother-to-Child HIV Transmission is Potentially Cost Saving', *AIDS Bulletin* 8 (1) (1999).
Willan, S., 'Will HIV and AIDS Undermine Democracy in South Africa?' *AIDS Analysis Africa* 11 (1) (June/July 2000).
Wilson, W., 'The Study of Administration'. *Political Science Quarterly* 2 (1987).
Winsbury, P., 'Where the AIDS War Can Be Won', *AIDS Analysis Africa* 2 (5) (1992).
Wissink, H., 'History and Development of Policy Studies and Policy Analysis'. In *Improving Public Policy*, ed. F. Cloete and H. Wissink. Pretoria: Van Schaik, 2000.
Wood, G., 'AIDS and the Insurance Industry', *AIDS Analysis Africa* 4 (4) (1993/4).
World Bank, *Confronting AIDS: Public Priorities in a Global Epidemic*. New York: Oxford University Press, 1999.
Yach, D., 'Development and Health: The Need for Integrated Approaches in South Africa', *Development Southern Africa* 9 (1) 1992.
Young, F., *Tool Box for Building Strong and Healthy Community Organisations Working in HIV and AIDS and Sexual Health*. Pretoria: HIV and AIDS and STD Directorate, Department of Health, 1999a.
Young, J., *The Exclusive Society*. London: Sage, 1999b.

Zazayokwe, M., 'Some Barriers to Education about AIDS in the Black Community'. *Social Work Practice* (1990).
Zuma, B., 'Cross-Cultural Counselling', *Positive Outlook* 3 (4) (1996).

Official documents

ANC, *National Health Plan for South Africa*. May 1994.
Government Gazette, R485, 23/4/99. Amendment to the regulations to communicable diseases and the notification of notifiable conditions.
Strategic Plan. *HIV and AIDS/STD Strategic Plan for South Africa 2000–2005*. May 2000.

Newspapers and news magazines

Associated Press, 24 April 2001.
Business Day, 10 September 2001.
Business Day, 11 May 2000.
Business Day, 6 October 2000.
Cape Times, 22 October 2004.
Citizen, 25 June 2001.
Finance Week, 24–30 October 1991.
Finance Week, 6–12 April 1989.
Financial Mail, 13 April 2001.
Financial Mail, 13 October 2000.
Financial Mail, 14 June 1996.
Financial Mail, 14 June 2002.
Financial Mail, 2 June 1989.
Financial Mail, 29 September 2000.
Financial Mail, 30 June 1989.
Financial Mail, 5 May 2000.
Financial Mail, 8 February 2002.
Financial Times, 19 June 2001.
Finansies & Tegniek, 13 September 1996.
IRIN, 27 July 2001.
Mail & Guardian, 12–18 May 2000.
Mail & Guardian, 16 August 1999.
Mail & Guardian, 20 September 2000.
Mail & Guardian, 26 October 2000.
Mail & Guardian, 31 March–6 April 2000.
Mail & Guardian, 4 June 2004.
Mail & Guardian, 10–16 December 2004.
Mail & Guardian, 25 February–3 March 2005.
Mail & Guardian, 24–31 March 2005.
Middle East Intelligence Wire, 7 February 2000.
Reuters New Media, 16 July 2004.
SAPA, 12 March 2000.
SAPA, 13 November 2001.
SAPA, 14 November 2001.

SAPA, 17 September 2001.
SAPA, 20 October 2000.
SAPA, 25 January 2002.
SAPA, 28 September 2003.
SAPA, 4 April 2001.
SAPA, 9 January 2001.
Sunday Herald, 18 July 2004.
Sunday Independent, 2 April 2000.
Sunday Independent, 12 December 2004.
Sunday Times, 16 July 2000.
Sunday Times, 18 July 2004.
Sunday Times, 9 July 2000.
Sunday Times, 13 March 2005.
The Star, 12 January 2000.
The Star, 4 March 2003.
Washington Post, 14 July 2000.
Washington Post, 15 March 2001.
Washington Post, 29 April 2004.
Washington Post, 5 July 2000.

Internet sources

Blaauw, D. and Gilson, L., Voices of National and Provincial Managers (2001). http://legacy.hst.org.za/sahr/2001/chapter14.htm.

Jack, E. Mbeki, 'Like PW on Tutu Issue' (2004). www.news24.co.za.

News24.com. TAC Slams ANC's AIDS Stance. *News24.com* (2005). www.news24.com.

News24.com. Condoms Clearly Don't Work. *News24.com* (2005). www. news24.com.

News24.com. HIV/AIDS Care Lagging in SA. *News24.com* (2005). www.news24.com.

News24.com. Death Stats Come to Life. *News24.com* (2005). http://www.news24.com/News24/South_Africa/0,,2-7-659_1664609,00.html.

Rahiman, F., A Regional Audit of HIV and AIDS, Human Rights and Other Relevant Issues. (1999). www.alp.org.za/view.php?file=/resctr/rpaprs/19990930_rpregaudfr.xml.

Schlemmer, L., *Thabo Mbeki's Strategy* (2000). http://www.hsf.org.za/focus20/focus20conts.html.

Stoppard, A., 'AIDS Strategy Develops Chinks in its Armour', *iClinic* (6 April 2000).

TAC, *Why the TAC is Going to Court Tomorrow and Holding Country-wide Demonstrations. TAC* (2004). www.tac.org.za.

UNECA, Compact for African Recovery: Operationalising the Millennium Partnership for the African Recovery Programme. *UNECA* (2001). http://www.uneca.org/conferenceofministers/compact_for_african_recovery.htm.

Index